More Praise

"Drawing on findings from infant development studies, neuroscience, and mindfulness, together with extensive clinical experience, Gill Westland cogently makes the case for psychotherapists to attend to the much neglected non-verbal domain as an essential aspect of the therapeutic process. I highly recommend this informative and accessible book, which should be read by both trainee and experienced practitioners."

—**Patrick Nolan**, The Irish Institute for Integrative
Psychotherapy, author of *Therapist and Client:*
A Relational Approach to Psychotherapy

"Gill Westland's book is an excellent introduction to contemporary individual psychotherapy, based on a solid, refined, and informed clinical experience in body psychotherapy. Westland leaves aside traditional rivalries between schools and modalities to convincingly show that verbal and body techniques are necessarily complementary and interdependent regulation systems. Any reader will find this clear description of practical psychotherapeutic issues highly instructive, and seasoned psychotherapists will refine their perception of how they interact with patients by reading this book."

—**Michael Heller**, author of *Body Psychotherapy:*
History, Concepts & Methods

A Norton Professional Book

VERBAL AND NON-VERBAL COMMUNICATION IN PSYCHOTHERAPY

GILL WESTLAND

W.W. Norton & Company
New York • London

For information about permission to reproduce selections from this book,
write to Permissions, W. W. Norton & Company, Inc.,
500 Fifth Avenue, New York, NY 10110

For information about special discounts for bulk purchases, please contact
W. W. Norton Special Sales at specialsales@wwnorton.com or 800-233-4830

Manufacturing by Maple Press
Production manager: Christine Critelli

ISBN: 978-0-393-70924-7

W. W. Norton & Company, Inc.
500 Fifth Avenue, New York, N.Y. 10110
www.wwnorton.com

W. W. Norton & Company Ltd.
Castle House, 75/76 Wells Street, London W1T 3QT

1 2 3 4 5 6 7 8 9 0

For my mother and late father,
with love

CONTENTS

PREFACE

For more than 30 years I have worked as a body psychotherapist, but I never set out to be one. It was through a series of meetings with significant people that I gradually became a psychotherapist. Individuals came at timely moments and awakened parts of me, which then opened up new possibilities, leading to outer changes.

After university, I trained as an occupational therapist. In my first job, one of my duties was to run relaxation groups for patients on the acute admission wards. To my dismay, patients did not feel calmer at the end of the sessions, as I had been taught they would. I was using a well-respected physiotherapy method, but briskly commanding someone to relax did not intuitively feel right to me. So I started asking the patients what they thought would help. They told me, "Well, if I sit up, rather than lie down, I might feel less vulnerable." "If I lie down, I feel more solid with my knees bent and my feet flat on the ground. The horrible feeling of ice in my chest also lessens." I learned to value their experiences more than the techniques and to work collaboratively with them.

Over time I developed relaxation groups that included slow stretching exercises, different relaxation methods, and patients choosing the positioning that suited them best. After each phase of the session, I asked them to reflect on their experiences and to give feedback to others. They told me what practices seemed to help and what seemed to make them feel worse. Working with this patient feedback, the relaxation groups began to improve. I learned to match what the patients said about themselves with what I observed in their bodies. If they felt less anxious, they would look less stiff and breathe more slowly.

Later, colleagues and I developed these ideas further into a training manual for relaxation group trainers working with patients in primary health care in the National Health Service (Westland, 1985; Howell & Whitehead, 1988). Patients reduced their use of tranquilizers and tobacco, and gained insight into their problems as well as hope, companionship, and reassurance (Kapila & Dixon, 1987). I think of this now as short- term group body psychotherapy.

At a conference I met Rita Maag, a biodynamic (body) psychotherapist who was presenting a bioenergetics workshop, a form of body psychotherapy (Lowen, 1975). Drawing on body psychotherapy, she could tell me why some people feel worse with standard relaxation techniques. My curiosity was stimulated, and I started training in biodynamic psychotherapy (Boyesen, 1980; Southwell, 1988). Biodynamic psychotherapy emphasizes implicit processes— experiencing, sensing, bodily processes, and feelings. During my training, I spent many hours learning how to "be with" fellow students as we participated in the highly experiential training. This was in stark contrast to making interventions and using techniques on clients. Nevertheless, learning was also going on explicitly, and both forms of learning were valuable. A major part of relating through "being with" another was learning how to become more embodied. That meant learning how to become aware of our own body sensations and how they changed with different thoughts, feelings, and movements, when alone or with others.

In the 1970s and early 1980s, when I was undergoing my training, psychotherapy was much more divided than it is today. Mainstream medicine, psychiatry, and psychoanalysis privileged top-down approaches, which stress the functions of reason, thinking, and talking. However, I was exposed to a variety of different psychotherapies, including bottom-up approaches that emphasize body-based sensory and emotional experiences, moderating levels of excitement, and physical movements as the route to change. No single approach seemed to have all of the answers. My understanding of different approaches and their contribution was helped by Ken Wilber's (1979) book, which put forward a map of how different psychotherapies are located in a "spectrum of consciousness." Each psychotherapy functions within a part of the spectrum and contributes in its particular spheres of consciousness.

During my training, I moved to Cambridge, UK to work in social therapy in psychiatry with David H. Clark (1964, 1981). He had a reputation for employing staff who questioned him and each other. His patients had mostly been diagnosed with schizophrenia and had severe problems. I readily joined with nurses, psychologists, and music, art, and drama therapists and others to run therapeutic groups for these patients. Once more I was challenged with how to relate to the patients and to find out what helped by asking them, and treating them as human beings rather than labels. It involved taking risks and being experimental without doing harm. In this context, I was able not only to bring different parts of myself together but also to integrate bottom-up methods into top-down mainstream thinking.

I duly finished my training and, somewhat sadly, I left the National Health Service when more hierarchical management styles were introduced after government changes. I moved on to develop a private psychotherapy practice. Alongside this I had two babies, and when visiting the United States was delighted to discover the pediatrician T. Berry Brazelton (1983) on morning TV. Brazelton clearly knew how to relate to babies and understood their individual differences. I recognized that elements of what he was doing with babies were very similar to my work with adult clients. He spoke softly and handled them sensitively. He read subtle changes in their bodies and especially in the autonomic nervous system, the body's regulatory system. He used these non-verbal communications to give each baby time to respond and to adjust to an interaction before starting another one.

In due course I became a trainer, supervisor, and consultant for the Chiron Centre for Body Psychotherapy (CCBP) in London. I enjoyed being in on the first 15 years of this newly formed center and guided it into membership in what became the UK Council for Psychotherapy (UKCP). UKCP regulates psychotherapy in the United Kingdom and the CCBP membership helped to establish body psychotherapy as a recognized profession in the UK. I also brought together the elements of the training into the center's first formal training manual, a step toward making what we were teaching accessible to a wider audience. My psychotherapy practice in Cambridge flourished and colleagues came to join me at Cambridge Body Psychotherapy Centre (CBPC). In parallel with our clinical work, we started a body psychotherapy training program, which duly became recognized by UKCP. Our latest achievement has been setting up the first body psychotherapy master's degree program in Europe. Now body psychotherapists are studying alongside students of psychodrama, music therapy, and drama therapy, providing opportunities for yet more dialogue and learning.

Behind any book there is a great deal of help and encouragement. I would like to express appreciation to Babette Rothschild for her encouragement to write the book in the first place. I would like to thank my editor at Norton, Deborah Malmud, who kindly and incisively guided me in improving the original drafts. I would also like to thank all of the staff at Norton involved in this book. They have been consistently warm, efficient, and courteous.

I would particularly like to acknowledge the support that I have had from my meditation sitting group, and the opportunities for discussion and learning from colleagues in the creative therapies group over many years. I would like to thank colleagues in the body psychotherapy profession and especially those at CBPC, CCBP and the London School of Biodynamic Psychotherapy, and the wider field within the European Association for Body Psychotherapy. At CBPC, Brett Walwyn, Sue Frazer, Alastair McNeilage, and Miriam Ware have lightened the load with their warm encouragement.

I am grateful for the learning gained from my individual psychotherapists and all of my psychotherapy trainers from different traditions. They have passed on their ways of being with people and provide a continuous thread back to their teachers. I would especially like to appreciate the late Dr. Johanna Brieger, the late Ian Gordon-Brown, Bernd Eiden, Jochen Lude, Rainer Pervöltz, Maura Forrester-Sills, and Franklyn Sills. I have learned enormously from clients, students, and my supervisors, and without them there would be no book. I would like to thank Janet Croft, Jane Frances, Ned Henderson, and Heather Reeves for their generosity in reading the manuscript and giving such detailed feedback. I am grateful for the diagrams done by Mary Hays. I would like to thank Clover Southwell for the many hours of sharing her wisdom and patiently responding to my many questions. Last, but not least, I would like to appreciate my husband, Richard, whose enduring love has kept me going, and our children, Tom and Holly, who have read parts of the manuscript and have been encouraging with their comments.

Verbal and Non-Verbal Communication in Psychotherapy

INTRODUCTION

SETTING THE SCENE

Words are powerful and the way that they are spoken can feel like a slap in the face, or like a gentle breeze inviting us to say more. As I was planning this book, I recalled an incident from childhood, when I was about 6 years old, that illustrates this. The names have been changed to protect confidentiality.

Douglas, a boy in my class, had some sort of problem. He rarely spoke, and mostly he sat by himself. Each morning, to take attendance, our teacher called our names and we replied, "Yes, Miss Duquemin" (an unusual name pronounced "duck-min"). When she called Douglas's name there was silence. One morning, Douglas surprised us all. "Yes, Miss D . . . D . . . Ducky . . . min," he stuttered quietly. This was significant because he had never responded before. Miss Duquemin could have recognized his achievement and been encouraging. She could have benignly corrected his pronunciation. Either of these responses would have appreciated Douglas and invited him to speak again at attendance time. Instead Miss Duquemin misconstrued his attempts at speaking. She glared at him and said sharply, "What did you say?" We all gasped. Douglas was not making fun of her and her unusual name. He just wasn't used to speaking and simply found her name difficult to say. Douglas looked frightened and confused. He never spoke again at attendance and not long after he was moved to a special school.

In psychotherapy, non-verbal communication such as Miss

1

Duquemin's glare and the sharp intonation in her voice goes on alongside the more obvious verbal dialogue in therapeutic interactions. When psychotherapists notice both their own and the client's verbal and non-verbal communication, fuller communication is going on. This book is especially about non-verbal communication. I explain what it is, how it works, and why paying attention to non-verbal communication, as well as verbal communication, is essential in psychotherapy. I discuss the roots in childhood of established patterns of non-verbal communication and offer ways in which psychotherapists can select and use non-verbal communication, as well as spoken language, to welcome and respond to clients' non-verbal communications.

The body is the source of non-verbal communication—a distracted gaze and slumped shoulders, a lively look in the eyes, or animated hand gestures. We can all see and come to understand this kind of communication through learning how to read our internal body sensations (including our intuitions) and couple them with our observations. This book provides grounding in and theoretical understanding of this non-verbal, bodily aspect of communication. I describe how to relate—at will, to a full spectrum of communications, non-verbal and verbal—and how to develop confidence in being intuitive, creative, and safe in interactions with clients.

VERBAL AND NON-VERBAL COMMUNICATION

Verbal and non-verbal communication are usually defined in polar opposition to each other, but they are closely enmeshed. Most communication happens non-verbally: about 90% is non-verbal and only 10% is verbal (McGilchrist, 2009a). Cognitive psychologists describe verbal and non-verbal communication as explicit and implicit communication. Explicit communication is conveyed in spoken language, whereas implicit communication is conveyed physically and not symbolized in words. Non-verbal communication includes the way in which verbal messages are delivered, but it goes far beyond this and includes a wide range of communications expressed by the body. Messages are carried in postures and movements (for example, stiff shoulders and heavy gait), gestures, facial expressions (lively and alert, dull and immobile), self and other touching, gazing, and personal mannerisms. Non-verbal communication includes changes in breathing (slow, irregular, fast), changes in skin color and hue (for example, blushing or turning pale), and involuntary movements such as shivering with cold, fatigue, or fear. The body is essential to non-verbal communication, and being able to see clients is important. If we cannot see the look in a person's eyes, the strain in his face, or the tightly folded arms and crossed legs, we cannot see that he is afraid and respond therapeutically.

Non-verbal communication also includes the way people speak, how loudly and fast they speak, their tone of voice, which words or phrases they emphasize, and where they pause and how long the pauses last. Spoken words—verbal communication—provide information and content, but the way the words are spoken carries their emotional meaning. This background communication of emotions non-verbally is called paralanguage. Paralanguage includes sounds such as ums, ahs, sniffs, sighs, gasps, shrieks, and nonsense babble. These sounds convey emotions in their intonation, pitch, and rhythms.

Words themselves make different sounds, and the choice of particular words is significant. Some words sound more harsh, others softer. Vowel sounds are softer than consonants, which are more clipped and sharp in the English language. We "wake up" with harder words such as *crash* and *crunch*; we become more mellow with words like *soak* and *wallow*. So spoken words carry content, but their form, how words are spoken, conveys emotional meaning. Indeed, "how a person speaks says as much, if not more, than *what they say*" (Pally, 2001, p. 71, emphasis added). It is the combination of the choice of words with the range of verbal and non-verbal elements that provides the personal qualities of communication.

Underpinning verbal and non-verbal communication is the general sense of someone's liveliness. This liveliness is conveyed by the way someone speaks, her general demeanor, and the silences that she leaves between words. This overall subjective impression of a person is captured in terms such as "dynamic forms of vitality" (Stern, 2010), "orgone energy" (Reich, 1970), and "life energy" (Boadella, 1987). Non-verbal communication conveys feelings, but it also helps regulate the body's physiology (Cannon, 1927; Reich, 1983; Stern, 1985; Schore, 1994; Trevarthen, 2003). Physiological and emotional regulation are closely linked and so physiological regulation also regulates feelings—amplifying or dampening them

3

down. Thumping the desk while breathing out and swearing discharges and controls anger; stroking one's hair and breathing out quiets anxiety.

A familiar scenario that illustrates non-verbal communication is when a client walks into the consulting room. The drooped shoulders, slow movements, gray and puffy face, dull eyes, and obvious low vitality alert us to possible depression. As the client speaks slow, whispered words, interspersed with long pauses, and sighs, she tells us without saying it: "I am depressed."

Although verbal communications account for far less than non-verbal ones in communication, Western society privileges the verbal over the non-verbal. Psychotherapy exists in this cultural context with a "hierarchy of knowledge" that regards verbal, objective, and rational knowledge as superior to intuitive, subjective, and unarticulated knowledge (Boyce-Tillman, 2005). Scherer observes:

> Therapy in clinical settings has continued to focus on the verbal rather than the non-verbal. There are many reasons for the continued prevalence of the verbal in therapy, including the intellectual influence of psychoanalysis and cognitive therapies, the ease of obtaining verbal reports, the need to classify behaviors and feelings into semantic categories, and the amount of effort and time required to observe and interpret non-verbal behavior. (2003, p. v)

Different psychotherapies have privileged either verbal or non-verbal forms of communication. Psychoanalysis has focused on the spoken word in the "talking cure," bringing the unconscious into consciousness, and gaining insight through interpreting transference. Body psychotherapies, creative arts psychotherapies, and humanistic psychotherapies have emphasized the non-verbal and finding forms to communicate it directly. These non-verbal communications occur through movements, sounds, music, or drawing. These psychotherapies have not always looked for ways of symbolizing and interpreting the non-verbal processes in words, in the belief that the verbal and non-verbal are not simply interchangeable. Body psychotherapies, in particular, have emphasized change happening in clients through learning new ways of regulating their emotions and their basic physiology with subsequent reorganization of the physical body. The changing trend across psychotherapies is toward integrating non-verbal and verbal approaches. In practice, of course, both forms of communication always occur. Taking heed of both broadens clinical expertise and what can be offered to clients.

UNDERLYING ASSUMPTIONS IN FULL-SPECTRUM COMMUNICATION

The approach that I am describing makes some assumptions. First, as we and our non-verbal processes are continuously changing, a *process approach* is called for, which emphasizes the subjective experiences of both client and therapist as they are happening moment by moment. These subjective experiences take precedence over techniques and theory in the therapeutic process. Figure I.1 shows the key elements of a non-verbal approach to psychotherapy.

During the therapeutic process, it is assumed that the therapist and the client influence each other continually and non-verbally. Psychotherapy is a two-person, intersubjective process in which the therapeutic relationship is jointly created and collaborative. When we relate collaboratively, we put ourselves alongside the client's subjective experiences. We are responsive to our client's communications, and clients respond to our communications. Metaphorically this takes the form of an improvised dance. In the dance there are times of one following and one leading, and times of moving together with no obvious lead, and no certainty about who initiates the next part of the dance. In the dancing, the momentum of the dance carries both of us along (Marks-Tarlow, 2013).

The therapist uses mindfulness practices, taken from Buddhist psychology, to develop sensitivity to bodily sensations and to develop the skills of detailed observation of clients. Mindfulness enables therapists to multitask—to relate to clients' thinking and the content of their sentences and to concurrently relate to the plethora of non-verbal processes going on in any moment. Having a mindful way of being lets clients know (non-verbally and nonconsciously) that we are receptive and inviting of them.

Another underlying assumption is a bodymind perspective, following Reich (1970, 1983), who assumed a functional identity between psychological and physical processes. Mind and body are not separate. Non-verbal communication is expressed and received by the body, both the therapist's body and the client's body. "Clinicians cannot afford to ignore the body—neither their patient's nor their own—because the body often receives and transmits what has not or cannot be put into words" (Wallin, 2007, p. 130). The therapist's stance is not only mindful and receptive, but also embodied. Non-verbal relating has to involve embodied relating. This entails having a subjective sense of the self as a living process and experiencing it through body sensations. Our thoughts, feelings, imaginings, and movements all arise in the body and have accompanying physical sensations. The way that these different parts of ourselves connect up gives us a different sense of ourselves. If we are tense, our movements will be restricted and our feelings limited in range. If we are more relaxed, we are likely to feel more at peace with ourselves.

A non-verbal approach makes emotional and physiological regulation central. Breathing is part of this regulation. Our breathing changes when we are by ourselves or with others. Breathing changes simply through noticing it. These changes happen without us controlling our responses. They are an automatic physiological response to focusing our attention on our breathing. Changes in a client's breathing, taken together with other observable physiological responses, such as the face flushing with embarrassment or the skin having goose bumps, tell us about our relationship with the client and how to pace the therapeutic process.

The way that therapists speak to clients is significant in non-verbal communication. Challenging statements can be said in a neutral tone of voice so that clients can hear what is said without protest. The words, "You are late. What happened?" said irritably, may feel critical. This may lead to the client merely justifying the lateness. The same words spoken with a curious tone of voice are likely to lead to a discussion and the unearthing of new information. Similarly, observing the way that a client is talking to us gives us guidance on how to proceed. Some clients, for example, do not pause between sentences. A way to help them is for us to ask about how they are feeling as they are speaking. Perhaps these clients feel as if their words are in control of them. It can be a revelation to discover that it is possible to pause, breathe in more fully, and then to continue speaking, and that this brings some relief.

Touch plays a key role in non-verbal communication for some clients. A kind touch can express more than words can say. Touch can also be a rapid way of bringing frightened clients into a calmer state. Sometimes touch communication is not appropriate. Then movements, sounds, and the use of creative media such as art (for example, drawing, painting) improvised dance, and music may be used by clients for self-expression. These non-verbal expressions of inner experiences stand in their own right as a form of communication. However, for some clients the use of creative media will be a route to finding words for their experiences.

The final underlying assumption is that psychotherapy is not only about the reduction of the symptoms that clients bring to us. The loss of symptoms is not to be underestimated, given the difficulties that many clients have with merely existing from day to day. However, no matter how traumatic someone's childhood or adult experiences, there is always in each of us "an organic impulse to heal, which can be experienced phenomenologically and that moves towards increased complexity and wholeness" (Johanson, 2014, p. 68). This force has been given different names, such as inherent health, essential self, or simply the life force, by different authors over the years. The term coined by Fosha for this innate impulse is *transformance*, which she describes as "the overarching motivation for transformation that pulses within us. . . . Innate dispositional tendencies toward growth, learning, healing, and self righting are wired deep within our brains and press towards expression when circumstances are right" (2009, p. 174).

So always in company with energy-draining symptoms is the vitalizing and healing life force. As symptoms begin to subside (and often before), the healing force, which has been obscured, reveals itself more fully. Our task is "to help our clients connect, or reconnect, with their own worthiness, their brilliant sanity" (Wegela, 2014, p. 5). *Brilliant sanity* is another term for inherent health. When clients are in touch with their life force, they come to know their inner capacities and resources. The life force is self-directing, and the process of healing is nonlinear and self-organizing (Capra, 1996; Maturana & Varela, 1987; Wilber, 1995). During the therapeutic process, we hope that our clients come to live life with more ease and with fewer symptoms, but also flourish, use their innate potential, and have more freedom.

The Therapist

Talking to the nonverbal
Choice of words
Level of consciousness
Content vs. process

Embodied relating
Contact
Intention
Mindfulness
Presence
Left-brain or
   right-brain
   based

**Verbal and
Non-Verbal
Communication**

**Expressive
media**
Art
Dance
Music

**Observing, relating to,
   and regulating**
Feelings
Autonomic nervous
   system responses
Energy/vitality

Touch

The Therapist and the Client

FIGURE INTRODUCTION.1 SUMMARY OF THE ELEMENTS OF A
NON-VERBAL APPROACH TO PSYCHOTHERAPY SHOWING WHAT THE
THERAPIST DOES, AND WHAT BOTH THERAPIST AND CLIENT DO.
THE TWO BUBBLES ABOVE THE CENTRAL "VERBAL AND NON-VERBAL
COMMUNICATION" ONE INDICATE WHAT THE THERAPIST DOES, THOSE
BELOW THE CENTRAL BUBBLE INDICATE WHAT BOTH THERAPIST AND
CLIENT DO.

CHANGES IN PSYCHOTHERAPY
AND THE CONTRIBUTION OF THIS BOOK

Over the last 40 years, psychotherapy has changed enormously. Changes have been driven by rapid developments in technology, new findings from neuroscience filtering through to psychotherapy practice, the interest of cognitive neuroscience in studying emotions, new information about trauma and retraumatization, and infant development studies. All of these studies have contributed to a better understanding of psychotherapeutic relationships, and especially the importance of non-verbal communication between therapists and their clients. We have come a long way from Freud's talking cure. As knowledge has expanded, it has brought into question long-held ways of philosophical thinking. The Cartesian mind-body split has been brought into question, and Schore (2012) has observed that we are in the process of what Kuhn (1970) would call a paradigm shift in psychotherapy.

Dialogue among disciplines is in vogue. Infant researchers are in dialogue with psychoanalytic psychotherapy; psychotherapies generally are in dialogue with neuroscience; body psychotherapy communicates with relational psychoanalysis; and experts in trauma are discussing across the range of psychotherapy modalities. As the limitations and gaps of particular psychotherapies are identified, it becomes possible for different disciplines to grapple with common problems in clinical work as never before. Accepting the shortcomings of a particular psychotherapy is not letting that side down. It opens the door for development and collaboration with others.

Central to this dialogue are studies of the brain and neuroscience. These studies provide an empirical basis for claims about non-verbal communication and provide a theoretical foundation for the development of theories of non-verbal communication. Where traditional psychotherapy, based on verbal communication, can raise skepticism and doubt about the objectivity of non-verbal communication, brain studies have shown that much of our psychological life takes place at a non-verbal level. The most significant change taking place in modern psychotherapy is the recognition that knowledge of the brain and body in relation to emotions and non-verbal experience is an essential aspect of the therapeutic process (Schore, 1994, 2012; Siegel, 1999, 2010). The work of forgotten analysts such as Sandor Ferenczi and Wilhelm Reich, who fell foul of verbal communication orthodoxy, is being revisited; their work on non-verbal communication is being re-evaluated; and some of their theories and practices are being incorporated into psychotherapy.

Sometimes dialogue and integration are happening in surprising places. Bringing the non-verbal practice of mindfulness to cognitive-behavioral therapy for the treatment of depression (Segal, Williams, & Teasdale, 2002) has been groundbreaking. The mindfulness dialogue has brought non-verbally focused practitioners such as contemplative psychotherapists and meditation and yoga teachers into the discussion. Steadily, psychotherapists are reaching out to others and expanding the "spectrum of consciousness" in which they work.

NEUROSCIENCE

Studies in neuroscience are making an impact on the theory and practice of psychotherapy. It is now well established that the left side of the brain functions rather differently from the right side of the brain. The former plays a larger role in language use and analytical thought, while the right side is more closely involved with emotional life and the body. It is in the right brain that non-verbal communication registers and originates. Some psychotherapists have used this information to reformulate psychotherapy and now speak of it as a non-verbal communication between the right brain of the client and the right brain of the psychotherapist, an intermingling and rapid interaction of non-verbal communication (see, for example, Schore, 2011).

The shapes and rhythms of non-verbal communications are formed implicitly in the first months of life. These early memories are called *implicit* or *procedural* memories, in contrast to *explicit* or *declarative* memories. Implicit memories are non-verbal. They are physically encoded in patterns of muscle tension, breathing rhythms, habitual movements, and general vitality. These physical patterns carry emotions and moods. The physical patterns are explored through non-verbal ways of relating to them.

Thoughts, physical sensations, and environmental factors can trigger partial recall of past experiences (from implicit memory) in the present. The recall is shown physically in the body. An illustration of this is a client who grew up in a violent family. As I raised my hands to make a point, he flinched and ducked his head. He knew that I was not going to strike him, but his body was back in his family home. He could not will himself to react differently, and his automatic response had to be explored through non-verbal means.

In a non-verbal approach it is being with the client that is most significant:

> At the most fundamental level, the work of psychotherapy is not defined by what the therapist explicitly, objectively *does* for the patient, or *says* to the patient. Rather the key mechanism is how to implicitly and subjectively *be* with the patient, especially during affectively stressful moments when the "going on being" of the patient's implicit self is dis-integrating in real time. (Schore, 2011, pp. 94–95, emphasis in original)

In this subjective being with the client—being to being—the client experiences different responses from therapists than those they had in childhood. These different responses, repeated often and over time, bring about a rearrangement of the structures of the brain. The change process in psychotherapy becomes one in which there is deep and fundamental reorganization of physical structures, especially in the brain. As clients become physically different, they feel psychologically different and form different relationships.

Brain scans of different types can reveal how the brain changes through psychotherapy, but much still remains unknown about the moment when new organization emerges, why it happened then, and what nudged it into existence. As Maturana and Varela (1987) tell us, living systems can never be directed to change. Taking our earlier dance metaphor, we can offer a different dance, but we cannot make clients change their dance. Interestingly, what we do know is that implicit memories can be transformed without clients having their attention drawn to them or being aware of them. Change can come without conscious insight (Lyons-Ruth, 1998; Marks-Tarlow, 2013; Schore, 2011).

PREVERBAL COMMUNICATION IN INFANTS

In observational studies, films of infants with their mothers, using split screens for observing the interactions, can be slowed down to microseconds. The painstaking analysis of these films has captured details of non-verbal infant-mother interactions not obvious to the naked eye in real-time viewing. Infant researchers have discovered that babies have non-verbal communicative capacities that were only guessed at before. These studies and the understanding that they bring are showing the importance of the non-verbal aspect of clinical work with adults. Adult clients who have experienced insecure or more traumatic attachments before they have developed spoken language require therapeutic relations that can reach these non-verbal levels of experience.

FRAGILE CLIENTS

Working with verbal emphasis, deliberately increasing anxiety, and inviting fantasy into the relationship and then offering interpretations of client-therapist interactions has been recognized as wounding, retraumatizing, and "attacking" for more fragile clients (Winnicott, 1991; Rothschild, 2000; Wilkinson, 2006; Wright, 2009; Heller, 2012).

Wright explains, "patients must have a capacity to separate and stand alone if they are to use interpretation without trauma" (2009, p. 32). He describes a patient from his practice:

> [She] experienced all my interpretations as dangerous attacks: and while I saw what I was doing as an invitation to insight, she experienced me as destructively critical. At these times she would block her ears so as not to hear me. At other times, perhaps when my voice was less "hard" and explanatory, she seemed to enjoy listening to me but would then treat the content of what I said as irrelevant. (Wright, 2009, p. 32)

Wright captures the essence of the problem here. He recognized that his verbal interpretations were intrusive for the patient and that the tone of his voice, the non-verbal dimension of his speaking, was part of the solution. The question, then, was how to work non-verbally with this client.

The collective term *fragile client* was coined by Patrick Nolan (2012) for those who may be diagnosed with borderline personality disorder, post-traumatic stress disorder, narcissistic personality disorder, and those with a predisposition toward psychosis. He wanted to find a less pejorative term for those with these diagnoses. What these clients have in common is a poor sense of self. They are thin-skinned, highly vigilant, and sensitive people. At least in the early period of psychotherapy, fragile clients need to feel "held" (Winnicott, 1960/1990c) and "contained" (Bion, 1962/1984) and understood. This is mainly accomplished through non-verbal communication.

THE BODY AND EMOTION IN PSYCHOTHERAPY

As we have already noted, the source of non-verbal communication is the body. Antonio Damasio's work has challenged the old idea of separation of mind and body and his somatic marker theory places the experience of emotions firmly in the body (Damasio, 1994). Trauma studies have raised the importance of attending to the physiology of the physical body in the consulting room (van der Kolk, 1994) and understanding what it is telling us.

Those using mindfulness practices within psychotherapy have highlighted the significance not only of therapists being aware of their bodies, but also clients developing awareness of their own bodies. When the physical sensations of the body are given attention, the "greater awareness of the body" helps clients understand "how better to deal with emotion" (Segal et al., 2002, p. 110). Rustin too has recognized that "the body as a source of understanding emotion is underutilized in mainstream clinical practice" and suggests that for some patients, "alerting them to attend to their bodies' signals gives them a way of accessing their emotions when language does not suffice" (2013, p. 82).

The monitoring of non-verbal, physiological body processes is now firmly in the consulting room. Ignoring these phenomena potentially does more harm than good (for example, Rothschild, 2000). With the increasing awareness of body processes in psychotherapy has come more understanding of non-verbal interactions.

THE SHIFT TO NON-VERBAL COMMUNICATION

The focus of psychotherapy is shifting. Traditionally the implicit, non-verbal aspects of interactions have only been the backdrop to the verbal discourse. In the consulting room, non-verbal communication is coming out of the background and solidly into the foreground. Meeting clients where they are, that is, engaging with and starting from the non-verbal, becomes the way to start psychotherapy. It means identifying with the client's non-verbal communications, while keeping a sense of ourselves—not becoming so identified that we lose ourselves. It is an intuitive and right-brained way of working. It entails being with clients and attending to the fine details of their non-verbal communication.

It was the psychoanalyst Wilhelm Reich (1897-1957) who moved away from listening to the content of clients' words and toward listening to their form. He came to regard the "how" of the words as more important than what was actually said. However, he did not ignore content altogether, but let it be more in the background. Reich observed, "Words can lie. The *mode of expression never lies*" (1983, p. 171, emphasis in original). Reich pointed out that *"word language very often also functions as a defense*: the word language obscures the expressive language of the biological core" (1970, p. 362, emphasis in original). And McGilchrist is also of the opinion that "language . . . is the perfect medium for concealing rather than revealing meaning" (2009a, p. 106). In Chapter 3 you will meet Tony, whose facility with words was such a defense.

And so, Rustin suggests, "you might use yourself to respond to the patient in the implicit realm of interaction simultaneously with the verbal exchange or as its own intervention" (2013, p. 41). By giving attention to the non-verbal, the therapist can see the underlying dynamic of the client. In the intricacies of this form of relating, what is impinging from within the client and pressing for expression becomes apparent (Boyesen, 1976). This drives the therapeutic process.

It can be daunting for therapists to know how to be with clients and not know where the interactions might lead. Mindfulness and awareness practices such as learning to be aware of our breathing enable us to anchor ourselves more solidly in our physical being and our subjective experiences. These are the basic skills for being with clients. Experiencing the bodily *tones* "bodily shade" of experiences through mindfulness fosters embodiment and integrates thinking, feeling, and acting. In this book we will learn how being embodied makes it possible to linger in moments of not knowing, moments when conceptually we do not know what is happening. These are moments to relate being to being, right brain to right brain, and are meaningful for clients as they tend to know if we are with them at a being level or not.

Each psychotherapy relationship and therapeutic process is unique. Giving attention to non-verbal communication enables psychotherapists to adapt their style for a tailor-made approach, rather than supposing that one size fits all. A tailor-made approach permits more spontaneity and has less surety. Starting from the uniqueness of each therapeutic relationship enables therapists to discuss with other professionals what they are actually doing, rather than what they think they should be doing to maintain orthodoxy.

This book is about non-verbal communication and yet, paradoxically, the book itself is in verbal form. Numerous exercises are presented to illustrate and teach the methods of non-verbal communication, and much can be learned in this way. But, as with all skills, these skills are most effectively learned with the aid of a teacher.

ABOUT THIS BOOK

I have assumed that the reader has no prior knowledge of any of the subject areas that are covered. Familiar terms in one form of psychotherapy are not necessarily known in others, and different authors use different terminology for roughly similar concepts. Technical terms and the vocabulary of specialized areas are explained in a straightforward way. I hope that this will encourage readers to research beyond their original training and draw inspiration from other perspectives.

I have written in a style that is intended to be evocative, inviting of subjective experience and embodied connection with the content. As in this chapter, I often start with an anecdote or a clinical vignette written in italics, attempting to take the reader into a more sensory relationship with the written word. I suggest that as you read the clinical vignettes that you notice your non-verbal responses to the text, as well as your thoughts and opinions. These clinical vignettes are composites. Often I have given the generally used term, but also offer an alternative that invites more personal connection with the topic to bring it "experience-near" (Kernberg, 1975/2004). Infant studies, for example, refer to babies as infants and have specific thinking about infants, but where possible, without obscuring the meaning, I write of babies or "the little one." The latter language is more suited to the consulting room.

Finding a language for non-verbal processes is not easy. I have stayed with the terms *verbal* and *non-verbal communication*, as communication is widely thought of in these ways. However, I agree with those who dislike this oppositional pairing of the non-verbal with the verbal, and the polarized thinking that it engenders (for example, Carroll, 2011), but to date I have found no satisfactory alternative. *Procedural process*, a term being used more frequently for non-verbal processes, does not have the right ring to it for me, although it is a step toward finding new terminology. The problem of finding new language for embodiment and the "psychotherapy body" has been discussed by Carroll (2011), and Panhofer and Payne (2011). No doubt in time new vocabulary will emerge to do justice to new ways of understanding the full spectrum of interactions within psychotherapy.

I write throughout from a bodymind perspective. The imperative to include the physicality of the body (rather than a symbolized body) in psychotherapy continues to be a theme across psychotherapy modalities. Mind and body are no longer considered separate, and the term bodymind has come into use to capture the new thinking (Totton, 2003). Sometimes I accentuate this unity of being by writing of embodied thinking, embodied emotion, embodied actions, embodied speech, and so on. Essentially I am writing about embodied relating. This draws attention to the fact that all of these processes take place within a body, the client's body or the therapist's body, and that understanding them depends on an understanding of their bodily dimensions—their embodiment. However, it would be clumsy to write *embodied* each time.

Embodied relating is not the same as thinking about the body. It is more than attempting to bolt on or add in the body as an afterthought in psychotherapy. As Totton observes, it is a "primary given," the ground of all psychotherapy (2014, p. 90). Embodied relating in psychotherapy requires a much more right-brain way of relating and requires therapists to cultivate a relationship with their own bodies through psychotherapy training and activities such as dancing, walking, meditation, yoga, and so on. Embodied relating is the difference between having a body and being in a body. Being embodied is a changing process representing shifts in our level of consciousness (Clover Southwell, personal communication, 2014).

I have followed Rustin (2013) in differentiating unconscious and nonconscious. This is a distinction that cuts across the verbal and the non-verbal. I use the term *nonconscious* interchangeably with *outside of awareness*. Typically the client's non-verbal communication will be nonconscious, whereas the trained psychotherapist will be conscious of non-verbal communication. *Nonconscious* also includes *not in symbolic form*. I use *unconscious* in the Freudian sense of repressed, but also in the Jungian sense of the unconscious containing elements of unknown experience that have never been conscious. Again, these may be brought to consciousness and expressed verbally, or there may be feelings or past experiences for which the client has no words, but may be expressed in movements or drawing.

I tend to use *emotions* and *feelings* interchangeably, and *affects* to refer to both. When it aids accuracy, I write of feelings as "the private mental experience of an emotion" and emotions as "the collection of responses, many of which are publicly observable" (Damasio, 2000, p. 42). So clinically emotions are observed on the outside and feelings are experienced inside. I use the term *therapist* to denote a practitioner of any form of psychotherapy working developmentally and relationally, and probably over time and at depth. I use *client* instead of *patient* as it is more familiar in my tradition and carries more of a sense of working with another, rather than an expert imposing something on someone.

Physical Positioning, Techniques, and Theory

I assume that interactions between therapists and clients are mostly happening face to face with chairs placed at an angle, unless otherwise stated. This does not preclude the use of the couch or the mattress (the equivalent of the couch in body psycho-therapy) for some clients. What I describe is intended to be used in context and according to training and basic common sense. I am assuming flexible use of furniture and flexibility about where clients and therapists position themselves. This could mean moving chairs closer or further away, but also includes standing up and walking around, if there is space to do this. Getting out of the chair can be challenging if it has not been in the original training of a psychotherapist. For clients who are relatively more stable in themselves, moving around can be introduced quite early in the psychotherapy. Then this mobility becomes just part of the range of possibilities. Physically moving around the room and changing positions is described further in Chapter 6 in a vignette with a client called Peter.

Sometimes I describe techniques for use with clients, but the idea behind them is that what are at first technical practices become honed skills through their repeated use, in the same way that learning to drive a car becomes second nature with practice, or practicing scales enables moving music to be played. Repeated practice means that gradually "techniques" become embedded in the therapist as skills and can be inserted seamlessly into the conversation with clients without being obvious. "Skills are embodied, and therefore largely intuitive: they resist the process of explicit rule following" (McGilchrist, 2009a, p. 121). We can often introduce a technique when what is required is being with a client. When this happens, clients are likely to feel objectified and react to this. Somewhat paradoxically, clients who feel the therapist is with them may be willing to try out a technique.

Psychotherapy theories, like techniques, are helpful for thinking about psychotherapy. However, in actual therapeutic exchanges, theory can give psychotherapists the illusion of knowing what is happening and distract them from relating in a human way with their clients. Again, theorizing about clients can be another way of objectifying them. Nevertheless, the conceptual knowledge of theory can give therapists the confidence that they know what is happening. This confidence enables them to put the theory aside and experience what is actually happening.

The ways of working that I describe may be unfamiliar to some readers, and some ways of working may require further training, but hopefully they point to possibilities for further investigation and development.

Regularity and Length of Meetings With Clients

I am assuming that therapists are meeting with their clients on the same day and at the same time each week. This does not preclude more frequent meetings for some clients. Regularity is important for building the reliability of the relationship. I am assuming that meetings are for one hour. Sixty-minute hours are more suited to a non-verbal approach. This gives clients time to slow down and adjust from verbal, social ways of relating to a more non-verbal subjective experience of themselves, and then, toward the end of the session, preparing for everyday relating once they leave the session. Shorter sessions keep the therapeutic process more conceptual. However, what is important is to find the session length best suited to each client (Braatøy, 1954), within the limitations of our diaries and livelihood and then to be consistent with it.

Usually weekly meetings are sufficient for many clients as non-verbal, embodied relating reaches them at a physiological, more fundamental neurological (nonconscious) level of their experience. This is what implicitly gives clients holding and containment. In a non-verbally focused psychotherapy, clients also require time in between sessions to physiologically "digest" the therapeutic process before being stimulated by further therapeutic interactions.

I recommend leaving gaps—of perhaps 15 minutes—between clients to briefly "let the previous client go" and to prepare for the next client using some of the awareness practices described in Chapter 3, which takes us into sensory experience and readiness for clients. Using gaps for awareness practices also builds our resilience, preventing burnout.

Widening the Repertoire

My hope is that this book will broaden the repertoire of different clinicians across modalities and offer additional ways of thinking about clinical work. The emphasis is on relating to non-verbal, bodily, emotional, physiological, implicit processes, which can be characterized as what Schore (2012) calls a right-brain-to-right-brain interactive approach to psychotherapy. Many books already have a verbal focus. This book is intended to supplement these books by addressing the non-verbal dimension of communication.

NON-VERBAL COMMUNICATION IN ACTION

The following is a clinical vignette, in italics, illustrating the role of non-verbal communication in a first assessment consultation. There are two participants in the non-verbal communication, the client and the therapist. I indicate the client's non-verbal communication by underlining, and the therapist's non-verbal communication by double underlining. As you read this and subsequent clinical vignettes you might try reading it with pauses every so often. In the pauses notice your feelings and any body sensations as well as any thoughts that you have. This helps with noticing different aspects of our experiences.

Caroline had e-mailed me because she was supposed to be completing a doctorate, but her writing had ground to a halt. She wanted to complete it, but she sat at her computer without inspiration and could write nothing. I liked Caroline from the start. She smiled and was friendly, but I noticed that her eyes were watchful. She was alert and a bit jumpy in her movements. Her eyes slowly scanned around as if she was checking for any threat. These body signals showed that she was fearful and did not trust her surroundings to be safe. From clinical experience, I knew these signals indicated that non-verbal communication would be important for her. She was a fragile client requiring non-verbal recognition of her alarmed state, which could come from me being with her in a right-brain-to-right-brain way. It would mean being receptive and responding to her non-verbal communications. From her particular sensitivity to me and her surroundings, I sensed that she would intuit if I was making contact with her, that is, relating to her non-verbal, subjective experience of herself. At the same time, I wanted to gather factual information to inform my clinical decision making about possible future psychotherapy with her.

I gave Caroline clear instructions on where she should sit and where I would sit. I reminded her of the length of our meeting, that it was intended to find out more about her and then to discuss possible psychotherapy together. This start created predictability, part of feeling safe. I kept my movements predictable as well and without too many gestures. I spoke more slowly than usual and adjusted to her pace of taking in information. She was quick to understand what I said, but I saw that she looked ready to flee with a slight pulling away in her shoulders, when I spoke. I gave her time to register that my words were not an attack. I continued when her shoulders eased.

*In a first consultation, I assume that the newness of the situation will be somewhat threatening, and it shows me how a potential new client responds to this. Caroline's sensitivity and physical responses indicated to me that something unusually frightening had happened to her. I deliberately collected factual information at first such as how old she was, her address, her occupation, living situation, and so on. This engaged Caroline's thinking (left brain), rather than her feelings. It reduced her anxiety and gave her time to adapt to the consulting room and myself. I could see that she was more comfortable in the room, when she leaned back in the chair and her speech became somewhat slower. We moved into talking about her doctorate. At first she told me the topic, and her deadline and factual information. Her speech was not emotionally laden until she talked about struggling to complete her PhD. As she did this she slowed her words. Our interaction had deepened emotionally and more of the non-verbal dimension was coming to the fore. I asked her about the **experience** of writing. "I can't stop thinking about it. I'm tired and can't sleep. I'm feeling bad about myself. I don't know why I can't just get on with it."*

She deepened into her emotional experience and put it into her words when she spontaneously said, "I don't know why I'm doing it anymore." Academic achievement was her parents', and especially her mother's, idea. Caroline had always found it easy to study and do well until now. She looked more distressed. Her upper lip trembled and her face reddened as her feelings rose up. Her speech became faster as she began thinking about why it was so hard to do what she had always been able to do. I saw this as her way of regulating her feelings that were coming up. Thinking about herself reduced the tremble of the lip.

I kept myself calm by being aware of my breathing and making sure that I was breathing fully (not breath holding), and lengthening my out breath from time to time. My calmness non-verbally communicated to Caroline and enabled her to go on. I continued to use Caroline's signals (e.g., feelings welling up) to pace our interactions. I paused in speaking at times to give Caroline time to be ready for another comment or question from me. I made none of this explicit to Caroline.

Our conversation shifted gear again, when Caroline said, "I feel lost." Tears spilled from the corners of her eyes and trickled down her cheeks. She lost some of her alertness and breathed more easily. She continued, "I don't know why I'm crying. . . . I don't know what I want anymore. . . . It was always so mapped out before . . ." I sat silently with her and sensed how frightening it was to feel lost. She looked much younger than her 20-some years. These words were the most significant of the whole session. Here Caroline's words and her feelings were congruent. They encapsulated her problem. Who was she, if not someone on the verge of a lifelong academic career?

HOW THE BOOK DEVELOPS

In this chapter I have set the scene for subsequent chapters. I have outlined developments in psychotherapy and the trend toward bringing non-verbal processes into the foreground. Chapters 1 and 2 provide the theoretical underpinning for working non-verbally. Chapter 3 develops theory, but is mostly about theory in practice. Subsequent chapters all build on the previous ones in layers. It is assumed that the content of earlier chapters is being applied to the clinical examples as a specific angle is emphasized in each one.

Chapter 1 describes the neurological underpinnings of communication. The basic structures and functions of different parts of the nervous system are described in a simplified way. The differences between the left and right hemispheres of the brain in verbal and non-verbal communication are discussed. "Top-down" and "bottom-up" processing—the higher functions of the cerebral cortex and subcortical instinctual structures interacting together—are considered. The role of the amygdala, the prefrontal cortex, and the autonomic nervous system in emotional processing are discussed. The discussion on mirror neurons sheds light on somatic resonance. Understanding from this chapter is applied with clients so that we can consider whether a client requires a more spontaneous emotional response from us or an explanation about something.

Chapter 2 describes how different views of babies affect child care, developments in the understanding of babies through observation, and the elaboration of attachment theories (correlated with character strategies). Infant communication from conception onward is described, along with the importance of face-to-face interactions. Self-regulation and soothing, infant cycles of activity related to levels of consciousness, and the "mixed blessing" of the development of spoken language are discussed. The importance of preverbal experiences (implicit processes) and the development of signature patterns of relating and future psychological problems are highlighted.

Chapter 3 describes cultivating the skills for being with and staying in states of not knowing with clients through mindfulness and awareness practices. Awareness practices are discussed for monitoring over- and underinvolvement, merging and separating, and being interconnected with clients. Therapeutic presence, intention, and adapting presence for particular therapeutic purposes are discussed. This includes adapting psychic (energetic) space for "short rein" or "long rein" relational holding, working with different levels of consciousness implicitly or overtly, and reflecting on the qualities of clarity, compassion, and spaciousness to guide the therapeutic process. The messages conveyed subliminally to clients by the consultation room and how to use furniture and furnishings with particular intent are considered. Contact, resonance, and meeting clients where they are (implicitly) are described, alongside themes of somatic resonance and reaction (somatic transference and countertransference), and attunement and misattunement. The Brahmaviharas with their interconnected inherent qualities of compassion, loving-kindness, joy, and equanimity are discussed as qualities to cultivate in the therapeutic process.

Chapter 4 discusses Western culture's privileging of verbal over non-verbal communications. Body, speech, and mind inquiry, drawn from contemplative psychotherapy, is introduced as a descriptive way of observing and thinking about the verbal and non-verbal communications of clients. "Dead" and alive words are discussed, along with words as defense and the significance of the "charged word." How psychotherapists can use spoken language to relate more to clients' left or right brains are considered. Using words that are not too usual or unusual is discussed, as well as using concrete, metaphorical, and poetic language. Masculine and feminine language is also considered. The chapter goes on to describe how to use the rhythm of words and sentences—tone, pitch, pauses, speed, emphasis, and linking words, gestures, gaze, presence, and sense of space for different therapeutic purposes, and especially how to keep clients in a "live streamed" flow of expressive words. Consideration is given to situations in which the therapist's words and gaze can be received as an attack. A discussion of communicating with clients to deepen emotional connection or reducing emotional overload is opened up in preparation for a more detailed discussion in Chapter 5.

Chapter 5 expands on the themes of Chapter 4 with discussion on therapeutic interactions considered in terms of breathing cycles. The four stages of the breathing cycle are used to describe the rhythmic nature of the therapeutic process as two individuals breathing separately and together. Each stage of the breathing cycle is considered, along with the detailed processes within therapists when they are speaking, after speaking, when listening to the client, and when the client has finished speaking. There is discussion on the breathing "signatures" clients develop in early insecure and traumatic attachments. Embodied language, pausing, timing, and pacing are considered. The chapter describes how clients can be taught both verbally and non-verbally to reflect on their own experiences of the different phases of the breathing cycle, including in interactions with the therapist. The intersubjective nature of these cycles is described.

The chapter then moves into ways of recognizing the nature of the unfolding relationship—flowing, disjointed (attuned or misattuned)—by observing breath and body language. Misattunements are discussed as inevitable, and ways of recognizing, exploring, meeting, soothing, and mending them are discussed.

Chapter 6 focuses on how to be with emotions and how to work with clients ranging from those who are emotionally overwhelmed to those lacking emotional expression. It discusses how to modify presence to communicate with particular levels of consciousness in clients. Tuning into the language and rhythms of clients and then shaping their "tune" by introducing different rhythms in a spontaneous improvisation is presented and elaborated on, with considerations about whether amplification or damping down of feeling is called for. How therapists can work with highly charged emotions and contain their own feelings is discussed and the importance of grounding, centering, and boundaries for both clients and therapists alike.

Emotions are described as energetic, physiological, and embodied movements, which are entwined with the autonomic nervous system. The metaphor of emotions flowing within a "river of life" is introduced, along with clients lacking emotional expression and being physically overbound (overcontained) or being excessively emotionally expressive and underbound (undercontained). The chapter discusses how a lack of a sense of self can be linked to lack of boundaries and being over- or underbound. The importance of recognizing the level of excitement and stress in clients, how to reduce the intensity of more stimulating, and sometimes disturbing physiological up-going (arousing) processes by making intentions explicit, naming experiences, using furniture and the physical positioning of therapists and clients, and using the body as a resource is discussed. The chapter also describes how clients can learn to expand their range of emotional expression and how they can learn to recognize authentic emotional responses in words and action (embodied speech).

Chapter 7 discusses free association of the body. It picks up on themes from Chapter 6, especially deepening into emotional expression. Obvious communications from clients, such as posture, gaze, and gesture, and then more subtle ones, are described. The use of "It and I language" by therapists is discussed at different phases of interactions. This also includes the use of paralanguage to speak to non-verbal communications. The chapter includes some caveats.

Chapter 8 discusses communication with clients through touch. Touch is the first language to develop, and impairments in attachment can affect the clients' capacities for touching and being touched. The chapter discusses the role of touch in different forms of psychotherapy. It calls for experiential training in therapeutic touch as a necessity, if touch is to be part of a therapist's repertoire. "Contactful touch," mindful touch, and intersubjective touching are discussed. Reasons to touch in psychotherapy are considered.

Chapter 9 discusses how to recognize the dominant communication modes of clients. Nolan's model of five modes of function and expression—cognition, emotion, body sensations, imagination, and motor activity—and Boadella's model of thinking/imagining, feeling, and acting are described for thinking about whole experience and fostering its development in clients. The chapter goes on to discuss how to use the client's dominant mode of communication, building on this, and then how to expand the client's range of communication possibilities. The use of creative media to bring the inside outside is discussed and its particular use with clients who have difficulties communicating through spoken language. The use of metaphors for linking thinking, somatic experiences, and feeling in a graduated manner to foster whole experience is also discussed. The conclusion speculates on the future of psychotherapy.

Chapter 1

NEUROLOGICAL FOUNDATIONS OF NON-VERBAL COMMUNICATION

A working knowledge of the basics of how the body processes information and how the brain and body work together helps us to understand our clients. It enables us to know when and how to speak, and respond to clients to encourage relatively more thinking or feeling. Neuroscience is a complex and new field and, as a psychotherapist, and not a neuroscientist, I have selected what seems useful for illuminating the practice of psychotherapy. Drawing on the evidence for the close integration of body, mind, and emotion, this chapter lays the neurological foundations for psychotherapeutic understanding and practice. For the clinician, the *function* (in simple terms) of the different parts of the nervous system is what is most important.

THE NERVOUS SYSTEM: THE SYSTEM OF COMMUNICATION

The body's main communication and control system, extending throughout the body and connecting with all of its organs, is the **nervous system**. It deals with masses of *information coming both from inside us* and *through our senses from the outside* as we relate to our environment. The nervous system has to process all of this

27

information pouring in, and respond to it swiftly for our safety and survival. Our responses to information coming in are expressed in movements of muscles and bones (the motor apparatus). "However global or imperceptible, all movement depends on the contraction of some muscle group somewhere in the body" (Greenfield, 1998, p. 41). We *receive from* and *then act on* the world. We are in constant movement.

Information processing happens in the context of various degrees of emotional and physiological excitation. This affects the relationship between the sensory information coming in and our movement outputs. If we are too excited (highly aroused), we may find it hard to focus on a task; we are easily distracted and overly sensitive in our reactions to minor occurrences. Tasks are most efficiently performed and new learning occurs when we are neither over- nor underaroused but are keeping within the middle range of arousal (Greenfield, 1998). So the task for therapists working non-verbally is to observe how (physiologically) stimulated clients are. We want some physiological arousal, but not too much. We adjust interactions with clients to keep them and us within the "window of tolerance" (Ogden, Minton, & Pain, 2006; Siegel, 1999). This might be, for example, waiting a moment longer before speaking to give a client time to become more at ease and therefore more receptive to us. There was an example of this with Caroline in the Introduction. The understanding of these states of arousal, their physical manifestations, and how they can be adjusted is an essential tool in the non-verbal engagement of therapists with their clients. This is discussed at length in subsequent chapters.

Sensory Information

Information from the world comes in through the major sensory organs for sight, taste, smell, and hearing, located in the head. The process of receiving information from the world is called *exteroception*. Seeing is important from birth onward in our relationships. Our hearing tunes into noises and then fine-tunes to listen intently and to differentiate the different sounds. The senses of smell and taste are often neglected in psychotherapy, but are significant for some clients. Traumatized clients, for example, may be particularly sensitive to smells in the consulting room (heavily perfumed flowers, a new carpet). In moments of recall they may taste and smell the past event in their telling of it. The sense of touch provides sensory information from the surface of the body through receptors in the skin. The sense of touch is actually part of a group of sensory modalities that includes vibration and temperature sense (Solms & Turnbull, 2002). All of the senses are communication channels. Clients will have preferences about the forms of communication and the sensory channels in which they receive information. Some channels may be developed more than others. For some clients, touch is their main sense channel for taking in information from the world and for feeling contact with the therapist (see Chapter 8). Anxious clients may mishear what is said to them, and sensitive clients may not like prolonged periods of being looked at.

Information from the sense organs registers information about our surroundings, but also has an emotional impact on us. The pitch of someone's voice makes us react with interest or aversion, depending on how we interpret the sound of the voice. The movements of the facial muscles carry emotional meaning. The muscles of the face can be controlled voluntarily, for example, when applying makeup or in shaving, but many facial expressions, such as blushing, occur without any voluntary control. Sometimes our faces convey feelings that we would prefer to hide. Conversely, facial expressions can be difficult to read. However, a genuine smile involves the small muscles around the eyes, as well as the mouth. Once more this highlights the importance of clients being able to see us and of us being able to see them.

The nervous system consists of the *central nervous system* and the *peripheral nervous system* (Figure 1.1). The peripheral nervous system has three parts: the *autonomic nervous system*, the *somatic nervous system*, and the *enteric nervous system*.

From a focused viewpoint, the smallest parts of the nervous system for receiving and transmitting information are nerve cells called *neurons* and *glial cells*. There are 100 billion neurons making trillions of connections with other neurons in a complex web (LeDoux, 1998). Each neuron has a cell body and two kinds of extensions from it, called *dendrites* and *axons*. *Dendrites receive* signals and *axons send* signals. Dendrites look like branches of trees, constantly moving and changing shape. Most neurons have only one

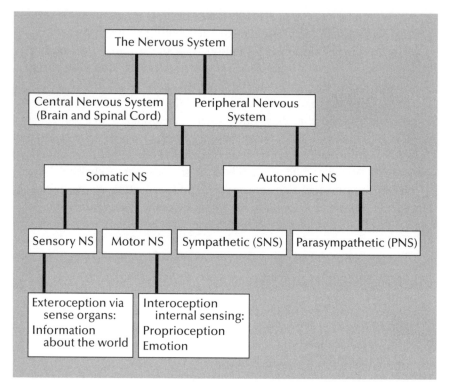

FIGURE 1.1 THE NERVOUS SYSTEM (NS).

axon. Axons can measure up to 1 meter in length for signals that must travel farther in the body. So it is the nerve cells that connect everything up in the nervous system. The axon of a neuron connects up with a dendrite of another neuron; the axon of that neuron connects with a dendrite of another axon, and so on. Dendrites, with all their branches, can accept many axon links, and multiple connections occur.

The receiving and sending of signals is done in milliseconds by electrical and chemical transmissions along the bodies of the axons and dendrites and across tiny gaps between the different neurons called *synapses*. Electrical activity in an axon triggers the release of a *neurotransmitter*, a chemical such as acetylcholine or dopamine, which triggers the next phase of the transmission of signals. The huge network of neurons takes information up and down the body.

Sensory information is taken to the brain by *afferent* axons, and *efferent* axons take information along motor pathways from the brain. This is the basis of "up-down" and "down-up" information processing.

Neural Plasticity

The connections between neural synapses are dependent on our experiences in babyhood, described as experience-dependent. Connections occur throughout adulthood from our experiences of the world and our interactions with others. Neuroscientists call this *neural plasticity*. When we focus on feelings in long-term dynamic psychotherapy, we provide opportunities for new experiences and new learning, with the potential for changing the structure of the client's (and our own) brain-body systems (Schore, 2003b). Changes can be tiny, but are cumulative and incremental. Unused synaptic connections wither (neuronal pruning), giving rise to the maxim "use it or lose it." We filter our experiences through the neural pathways that we have, but "as neurons fire together, they wire together." This is called Hebb's law (Hebb, 1949). Some emotional arousal increases neural activity and learning, and consolidates changes. As new synaptic connections are formed and others die off, this leads to psychological changes.

THE CENTRAL NERVOUS SYSTEM

Let us turn now to the *central nervous system*, which consists of the *brain* and *spinal cord*. The brain is soft and gelatinous and bathed in cerebrospinal fluid. It is encased in the bones of the skull for its protection. It is worth noting at this point that the terms used for different parts of the brain are not internationally consistent and therefore can be confusing, when reading different authors. I have included the most commonly used names in the literature for cross-referencing.

The brain connects two worlds—the world inside us and the world outside. The brain mediates between these two worlds so that our basic needs are met. Staying alive depends on how successfully the brain does this. What is interesting is that it is up to us how we respond (neurologically and physiologically) to the world;

the outside world pays no attention to what we may need, except when we are babies (Solms & Turnbull, 2002), or perhaps in special circumstances, such as when we are ill. In psychotherapy, however, we can purposely adapt how we respond to clients. This in turn enables clients to respond differently to the world and to survive in a more optimum way.

The brain has three layers. The outer layer (or upper brain) is the *cortex*, named after the Latin for tree bark, as it resembles bark. The cortex is also called the *cerebral cortex*, the *cortical level*, and the *neomammalian brain*. The central layer, the *midbrain* (also called the *paleomammalian brain*) includes the *limbic system*, often called the *emotional brain* and sometimes the *visceral brain*. The bottom layer, the *brain stem*, also called the *reptilian brain*, is a stalk-like structure sitting on top of and tapering into the *spinal cord or column*.

A way of visualizing the brain is to make a fist with the right hand, with the thumb inside the fist, and then wrapping the fingers of the left hand around the top of the fist. The right arm is the spinal cord and the fist made by the two hands represents the three layers (Rothschild, 2000; Siegel, 1999). If you do this, it will give you an idea of how the structures relate to each other and give you a sensorimotor feel for it.

Different levels of the central nervous system relate to different levels of control of the body. The "higher" (cortical) parts have more abstract and complex functions. The "lower" (subcortical and brain stem) parts regulate basic, but vital functions such as breathing, heartbeat, digestion, and temperature control that we are usually unaware of. Observing and responding to basic subcortical functions such as breathing form a central part of working therapeutically with a non-verbal focus. We shall learn more about breathing as a main focus of the therapeutic relationship in Chapter 5.

Communications with the brain travel *vertically* from the rest of the body to the brain and from the brain to the rest of the body—*bottom up and top down*. They *also move horizontally in the brain—left to right and right to left*. For most tasks, the whole brain is active, with parts of the brain working in parallel for the completion of different functions. However, for particular tasks, specific parts of the brain may be more active than others. Our clients are likely to have difficulties with both vertical and horizontal processing, and this is what we keep in mind in our interactions.

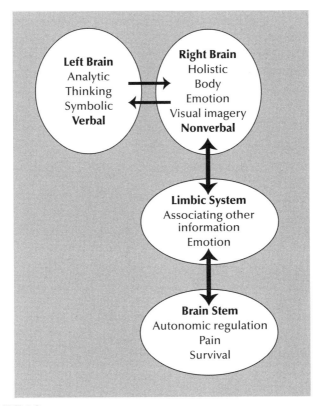

FIGURE 1.2 TOP-DOWN AND LEFT-RIGHT PROCESSING.

The Spinal Cord

Reflex actions, such as pulling away from a hot surface, that happen before the brain has registered that something is too hot to touch are controlled by the spinal cord. The spinal cord carries information from the peripheral parts of the body back to the brain and links the brain to different parts of the body. It also plays a part in controlling blood pressure, digestion (gastrointestinal activity), and sexual responses.

The Brain Stem

The brain stem links the brain to the rest of the body. It regulates basic internal functions such as breathing, heart rate, and temperature to maintain an optimal internal milieu. Near the top of the brain stem at the back of the head is the *cerebellum*, which is involved in balance, concentration, memory, and language. The spinal cord and brain stem are the most basic systems for our survival and, unsurprisingly, are fully functioning at birth. They play a key role in regulating emotions but cannot be consciously controlled.

The Midbrain and Limbic System

The Limbic System

The limbic system is a theoretical construction rather than a precise anatomical structure. Thus, what exactly belongs in the limbic system is debated by neuroscientists (Siegel, 1999) and how it is implicated in emotion is disputed (for example, Panksepp & Biven, 2012). Parts of the limbic system lie between the cerebral cortex and above the brain stem, but also include some cortical structures. Generally included in the limbic system are the *amygdala* and the *hippocampus*, the *thalamus* and the *hypothalamus*, the *orbitofrontal cortex* (OFC), and the *middle prefrontal cortex*. These structures are conventionally described in the singular but exist on both sides of the brain.

The *limbic system*, along with the brain stem, controls most of our bodily activities and ensures our basic survival by *regulating the autonomic nervous system*. Key for our relationships and for non-verbally focused psychotherapy is that *the limbic system processes social experiences and regulates our emotions* (although other parts of the brain are also involved with emotions). The limbic system navigates between basic internal needs and interactions with the outside world, and so plays a large part in the integration of brain activities.

The Amygdala

Daily life events, including everyday stressful ones, are processed by the *amygdala*, which acts like an alarm bell. An illustration of this is that if we glimpse in our peripheral vision an unexpected shadow, we can startle. This stimulates the preparation of the *flight-or-fight response* to the potential threat. Again, these sudden "gut reactions" of alarm are essential for our survival and well-being as they orient us to danger. Another significant function of the amygdala is its involvement in *emotional experiences and attachment*.

The amygdala is functioning at birth, and is involved in the *memories of early attachments*. These memories are implicit (nonconscious) and are part of what makes us feel like ourselves. Clients cannot retrieve implicit memories by asking questions such as, "When did that happen?" This is because these memories are encoded before babies have speech and so are not available in language. However, the memories can be deciphered through exploring sensations, impulses, and movements with clients. In psychotherapy, one of our hopes is to increase positive implicit memories and decrease unpleasant ones.

The Hippocampus

The *hippocampus* moderates the amygdala and acts more slowly. It is the hippocampus that appraises the shadow above that made us startle, and decides whether it really is something to be feared or not. Perhaps it was merely the movement of a tree and nothing to be afraid of. The hippocampus, along with the cerebral cortex, is also involved in explicit (conscious) memory. Explicit memories can be put into words, enabling clients to respond to questions like, "When did that happen? And then, what happened?" creating a sequential narrative of events. Knowing whether to ask clients when and what happened or to find other ways of exploring through more physical methods is a key choice in non-verbally based psychotherapy.

Significantly, the hippocampus is immature at birth and only develops in the second and third year of life. This means that stressful and traumatic relationships in babyhood are not available verbally; our clients will not be able to tell us about early memories in words. If the hippocampus is underdeveloped in our clients, they may describe themselves as jumpy and be excessively alert (hypervigilant). This is because stressful relationships in babyhood giving rise to amygdala reactions have not been moderated by a fully functioning hippocampus. For such overalert clients, finding safety in psychotherapy is important and transformative. Caroline in the introduction was such a client, who became calmer because of my non-verbal communication of safety to her.

The Thalamus and Hypothalamus

The *thalamus* is in the midbrain and surrounds the limbic system. It acts as a relay center, passing sensory information on to the cortex. The *hypothalamus* provides an essential connection between the body, the emotions, and the mind. It regulates the functioning of internal organs by communicating with the *autonomic nervous system* and the *pituitary gland*. Together they control the *hormonal system* and activate other glands. Glands secrete hormones into the bloodstream to various organs in the body concerned with digestion, blood circulation, and heartbeat. The hypothalamus controls the responses to danger in what is called the *hypothalamic-pituitary-adrenal axis* (HPA) by producing the stress hormone cortisol. The hypothalamus interacts in both directions with the amygdala, thereby closely linking bodily reactions and emotions.

The Prefrontal Cortex

The *prefrontal cortex* (PFC) also modulates emotions as well as physiological and behavioral processes. It is involved in *the self-regulation of positive feelings*. The prefrontal cortex subdivides into the *dorsolateral cortex*, the *orbitofrontal cortex* (OFC) (also called the ventromedial), and the *middle prefrontal cortex*. The *dorsolateral cortex* connects with the hippocampus and the left brain and is involved in enabling us to *think about experiences*. At this level of brain processing, verbal communication can take place, emotions can be named, and feelings expressed in words. In Chapter 6, I describe Suzy, who had a traumatic childhood. Putting her feelings into words was an ongoing theme in our psychotherapy together. She was flooded by her feelings, and naming them was part of reducing their overwhelming nature. The *middle prefrontal cortex* connects the body, brain stem, and limbic system (the amygdala) and the right brain. It houses the *anterior cingulate cortex,* the *insula,* and the OFC.

The Anterior Cingulate Cortex, Insular Cortex, and OFC

The *anterior cingulate cortex* (or *gyrus*) plays a central part in our psychological makeup and processes. It regulates the amygdala, the autonomic nervous system, and emotions. It plays a major part in *homeostasis*, the process of maintaining physiological balance in the body. In addition, the anterior cingulate plays a key role in attachment, empathy, and feeling a sense of affiliation with others.

The *insula* (or insular cortex) provides a *basic sense of self* by telling us about our *internal body states and sensations*. This is called *interoception* (Porges, 2011). Sensing our own and helping clients sense their internal bodily states by becoming aware of body sensations is part of working with a non-verbal psychotherapy focus. It includes *proprioception*—knowing about our movement and where our joints are, essential information for balance and coordination. In psychotherapy we tune into our body sensations in response to our clients as part of the process of knowing implicitly what might be happening for them. I discuss this further in Chapter 3. Often clients with traumatic histories will have to be taught interoception. Gut feelings (visceral feelings) and somatic body states associated with emotions are processed in the *insula*. Somatic sensations underpin our emotions. They are essential for knowing how we are feeling and being able to know the emotions of others (see Chapter 5). In childhood the insula learns to integrate information (implicitly) about internal body states and external sensory information (Marks-Tarlow, 2013).

The OFC plays a major role in *emotional regulation* through *reading facial expressions, gestures, and tone of voice*. It also has an integrating function and is another structure for modulating the amygdala. The OFC is significant in mother-baby bonding (Schore, 1994). Damage to the OFC and lack of development leads to difficulties with responding to social signals and in managing our feelings. In an emotionally focused psychotherapy, the therapeutic experience is likely to change the OFC (Schore, 2003b). As emotions are regulated, they become more manageable.

The Cerebral Cortex

The cerebral cortex has an overarching role. It receives and organizes experiences from the environment. It takes care of managing conscious thought processes, memory, and planning. It also evaluates and judges, and is shaped by the interactions of our social and physical worlds. However, it is not in overall control of bodily activities (Cozolino, 2002; Uvnäs Moberg, 2003).

Lobes

The cerebral cortex is divided into two halves or hemispheres and further subdivided into four major parts called *lobes*. Again these structures are usually written about in the singular. These are the *occipital lobe* (at the back of the head), the *temporal lobe* (behind the temples), the *parietal lobe* in front of the occipital lobe, and the *frontal lobe*.

The occipital lobe receives and processes visual information. The temporal lobe processes auditory information, and is involved with receptive language—(listening and understanding)—and memory. The parietal lobe integrates information from touch, gives us a sense of our body in space, and links sensations and motor activity. The frontal lobe is known as the executive brain and is involved with expressive language, motor activity, and reasoning (Cozolino, 2002). Located within the frontal lobes is *Broca's area*, named after Paul Broca, who discovered that this area was one of the parts of the brain concerned with language. Psychotherapy focused on feelings seems to alter the functioning of the frontal lobe so that the amygdala becomes less reactive in clients in whom it has been overactive (Schore, 2003b; LeDoux, 1998)

Mirror Neurons

In Broca's area, in the *pars opercularis* are specialized nerve cells called *mirror neurons,* which were discovered in the 1990s (Gallese, Fadiga, Fogassi, & Rizzolatti, 1996). Mirror neurons become active when we do a task or when we see someone else do it. When the activity is not directed to an object, the left hemisphere is active; the right is active when there is an object. Through mirror neurons we understand the intentions of others. They connect us with others and help us in relationships by enabling us to anticipate the actions of others (Siegel, 2010). They are implicated in the neurobiology of empathy and provide a ready explanation of our ability to "pick up on others' feelings" and feel that another person is on our wavelength. Mirror neurons provide an empirical basis for resonance, the ability of psychotherapists to sense what someone else is feeling. They are one route through which non-verbal communication takes place, and for clients mirror neurons offer a route for internal change simply by unconsciously "observing" therapists' behavior.

Differentiated Halves: The Left and Right Sides of the Cortex

The cerebral cortex is divided into two halves called hemispheres. The two hemispheres, the left and the right, have differentiated functions, called *lateralization* (Figure 1.3). The two sides of the brain are connected with and communicate mostly via the *corpus callosum*, but also through some regions below the cortex. Although there is specialization in the two hemispheres of the brain, both are involved in any activity.

The Right Side of the Brain (Cortex)

The *right hemisphere* or side of the brain is longer, wider, and larger than the left hemisphere. It modulates emotional arousal, regulates stress, and processes novel information. It is involved in non-verbal communication and is concerned with *implicit* or *procedural memory*. It takes in whole situations and is active in shared meaning between people (intersubjectivity), humor, empathy, creativity, intuition, visual imagery, and metaphor (McGilchrist, 2009a; Schore, 2012). The right brain develops throughout life. It receives non-verbal communications coming from facial expressions, through the eyes, voice tone, gestures, posture, and the timing and intensity of communications. Most importantly, the right brain matures earlier than the left brain and is dominant for the first three years. This means that the way mothers communicate non-verbally has a major impact on their babies and the way that their brains develop.

The Left Side of the Brain (Cortex)

The *left brain* is concerned with the verbal, conscious, and rational. It is oriented toward details. It processes serial information and focuses on things and objects. The left and right sides of the brain process information differently and have difficulty understanding each other's perspective on the world. In psychotherapy, clients ask, "Why do I feel this way?" This is a left-brain question. The right brain, meanwhile, wants to explore body sensations and feelings. If it could speak it would say, "I know why I am like this, but it does not change anything. I want someone else to really get me and to feel how it is to be me." We could say that the left brain corresponds to the "what" of communication and the right brain with the "how" (McGilchrist, 2009a).

The brain, with its left and right hemispheres, gives rise to two different ways of viewing the world, "two fundamentally opposed realities, two different modes of experience" (Figure 1.3;

McGilchrist, 2009a). McGilchrist writes that the two parts of the brain need to cooperate, but instead they are involved in "a sort of power struggle, and that this explains many aspects of contemporary Western culture" (2009a, p. 3). Our world is increasingly dominated by left-hemisphere ways of doing things and making sense of things, leaving us with feelings of alienation. McGilchrist, imagining a world with the left hemisphere in charge, writes, "there would be a loss of the broader picture, and a substitution of a more narrowly focussed, restricted, but detailed, view of the world, making it perhaps difficult to maintain a coherent overview" (2009a, p. 428). Our bodies would be relegated to objects to manipulate to suit our passing whims about our appearance. This world would be more mechanical and technical. We would lose "knowledge that came through experience" and suffer a "loss of the sense of uniqueness" (McGilchrist, 2009a, p. 429).

For any particular client, there is a choice to be made about com-

	Left Brain	Right Brain
Attention	Focused and abstracted from context Local, narrow, selective	Broad, global, flexible Wholes in context, then left divides into parts Intensity aspects of attention, e.g., alertness, vigilance, sustained attention
Vision		Peripheral, attention to the edges of awareness
Learning	Prefers routine and what it knows	New learning, then moves to left brain
Emotion		Bodily experience of emotions
Language	Focus on highly related words Processes language	Broader range of words; processes nonlinear aspects of language; understands the clues in the context of communication, e.g., metaphor and humor

FIGURE 1.3 THE FUNCTIONS OF THE LEFT AND RIGHT BRAIN.

municating more frequently to the left or right hemisphere, and finding ways to get the left and right hemispheres communicating. Emotional health depends on both sides of the brain.

THE PERIPHERAL NERVOUS SYSTEM

The *peripheral nervous system* is outside the central nervous system and has nerves (axons bundled together) leading to and from the skin, muscles, and internal organs such as the liver and kidneys. Those moving in an *incoming direction* are called *sensory nerves. Outgoing nerves* are called *motor or somatic nerves.* The peripheral nervous system divides into the *somatic nervous system* and the *autonomic nervous system. The autonomic nervous system* further subdivides into the *sympathetic nervous system* (SNS) and the *parasympathetic nervous system* (PNS).

The Somatic Nervous System

The *somatic nervous system* has *sensory* and *motor nerves.* Movement of muscles is controlled from the central nervous system, but as we saw earlier, reflex movements are controlled from the spinal cord. Sensory nerves allow the body to interact with the environment and sense what is going on. They register, for example, fullness or emptiness in the stomach, and the state of our breathing. They pick up information from receptors and carry the information back to the central nervous system. Skin receptors, mentioned earlier, register information about touch and pressure and can differentiate a light touch from a heavy one.

How fast information travels to the central nervous system depends on the thickness of the nerve fibers. Acute pain and touch are conducted via thick, fast-conducting fibers. A thin and slow-conducting nerve fiber was discovered in the early 2000s. It conveys messages of pleasant sensations and is activated by regular touch (Uvnäs Moberg, 2003). All sensory information passes through the spinal cord on its way to the central nervous system. It is only then that the information is consciously known and processed. On its way to the cerebral cortex, however, the signals from the sensory nerves also pass through the limbic system where the body may react to signals outside our awareness.

The Autonomic Nervous System

The *autonomic nervous system* (ANS) is not usually under voluntary control and its activity cannot be controlled in the way that movement can be controlled. It keeps our heart beating, digests our food, keeps us breathing, and maintains our temperature as our circumstances change. The two parts of the autonomic nervous system, the *Sympathetic Nervous System* (SNS) and the *Parasympathetic Nervous System* (PNS), tend to work opposite each other. If you imagine a see-saw, as one end dips the other end moves up to maintain balance (called homeostasis). The autonomic nervous system makes continuous adjustments to keep equilibrium, meeting the demands of life and maintaining health and well-being. Prolonged overactivity of the SNS, without coming back into balance with the PNS, results in stress-related medical conditions. This relation between the mind and body has long been recognized.

The Sympathetic Nervous System
The *sympathetic nerves* go from the *spinal cord*, particularly from the chest and groin area, to organs and muscles. The most important substance transmitting the signals is noradrenaline. The SNS is associated with states of arousal and action. The SNS uses up energy and is best known for its role in the flight-or-fight response, when we feel threatened.

Parasympathetic Nervous System
The parasympathetic nerves begin at the brain stem and the lower part of the spinal cord. Those from the brain stem meet in the vagus nerve, a large nerve that goes to several organs. The terms PNS and vagus are often used interchangeably (Stauffer, 2010). The main substance transmitting the nerve signals is acetylcholine. The PNS is linked with feelings of "calm and connection" (Uvnäs Moberg, 2003). It is energy conserving and involved with rest, relaxation, recuperative processes, and healing. It is active in processes such as cooperating in teamwork and bonding with others.

The autonomic nervous system is important for observing one's own and the client's level of excitement or relaxation. It can be observed in clients and felt in oneself. When clients feel safer, their breathing is more regular, and their skin is likely to be pink and warm. The relaxed therapist will notice his or her own slower, fuller breathing, may feel warm and hear rumblings from the digestive system. Observations of the ANS are used extensively in non-verbal relating (see especially Chapters 5 and 6).

There are some circumstances when both the SNS and the PNS are activated by the limbic system. This is the freezing (tonic immobility) response. Freezing occurs when there is a threat to someone with no way of escaping or death seems imminent. Freezing can be seen in clients with traumatic histories. It is important to recognize this to be able to work safely with them (Rothschild, 2000).

Enteric Nervous System

Much remains unknown as yet about the enteric nervous system. It has been called the "second brain" (Gershon, 1998) and has as many neurons as the brain. There is some speculation that it is implicated in the "digestion of emotions," so-called psychoperistalsis (Boyesen, 1980). Peristalsis is the movement of the muscles action in the digestive system and usually denotes PNS activity. The rumbling sounds of peristalsis, called borborygmi, seem connected with interactions in psychotherapy. So, for example, the Jungian analyst Heuer regards his patient's tummy rumbles as acting as a "spontaneous commentary" on the relationship. Sometimes the sounds come "as if in response to an interpretation I have offered" and are a "bodily confirmation." Sometimes the sounds come immediately after the patient has spoken, "underlining the importance of what has been said" (Heuer, 2005, p. 113). Heuer suggests that peristalsis can offer feedback and in silences, peristalsis gives reassurance that the patient is emotionally digesting. Sometimes peristaltic sounds occur in both analyst and patient, when there are silences on the verbal level in a "psychoperistaltic dialogue". At these times, "words would only be an obstacle to the dialogue happening on a deeper corporeal level" (2005, p. 113). Peristaltic sounds can inform a non-verbal approach, and we return to them in later chapters.

CONCLUSION

Key aspects to keep in mind in a non-verbal approach are the functions of the left and right brain, understanding what experiences clients cannot retrieve in words because they are encoded in the subcortex, and the overall balance of thinking and feeling. Monitoring the physiological arousal of ourselves and our clients is of central importance. This includes monitoring the balance between high and low arousal related to the processing of information in therapist-client interactions (Figure 1.4). This gives a fluctuating sense of self. These key aspects guide us in how to respond to clients, to balance thinking and feeling. In Chapter 2 we will look more specifically at neurological development in babies and how babies develop through interactions with their parents.

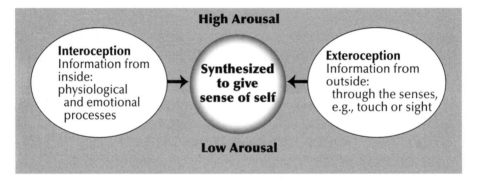

FIGURE 1.4 LEVELS OF AROUSAL RELATED TO INFORMATION PROCESSING FROM INSIDE AND OUTSIDE THE BODY RELATED TO THE SENSE OF SELF.

Chapter 2

HOW BABIES RELATE

INFANT DEVELOPMENT AND COMMUNICATION

The way that babies have been regarded at different times in history has led to different forms of baby care. I illustrate this by describing the Truby King baby and the Daniel Stern baby. The relationships that parents establish with their babies lay the foundations for adult relationships.

INFANT DEVELOPMENT

The Truby King Baby

A real Truby King baby, then is one whose mother brings it up strictly according to the Truby King system—**a baby who is completely breast fed till the ninth month** and then weaned slowly on to humanized milk. . . . Truby King babies are fed four-hourly from birth, with few exceptions, and they do not have night feeds. A Truby King baby has as much fresh air and sunlight as possible, and the right amount of sleep. His education begins from the very first week, good habits being established, which remain all his life. (Truby King, 1941, p. 4, bold in original)

> A little crying every day is good for the normal, healthy baby, causing him to breathe more deeply. . . . Beware of the "spoilt" cry! A baby who cries simply because he wants to be picked up and played with must be left to "cry it out." (p. 168)

Frederick Truby King, medical superintendent of a New Zealand mental hospital, devised these methods of care for babies in the later part of the nineteenth century, and together with his daughter, Mary Truby King, through her Mothercraft classes, spread these ways of baby care throughout the developed world. Truby King advocated breast-feeding to prevent malnutrition and disease, factors in high rates of infant mortality. At birth babies were separated from their mothers for at least 6 hours so that they could both rest after the strenuous process of birth. The babies were fed at regular intervals, including being awakened from sleep for feeds. By 10 months babies were expected to be out of diapers, having been trained from day one to urinate and defecate on demand by being "held out" i.e. being held up away from the mother's body without any clothing after feeding until they defecated and urinated. Truby King babies had their internal rhythms set by their mothers from the start and were not seen as communicating little beings. The remnants of these methods of baby care survive today. These imposed cycles of care are unlikely to correspond with the natural cycle of babies, and being fed repeatedly at times when babies are not hungry leads to deadening and alienation from "gut feelings" (Pervöltz, 1982, p. 129).

The Stern Baby

In stark contrast, Daniel Stern's baby has an inner life of raw, tonal experiences and emotions. Stern introduces us to baby Joey:

> Imagine that none of the things you see or touch or hear have names, and few memories attached to them. Joey experiences objects and events mainly in terms of *feelings* they evoke in him, and the opportunities for action they offer him. (1998, p. 13, emphasis in original)

Stern describes Joey gazing at sunlight on a wall:

> *A space glows over there,*
> *A gentle magnet pulls to capture,*
> *The space is growing warmer and coming to life.*
> *Inside it, forces start to turn around one another in a slow dance.*
> *The dance comes closer and closer.*
> *Everything rises to meet it.*
> *It keeps coming. But it never arrives.*
> *The thrill ebbs.* (1998, p. 17, italics in original)

At 6 weeks Joey is curious and knows what he likes to look at. He gets excited by what he sees. His excitement "increases his animation, activates his whole being." Sometimes he gets almost overexcited, but changes his response. The patch of sunshine is a "gentle magnet whose force he feels" (Stern, 1998, p. 18). Stern's baby is an initiating and engaged baby, who is fascinated by his surroundings. His curiosity ebbs and flows as he interacts with his environment.

Babies today are seen as socially engaged, active, and responsive. Truby King babies, fitting into routines with no thought for their emotional needs, are less common. Over time, new ways of perceiving babies have come from infant studies. These findings have percolated into adult psychotherapy, leading to the revision of theories, and changes in clinical practice (Holmes, 1993; Schore, 1994; Siegel, 1999; Stern, 1985; Wallin, 2007). They point to the significance of babies communicating non-verbally, well before talking develops.

Babies whose internal and interactional rhythms (emotional and physiological) are set by parents in the Truby King style are likely to have difficulty regulating themselves, and this is likely to continue into adulthood. However, even knowing that babies communicate does not stop repeated miscommunications, leading to adult problems. In babyhood our relationships with our caregivers establishes our relational signature, which is the basic pattern of relating to others and is rhythmic in nature.

The relational signature, like a signature tune, reveals itself physically, psychologically, emotionally, energetically, physiologically, and in our thinking. It manifests in non-verbal communication as rhythmic patterns of interaction like a dance. Signature patterns of relating can change through our different life experiences. However, the signature patterns of relating that our adult clients bring to therapy will indicate the likely style of their baby-parent interactions. These give us pointers to where clients may be experiencing difficulties. Being able to tune into the signature patterns of clients quickly (as with Caroline in the introduction) establishes non-verbal communication from the start and begins to modify the signature patterns.

A HISTORICAL PERSPECTIVE ON BABIES AND COMMUNICATION

Until the 1960s, medicine, psychiatry, and psychoanalysis believed babies only communicated minimally prior to the acquisition of speech. Without spoken language, babies could not initiate and participate in relationships with others, and without language, babies could not think or remember events. At that time communication was seen as verbal and about processing information in thoughts (cognitively) (Malloch & Trevarthen, 2010a). Knowledge about babies and young children came from experiences of working with adult patients and disturbed children in psychoanalysis. Information from these settings was then extrapolated into psychological theory.

Child Observation

Different ways of perceiving babies developed in complementary areas. The new theories and research findings did not emerge sequentially, nor were they always welcomed by those holding different ideas. A major innovation occurred when, at the invitation of John Bowlby, Esther Bick pioneered psychoanalytic infant observation from 1948 onward at the Tavistock Clinic (Rustin, 2009). Students of child psychoanalysis began to observe real babies over time, at home, with their families. The observers were instructed to simply look, to notice their feelings, and were discouraged from explaining or making formulations about their observations until later on, and even then only tentatively (Reid,

1997). By the 1970s, infant observation had become a core require-
ment of most psychoanalytic training in Britain and had extended
into the training of doctors, social workers, and clinical psychologists. Later on observation was extended to older children and
now includes observing babies in single-parent families, families
with same-sex parents, and multicultural families, perhaps with
English as a second language (Rustin, 2009). The perspective of
observation broadened in one study combining Laban movement
analysis, pioneered by Rudolf Laban (1879 -1958), with a psychoanalytic stance (Bloom, 2006). Both the "clinical infant" inferred
from clinical practice and the "observed infant" from developmental psychology contribute to a comprehensive understanding of
adults in psychotherapy (Stern, 1985, p. 14).

The Work of the Harlows

Meanwhile, in the United States in the 1960s, Harry and Margaret Harlow conducted what have become classical experiments
with baby rhesus macaque monkeys. They aspired to challenge
Freud's theory that the need for nutrition was paramount in the
baby-mother relationship. To this end, they separated baby monkeys from their mothers and put the baby monkeys in cages in
which they could choose to approach a surrogate wire monkey
with a feeding bottle full of milk, or a surrogate with a soft material
covering. The monkeys moved toward, and then clung to, the soft,
padded surrogate mother monkey, even though it had no feeding
bottle. According to Freud's theory, the monkeys should have chosen the surrogate mother with the milk. Instead the experiments
showed that contact and comfort were of primary importance. It
was the physical contact with the soft padded surrogate mother that
gave the baby monkey some basic security.

The Harlows found that basic security was necessary to negotiate
the next phase of development. They conducted further experiments in which they socially deprived the baby monkeys in different ways. From these experiments, they concluded that not only
were infant-mother relationships significant for later development,
but also those with their peer playmates. The socially deprived baby
monkeys were unable, in varying degrees, to relate to others, were

averse to physical contact and aggressive (Harlow & Harlow, 1966). This work, and other studies in the emergent science of ethology, observing animal behavior under normal conditions, showed that social bonding among animals was not necessarily connected with feeding (for example, Lorenz, 1953). These studies influenced psychoanalysts, the most notable being John Bowlby, part of the British object relations grouping.

Object Relations Theory

Object relations developed in Britain out of Freudian theory, with its roots in the thinking of earlier analysts such as Otto Rank and Sandor Ferenczi. *Objects* in this context are persons or parts of persons. The grouping was not a coherent one, with diverse and sometimes conflicting perspectives. It did agree that *relating and contact take precedence over nutritional needs in babies*. They challenged Freud's theories about instinctual drives and took the psychoanalytic focus away from the oedipal scenario toward preoedipal development and to the needs of the developing infant (Gomez, 1997). Included in the object relations grouping were Melanie Klein, Douglas Fairbairn, Donald Winnicott, Michael Balint, Harry Guntrip, and John Bowlby.

Ego and Self Psychology

Similar strands of development were happening in the United States in psychoanalysis and changing clinical work. A notable development was the school of ego psychology (especially between the 1940s and 1960s), which emphasized the individual's experiences and significance was given to inadequate early attachment leading to poor ego development. Within the United States, self psychology also blossomed from the work of Heinz Kohut, who saw adult problems arising through lack of early empathy. This moved the therapeutic stance away from the analyst being an outside observer to one of "empathic immersion" in the patient's intrapsychic world. The analyst now became an experiencing participant.

ATTACHMENT THEORY
John Bowlby

Back in the United Kingdom, Bowlby saw the bond (attachment) between a baby and its mother as a natural, healthy function. He became convinced that separation and loss were precursors of disturbance in later life, believing that the key component was disruption of the relationship with the caregiver. Bowlby illustrated his burgeoning theories in a film made by Robertson and Robertson (1969), which has had a lasting impact on how sick children are treated in hospitals.

In the Robertsons' film, Bowlby's three phases of protest, despair, and detachment, which occur when a child is separated from her parent, are discernible. On being left in the hospital ward by her family, the 2-year-old girl, Margaret, protests and demands, "I want my Mummy!" Later she becomes despondent, and then an outwardly docile "good little girl" who has successfully adapted to being away from her parents. However, closer scrutiny shows that she is increasingly hard for the nurse to engage socially. She has "shut down" and become "detached" from the nurses and her surroundings. Separations such as this evoke in a child a gamut of feelings with high states of physiological arousal that are not always obvious.

During his life, Bowlby created and evolved attachment theory with his colleague, Mary Ainsworth, and it has become theoretically independent from object relations theory. The term *attachment* refers to the baby's connection to the mother, called the primary caregiver, who can also be the other parent or any other key person caring for the baby (e.g., grandparents, nannies, or day care workers). When a baby or young child feels threatened, she is afraid and begins to look around (attachment or proximity-seeking behavior) for her mother (the attachment figure). She wants to feel safe, secure, and protected by getting physically close to her mother. A threat can be something unfamiliar, being alone, or a sudden change. *The more predictable and available her mother is, when she is needed, the stronger the sense of secure attachment the baby and young child will develop.* Babies have many repeated experiences of being with their mothers, which develop into *internal working models* within the baby. These are internalized patterns of relating with the mother (Bowlby, 1979, p. 117). Styles of making contact with others (attachment behaviors) are derived from these first internalized patterns of relating with the mother. They are discernible throughout life and come to the fore in situations that are stressful, such as times of loss, novelty, illness, and fatigue. The psychotherapy situation is one such situation, particularly in the begining.

Mary Ainsworth

Ainsworth's groundbreaking work was observing infants in their homes, then in experimental situations, and in classifying attachment patterns. She observed babies aged between 1 and 24 months in Uganda and in Baltimore and evaluated the mothers' sensitivity to the communication signals of their infants. Her new approach was looking at *patterns of behaviors* between mothers and babies, rather than counting the number of times a behavior occurred. She found that some mothers were perceptive and nuanced in their responses to their babies and deemed them "highly sensitive." She found that *babies with sensitive mothers were secure*. They cried little, and when their mothers were in their vicinity, they explored confidently.

In the Baltimore study she observed mothers and their 3-month-old babies in commonplace interactions, for example, how the mothers responded to crying and how they touched their babies, perhaps during feeding. She found that mothers who responded promptly had smooth, cooperative interactions with their babies. Furthermore, "when the mothers meshed their own playful behavior with that of their babies, infants responded with joyful bouncing, smiling and vocalizing" (Bretherton, 1992, p. 16). Ainsworth concluded that if mothers were responsive to their babies, the babies developed confidence in their ability to influence what happened to them. Interestingly, harmonious relationships observed at 3 months were also found at 1 year. These babies actively communicated through facial expressions, gestures, and vocalizations, and continued to cry less.

Ainsworth developed her work by looking at mother-baby interactions in a laboratory procedure called the Strange Situation (Ainsworth, Blehar, Waters, & Wall, 1978). The Strange Situation was designed to activate the attachment behaviors of 1-year-olds by placing them in stressful situations that approximated common situations in everyday life. The situations were low stress at first, and then incrementally more stressful, but were never intended to be overwhelmingly stressful. The babies' attachment system revealed itself in the use of the mother as a secure base from which to explore, the distress activated in brief separations, and the level of fear on encountering a stranger. The Strange Situation has become a standardized and reliable measure for revealing and rating a 1-year-old's attachment to his parent.

The experiment takes 20 minutes and is videotaped and rated afterward. The experimenter observes both the child's and the mother's reactions in the different parts of the experiment. There are eight episodes of brief separation and reunion, each lasting 3 minutes, but sometimes less:

1. The baby and mother are taken to a laboratory playroom with toys by a researcher. The researcher leaves the room.
2. The mother does not participate as the child explores.
3. A strange woman (unknown to the baby) enters the room. She speaks with the mother, and then approaches the child. The stranger plays with the baby. The mother is asked to leave the room.
4. The stranger and the baby are left together.
5. The mother returns. The stranger slips away and the mother is instructed to interest the baby in the toys.
6. Next the mother leaves the room and the baby is alone.
7. The stranger returns.
8. The mother returns and the stranger slips away.

From observing the baby's behavior after each of these episodes, Ainsworth identified three main groups. **Securely attached infants** (Group B) had mothers who enjoyed being with them. They were easily accessible to their babies and responded promptly to any distress in them. They were spontaneous and free in their emotional expressions. These mothers were also cooperative rather than interfering, and the timing of their interactions was finely tuned. In the Strange Situation, their babies were visibly upset when they left them. On their return, the babies indicated clearly that they wanted attention and they got it. After reassurance, their babies went on happily exploring and playing. These babies were confident and more independent because they had a basic trust that when they needed comfort their mothers would be available. They could use their mothers as a secure haven when distressed, and had a secure base from which to venture into the world.

Ainsworth also found two forms of **insecure attachment**: *insecure-avoidant* (Group A) and *insecure-resistant/ambivalent* (Group C). Babies in the **insecure-avoidant attachment** group showed minimal response to the separations and reunions in the Strange Situation. Their mothers *avoided gaze and eye contact* with them and *moved away* when their babies approached them. These mothers were not emotionally expressive. They also *shied away from physical contact* and they gave their babies unpleasant experiences of bodily contact when they did touch them. They were rigid, interfering, and insensitive to the baby's signals. This group of babies was anxious, but they were not soothed, if picked up. Outwardly it looked like the baby was indifferent to being held and put down.

Insecure-resistant/ambivalent (Group C) babies were distressed immediately when their mothers left them in the Strange Situation. Their mothers were insensitive but less obviously rejecting than Group A mothers. Group C mothers were less averse to physical contact, but were inept at holding their babies. Holding their babies was functional and for performing routines that required physical contact. In the Strange Situation, the babies took longer to soothe than the insecure-avoidant grouping, and the babies combined angry resistant movements with clinging and staying close to the mothers.

Further Attachment Studies

Subsequently Mary Main and Judith Solomon (1986) looked again at the videotapes of babies who had not fitted into the A, B, and C attachment categories. They identified another grouping: **insecure-disorganized/disoriented attachment** (Group D). When these babies were separated in the Strange Situation, they exhibited contradictory behaviors such as both seeking contact and strongly avoiding it, or expressing strong distress but moving away from rather than toward the mother. They avoided contact or froze. They stumbled and made asymmetrical movements, and they combined slow movements and freezing even when the mother was present. These babies had fearful facial expressions and bodily postures indicative of fear, such as hunching the shoulders up, when the mother was present. They were confused and had rapidly changing expressions of feelings. These babies had mothers who were either frightened or frightening. The mothers, for example, growled, hissed, and stalked their babies on all fours. This was not playing with their babies (Hesse & Main, 1999). The insecure-disorganized/disoriented attachment grouping is most vulnerable to later pathology and is strongly linked with borderline personality disorder, dissociation, and post-traumatic stress disorder in later life (Beebe, Lachmann, Markese, & Bahrick, 2012; Beebe, Lachmann, Markese, Buck, et al., 2012; Fonagy, Gergely, Jurist, & Target, 2002; Schore, 2003a).

Further studies were conducted by Main, who went on to devise the **Adult Attachment Interview.** Parents were interviewed about their own childhood to find out about their attachment patterns. Main identified three groups. Group 1, **Autonomous**, had had secure parenting. Group 2, **Preoccupied**, found it difficult to organize a narrative of their childhood and had differing versions of events in their narratives. Group 3, **Dismissive**, had poor memory of their childhood. Those in Group 3, when speaking generally about their childhood, tended to have an idealized view of it. Based on these interviews, it was possible to predict what sort of attachment their babies would make with them. This work has implications for how attachment interactions may have been transmitted intergenerationally to our clients.

No new attachment styles have been found, suggesting that these groups represent basic responses to threat, designed to increase the chances of survival by fighting, fleeing, or freezing, and approaching to find safety (Holmes & Farnfield, 2014). Across cultures, attachment studies have found that most infants (65%) are securely attached (Prior & Glaser, 2006). Those fitting into Group D are likely to have some characteristics of Groups A and C, meaning that they have some organization within their disorganization (van Rosmalen, van Ijzendoorn, & Bakermans-Kranenburg, 2014). There is some evidence that these proportions change in different cultures. In Germany, the United Kingdom, and the United States, for example, more infants fit into Group A (for example, Crittenden & Claussen, 2000, cited in Holmes & Farnfield, 2014). In Italy, Israel, and Japan, more infants fit into Group C (for example, Crittenden & Claussen, 2000, cited in Holmes & Farnfield, 2014). Studies continue to be done from a Western idea of the family group. It is the 35% of babies who are insecurely attached who are likely to become our adult clients. However, internal working models are not absolutely fixed and change over time through life experiences and the brain's neuroplasticity. Even so, traces of early attachment styles survive into adulthood. Additionally, when too many demands are placed upon him, the most securely attached baby can become an overwhelmed adult.

Pointers toward the attachment patterns of clients reveal themselves from the first point of contact, whether this is in an e-mail, a phone call, or a letter. Those with early disorganized attachment, for example, may share copious intimate details about themselves via e-mail without having gone through the early stages of getting to know the therapist and deciding if they are trustworthy. In psychotherapy, the regular schedule of meetings with clear beginnings, endings, and vacation breaks is likely to activate early attachment patterns. Knowing how to respond to cues, often given non-verbally by clients, enables psychotherapists to support clients well enough for psychotherapy not only to begin, but to negotiate the stresses of many repeated beginnings, endings, and moments of misunderstanding.

Interactions with mothers in the first months of life, well before speech develops, form internal working models. These interactions are nonconscious and are encoded in implicit or procedural memory. They form a person's repertoire of feelings and their regulation (Schore, 1994). Clients with insecure early attachments are likely to have difficulties in their relationships. Their thinking may be rigid or confused; their range of feelings and the capacity to express them may be limited. Their level of physiological excitement may be restricted, overactive, or without easy transitions between highly excited states and calmer ones. Their movements, gestures, posture, and facial expressions, collectively called "physical tendencies" (Ogden et al., 2006) will be restricted, lacking in gracefulness and easy flow. Movements are made by muscles, and their muscles will be excessively tense (hypertonic) or undertoned (hypotonic), and their basic vitality will be reduced (Marcher & Fich, 2010).

Clients with early insecure-avoidant attachment patterns withdraw from others, when distressed. They feel safer by themselves. Asking for help is difficult and often not even considered; help is not expected. Making the first contact to seek psychotherapeutic help represents an immense step. They may be unobtrusively watchful but find it hard to look at people. They may prefer to direct their gaze away from the therapist toward objects in the room. Their eyes may look at you, but there is a sense that there is no one at home looking out, as their eyes look dull and blank. This means that their intake of social cues in relationships is impaired. Expressing anything negative is particularly difficult. In Chapter 6, I introduce Peter, who fits this attachment style.

Clients with early insecure-ambivalent attachment patterns tend to be overclose and clinging, and have entangled relationships with others. They find being apart difficult. They can usually let their tears flow. Clients with early disorganized attachment may have freezing and dissociated responses when under duress. They may go very still or respond robotically and seem somewhere else in the consulting room. Caroline in the introduction had some of these features, and we shall meet Lily in Chapter 4 and Suzy in Chapter 6 with some features of early insecure-disorganized attachment. Clients may have mixed styles of attachment with one style predominating.

Those with early insecure attachment histories correlate with *DSM-V* diagnoses for personality disorders (for example, Montgomery, 2013). The genesis of narcissistic personality disorder belongs to the later half of the first year and an early insecure-avoidant style. The genesis of borderline personality disorder belongs earlier in the first year and is associated with insecure-disorganized attachment, where abuse and neglect are more present (Schore, 2002). Tony in Chapter 3 has narcissistic aspects, his learned way of protecting himself. Personality disorders were described by Reich (1970) as character structures and have been elaborated on. They are also known as character strategies or styles. They describe the way children and adults protect themselves from external threat from both psychological and physical perspectives (Johnson, 1994;

Kurtz, 1990; Lowen, 1971). The most relevant to this discussion are the schizoid and oral strategies described by Kurtz (1990) as "sensitive-withdrawn" (schizoid), "dependent-endearing" (oral), and "self-reliant-independent" (a variant of oral). Kurtz's categories are descriptive and fit a non-verbal approach well. The schizoid strategy correlates with insecure-avoidant attachment and oral strategy with insecure-ambivalent/resistant attachment. Like early attachment styles, character strategies overlap, but clients tend to have some more frequently used strategies.

INFANT COMMUNICATION

Contemporary studies agree that newborns arrive ready to communicate, and their early relationships affect later pathology. Different authors focus on different aspects of the mother and baby relationship, with some authors emphasizing brain development, while others explore emotional and physiological regulation, rhythms of relating, and the developing senses of self.

Before Birth

Even at conception Sills (2009) tells us that the "single-celled being" (Laing, 1977 writing poetically) is sensitive to the environment and speculates that stress even at this early stage of life may lead to becoming hypersensitive after birth and may be an important factor in the processes of insecure attachment. The first bonding happens 6 days after conception, when the embryo implants itself in the uterine wall of its mother. Stanley Keleman writes of the basic "conversations" that occur even on the uterine level between the little being and the mother:

> I am part of you yet I am not part of you. I need to be part of you for my own well-being and growth, so don't get rid of me even though I seem to be a foreign body. Can you accept who I am even though I am not you? (1986, p. 3)

By the end of the first month, this new little being has already formed a primitive brain and at 5 weeks there are two identifiable bulges, the foundations of the two hemispheres of the brain. At only

6 weeks old and less than 2 centimeters long, the little one makes circular movements, which become increasingly complex. It can hear, and its skin is touching and being touched by the surrounding environment. By 14 or so weeks, mothers can feel a baby's movements and sometimes see them too, as the abdomen moves. This is when a mother knows for sure, from her own experience, that she is carrying a child. As she feels her baby's separateness, conveyed by his independent movements, she recognizes the possibility of a relationship with her baby (Brazelton & Cramer, 1991).

At 20 weeks the little one's hearing capacity is completely developed. He can perceive the medium- and high-frequency sounds of his mother's voice. The mother's voice, with its particular timbre, rhythm, and musical qualities, lays the foundations of the baby's future "linguistic code" (Tomatis, 1987, p. 55, cited by Maiello, 1997). Maiello (1995) speculates that the mother's voice creates prenatal sound memories, and she puts forward the idea of sound as a "sound-object." Sounds also create, for the developing baby, the early beginnings of differentiation of "me" and "not-me." This comes from alternating periods of hearing the mother's voice followed by its absence (Maiello, 1997). By 26 to 28 weeks the little one not only hears, but also responds to sounds. A loud sound induces a startle response, and movements generally increase with exposure to light and sound (Brazelton & Cramer, 1991).

S/he can also hear the low-frequency sounds of the rise and fall of the mother's breathing, heartbeat, and the noises of her digestion. These maternal processes are governed by the autonomic nervous system and affect the little one. The autonomic nervous system activity has accompanying rhythmic waves of surging adrenalin rushes followed by periods of more tranquil activity, such as when the mother is resting and digesting a meal. If a mother is stressed, drinking alcohol, or taking sedatives, this also has an impact on the little one.

At Birth and After

Bonding and Attaching at Birth

During birthing, the hormone oxytocin is secreted from the pituitary gland and speeds the labor up. Babies who have had positive experiences in the womb and a stress-free birth will, if placed on the mother's belly, gradually move themselves up to the mother's chest. The baby will root around with his mouth and hands to find the mother's nipple. In response, the mother's chest warms up as she releases oxytocin in repeating pulses. The close skin-to-skin contact calms both the mother and her baby. If babies are allowed to stay on their mother's chest, they cry less. The baby's hands and feet also warm up. The warmth of the mother's chest correlates with the temperature of the baby's hands and feet (Uvnäs Moberg, 2003).

During this first direct experiencing of the world, babies look intently. As the newborn finds her mother's eyes, mutual eye contact occurs. This is described by Uvnäs Moberg (2003, p. 97) as "indirect touch." Hearing and smelling are also important in this first experiencing of each other. Newborns know the smell of their own mother's milk (Stern, 1985).

For the mother and baby who have had a difficult, perhaps traumatic birth, or for a depressed or particularly anxious mother, this early bonding outside the womb is far more challenging. It can set the pattern of future relating together. Depressed mothers are less sensitive to their babies, are off key in their responses, and their interactions with their babies are distorted. They are distinctly less attuned than nondepressed mothers, and the timing and pacing of their interactions is impaired. The tone and loudness of their voice, their patterns of intonation sequencing, and the repetition of these is out of sync. Of note is that they also have more falling intonation contours in their vocal expressions (Marwick & Murray, 2010).

Babies experience the qualities of their experiences globally and have "perceptual unity." Their world is a sensory one of touches, sights, sounds, and smells in which they come to recognize and integrate their own relating and patterns of relating with others. Stern tells us, "they can perceive amodal qualities in any modality from any form of human expressive behavior, represent these qualities abstractly, and then transpose them to other modalities" (1985, p. 51).

Self-Soothing and Self-Regulation in the Early Days

Newborns seek sensory stimulation and have some basic capacities for comforting and calming themselves, called *self-soothing*. They use these capacities when they are uncomfortable or distressed, but they also require relationships with adults for physiological regulation.

The Brazelton Neonatal Behavioral Assessment Scale (NBAS), developed by T. Berry Brazelton (Brazelton & Nugent, 2011), can be used from day 1 to assess a baby's self-soothing capacities together with the particular personality differences he is bringing to his family. A trained health practitioner, who is sensitive to the signals of the baby's autonomic nervous system, carries out the NBAS in the presence of a parent. The NBAS shows how the baby responds to different kinds of stimulation, such as light or sounds. One stimulation test is to shine a light onto the sleeping baby's closed eyes. The baby's eyelids may flutter rapidly, then flutter less and stop as he becomes used to it (habituated to it). After each form of stimulation or procedure, the assessor waits until the baby has recovered internal equilibrium—indicated in this example by the fluttering of the eyelids stopping—before stimulating the baby further. The NBAS reveals the sensitivity of the baby to stimulation and how well he is able to adapt to it. It shows the baby's efforts at calming himself and indicates what extra help a particularly sensitive baby may need to thrive. This could be the reduction of stimulation coming from sounds, light, and activity in the environment.

Sometimes babies get distressed and cannot calm themselves very easily. Mothers are needed then to help calm their babies—perhaps gently restricting the baby's movements to interrupt the escalating arousal that comes with distress. Babies's poorly controlled movements are what keep them overstimulated. Mothers also speak softly and slowly, handle the baby tenderly, and use distracting activities to soothe him. As we have already seen, a mother who is sensitive and responsive to her baby's intolerance for stimulation makes a huge difference. Babies that are more difficult to soothe and have difficulties with regulating their feelings are prone to problems of concentration and difficulties with learning that can be lifelong (Pally, 2000).

Cycles of Activity and Responsiveness
Before her baby was born, a mother may have noticed and predicted her baby's behavior. This may seem closely related to her internal state, with periods of activity followed by rest. She may also have noticed that she is not always in tandem with her baby and

that her baby has "intrinsic physiological properties" (Brazelton & Cramer, 1991, p. 27). Newborns enter into cycles of different states of consciousness. These states indicate how available the baby is to others and whether stimulation is appropriate or not. These states are a basic regulatory system. Babies who can stay in control and regulate their different states of consciousness can take in and respond to the world around them. For the mother to communicate with her baby, she must recognize the newborn's states of consciousness and whether he is receptive to communication or not (Brazelton & Cramer, 1991). Brazelton identified six states of consciousness:

1. Deep sleep: the baby is in deep sleep, and is relatively unreachable by outside stimuli. Deep sleep provides rest and organizes an easily overwhelmed nervous system.
2. Active sleep: the baby is in lighter sleep, and movements of the eyes will be evident, although the eyes are closed. The breathing is shallow, sometimes irregular, and there will be facial movements.
3. Drowsy, in-between state.
4. The baby is awake, relatively quiet but inactive; the eyes are "bright and shining."
5 Alert, but fussy state: the baby is available to external stimuli, can be soothed or brought to an alert state, but too much stimulation makes the baby fussy again. The baby's movements are jerky and disorganized.
6. Crying, which has four types: pain, hunger, boredom, or discomfort. Crying is the baby's way of communicating, and parents are wired to feel compelled to respond (Brazelton & Cramer, 1991, pp. 64–65).

In active sleep, babies may be responsive to their environment. Wilkinson (2010), in her baby observation, describes the 6-week-old sleeping baby fluttering his eyelids and registering his mother as she leaned over his cot.

Affect Attunement, Moderating Physiological Arousal, and Expanding Emotional Range

Mothers communicate with their babies by how they look at them, touch and handle their bodies in feeding, bathing, and dressing, how they carry them, and their manner of speaking to their babies. Sensitive mothers are attentive to babies' feelings and how babies communicate their needs. *Tuning into their babies' internal state and responding to it is more important than responding to the babies' obvious, overt behavior.*

Terms such as attuning, synchronizing, matching, and mirroring are used by different authors to describe this tuning in and carry nuanced meanings about mother-baby interactions. *Affect attunement*, the term coined by Stern (1985), captures most inclusively the *intuitive process of resonating with the background non-verbal communicating going on.* Stern asserts that affect attunement is different from empathy. Empathy involves "the mediation of cognitive processes" (Stern, 1985, p. 145), while attunement does not. Nonetheless, affect attunement and empathy are interchangeable in initial interactions. Both describe emotional resonance. However, "attunement takes the experience of emotional resonance and automatically recasts that experience into another form of expression" (Stern, 1985, p. 145). Affect attunement also includes vitality affects.

Affect attunement and *attunement* are the chosen terms in this book as they have relevance for our work with adult clients. When we are *connecting non-verbally with our clients, we are resonating with, and in tune with, them.* When we tune into or *make contact non-verbally* with clients, "it feels like an unbroken line," and we "keep the thread of communion unbroken" by seeking it out of the shape of its "animation" (Stern, 1985, p. 157). This is the essence of non-verbal relating with clients.

Regulation

As mothers and babies interact, they engage in an emotional, energetic, and physiological regulatory process together. As they regulate each other (interactive regulation), they also regulate themselves (self-regulation). In interactive regulation, a baby and mother are simultaneously influencing and being influenced in their level of arousal. If a mother is to regulate her baby, she must be able to manage her own feelings.

Some of the interactive regulatory processes are observable; others are more hidden in the non-verbal realm. Regulating breathing is a basic aspect of regulation. Mothers help their babies to establish their emotional range. They magnify positive states and reduce negative ones. As babies are sensitively regulated, they acquire a sense of safety, and their curiosity is fostered. This fuels further exploration and discovery. In Chapter 5 we shall look more closely at the psychotherapy process as individual and joint regulation and the use of breathing to guide the process.

Secure attachment in babies can be predicted at 4 months depending on the coordination between the mother and baby. Secure attachment is predictable, if there is midrange coordination between baby and mother. Coordination can be thrown off balance if the interactions are too tight, giving insufficient room for uncertainty, or too loose (Beebe & Lachmann, 2002). However, counter to what might be expected, Beebe and Lachmann (2002) speculate that for empathy the full range of coordination possibilities is probably best, including too tight and too loose coordinations. This is provided that movement across the range is maintained. This gives fleeting moments of the baby and mother missing each other, but then finding each other again. Full-range coordination also allows for more major ruptures and repairs. I consider "long and short rein holding" and the inquiry clarity, compassion, and spaciousness to assist with our "coordinations" with adult clients in Chapter 3.

Brain Development

From day 1, newborns move and their senses are functioning in a rudimentary way. As we have already noted, a baby's brain stem and limbic system are fully functioning at birth, but the cortex is not yet fully developed. The cortex develops over the next 20 years, throughout babyhood, childhood, adolescence, and early adulthood in interactions with the parents and the world.

The attachment relationship directly influences the development of the right brain and the unconscious (Schore, 1994). There are *sensitive periods* during which it is essential that the baby receives certain sorts of stimulation for his perceptual capacities to develop. Without this stimulation within a certain time frame, the connections between neurons do not occur and unused neural paths die off (Pally, 2000). The sensitive period for emotional development is between 6 months and 1 year, and the main element of this is the regulation of the baby's high states of positive affect by the mother (Schore, 1994).

Language Development

Newborns use their voice and make sounds. Making sounds is coordinated with breathing. Stresses in mother-baby interactions disturb the rhythmic pattern of the baby's sounds. Adults respond to the sounds of babies in high-pitched, soft, continuous tones, suited to the baby's auditory system. The actual words and their meaning (semantic meaning) are less important than the sounds with their tones, rhythms, and patterns of rising up or dropping down used to soothe or excite the baby. The sounds, gestures, words, and rhythmic interactions (protoconversation) used by mothers lay the foundations for taking turns in conversations in adult life (Bateson, 1975). Adult clients often have difficulty with turn taking, responding either too quickly or slowly, and with mixed patterns.

Maiello (1997) described her observation of Diana, a 3-week-old baby being spoken to by her mother about the pain of her long labor. She tells Diana that she is sorry for screaming. The mother's words and touch carry her emotional meaning. She speaks with a relaxed, soft voice and holds Diana to her chest. Diana gets hiccups but is "not too bothered," and they pass with her mother's attentive care. Diana's mother uses her voice and the holding to help Diana process and heal the recalled distress. Baby Diana has hiccups, suggesting that she is in touch with her mother's distress around the birth, but they stop as the emotional conversation goes on (Maiello, 1997). In a similar way, using simple, adult language, it is possible to speak to the distress in clients and to help them find calm (Chapter 4 considers more specifically how to talk with clients).

Vocal Range in Babies

The voice range of babies is between A to B with some notes going as high as C (Pierrakos, 1969). By 4 months, babies express the basic emotions of fear, rage, and love in sounds. Fear is the sound O-AAAA, love is OOOO-A. Rage is expressed in breath holding (Pierrakos, 1969). Vocalizations between babies and their mothers are not random. They have definite rhythms and a melodious feel to them, called "communicative musicality" (Malloch & Trevarthen, 2010b). With adult clients, we can "talk their music" rather than the content of their words (see Chapters 4, 5, 6, and 7).

By 8 weeks babies engage in shared, improvised sound duets with their mothers. Together they construct a story, with the babies initiating and responding intentionally to their mothers. The lead moves back and forth between the mothers and their babies with a sense of give and take. An illustration of this is that observations of baby Laura in conversation with her mother showed a narrative unfolding with an introduction, a development, a climax, and a resolution, similar to a dramatic performance in four acts (Malloch & Trevarthen, 2010a).

Vocal communications happen in more than one modality simultaneously. So a mother tapping her child gently on the back will also make sounds in the same rhythm as the tapping movement. When this does not happen in predictable ways, it is disturbing for the baby (see an example in Chapter 8). Movement is essential for the sharing of feelings. Babies and mothers share their feelings through touching, making sounds, looking at each other, and changing facial expressions. This all happens before babies have speech.

Communicative musicality also happens between adults as well as babies. It manifests *in* spoken words and also in wordless communications. It is the emotional narrative of conversations. The musicality "energises meaning in communication" and "embraces the part of ourselves that seeks companionship and serves the need in us to relate to others" (Malloch & Trevarthen, 2010b, p. 4).

Looking and Gazing

Babies are born with the capacity to share attention and awareness, and intention and emotions (innate intersubjectivity). They not only gaze around, but can also follow objects with their eyes. They show distinct preferences for looking at people rather than things and seek out the mother's face and especially her eyes (Brazelton & Cramer, 1991). It is the face-to-face interactions that help mothers to regulate their babies' excitement and engagement with others. They fine-tune the intensity and time spent in gazing at their babies and their general activity level to keep the baby in a state of well-being. This is done nonconsciously. Babies shape parental reactions to them with their movements. They do this by turning their heads toward them or away. Their eyes also say "yes, more," and "no, I've had enough" (Brazelton & Cramer, 1991). Our clients do this too and non-verbally show us when they have had enough or want us to continue. Wright's (2009) client, in the introduction, showed in her body language (blocking her ears) that she had had enough of his words.

For a mother to put her baby first and be sensitive to his communications, she has to suspend her own needs in favor of those of the baby. When he signals that he has had enough, she has to be able to fine-tune her own feelings and her own level of excitability. This gives her baby space to recover and find his equilibrium. Then, when he wants more excitement, she has to be ready to engage with him. Over time, the more that the mother responds, in a predictable way, to the baby's signals, the more attuned their interactions become. They learn the rhythms of each other and modify them to fit with the other.

The mother facilitates the baby's capacity to process information by adjusting the amount of stimulation, variations in it, and the timing of stimulations to the baby's particular temperament and physiological ability (Schore, 2003c).

So-called facial mirroring or matching is a two-way process going on between the mother and baby, with each simultaneously regulating the facial mirroring of each other. The mirroring or matching is not exact, more a sense of *"moving in the same affective direction"* (Beebe & Lachmann, 2002, p. 95, emphasis in original). This happens very rapidly, between ⅓ of a second and 1½ seconds, and is probably based on predicting the unfolding sequence of the other's behavior, rather than a stimulus followed by a response. Where the communications are continuously and jointly modified, the experience of being "matched" contributes to "feeling known, and someone is on the same wave length" (Beebe & Lachmann, 2002, p. 98). This applies in psychotherapy too.

Babbling, Movement, and the Beginnings of Words

Let us turn now to the change from making sounds to speaking in words from 6 months, when babies begin to produce words. Words emerge from the musical rhythms of baby sounds and are carried on the breath. Babbling is combined with rhythmic movements of the arms and legs, and especially the hands. Indeed, babies make more vocalizations when making rhythmic movements than not (Iverson & Fagan, 2004). In these early combinations of gestures and speech, gestures are mostly pointing and reaching ones (deictic gestures). Their purpose is to share experiences (declarative communication). The gestures start before the vocalizations linked with them and link in with the vocalizations (Esteve-Gilbert & Prieto, 2013). Then as single words emerge, these are also combined with gestures. I pick up this theme with clients in Chapter 7.

Rational, intellectual speech (propositional speech) moves toward the left hemisphere of the brain, and emotional speech moves more strongly into the right hemisphere (Malloch & Trevarthen, 2010). Gradually, between 18 months and 4 years, the child finds more and more words. The new words are filled with emotion expressed in the tone of the child's voice, and his accompanying movements and gestures. During this period, the child, with help, can begin to tell a story and speak about past events. These narratives come out of a growing "conceptual self-awareness," combined with "an embodied self-awareness in the subjective emotional present and in the subjective emotional past" (Fogel, 2009, p. 250). This is the essence of finding one's voice, i.e. using words to express confidently and authentically embodied feelings. "Too often, we lose our voice because our feelings are unacceptable and need to be suppressed" (Fogel, 2009, p. 251).

Being able to use language is a "mixed blessing," as it brings loss of perceptual unity. The young child links in socially and culturally with others and learns to fit in, "but at the risk of losing the force and wholeness of original experience" (Stern, 1985, p. 177). Language comes to function as the "official version" of experiences (p. 176). Feelings, actions, and breathing get split off from meanings (Pierrakos, 1969). Ashley Montagu concurs:

> The one-dimensionality of the word becomes a substitute for the richness of the multidimensionality of the senses, and our world grows crass, flat and arid in consequence. Words tend to take the place of experience. Words become a declarative statement rather than a demonstrative involvement, something one can utter in words, rather than act out in personal sensory experience. (1971/1986, pp. xv–xiv)

Attachment and Emotional Expression in Words

Children who are securely attached are more emotionally expressive with their early words and sentences, and combine them with body movements. Their vocabulary has a more sophisticated range for emotions and body sensations. In contrast, insecurely attached children talk less about emotions and, when they do talk about them, tend to speak more about their own negative emotions than positive ones (Fogel, 2009). Our clients who were insecurely attached will exhibit particular difficulties with linking body sensations, feelings, thoughts, actions, and words together in an integrated manner.

CONCLUSION

Understanding child development gives us clues about the developmental deficits that our clients may have experienced. Early insecure attachments may not exactly correlate with how our clients relate with us in the present, but by noticing their signature relational patterns we are guided in how to interact with our clients. We can observe their non-verbal communications, coupled with our internally experienced sense of them to pace our relating. In so doing, clients learn how to regulate their emotions and physiology. We can gauge how receptive clients are for communication and ascertain whether they have taken something in and whether they are ready for more stimulation from us, whether through our words, looks, or movements.

Insights from infant studies and neuroscience guide us in whether relatively more non-verbal, right-brain to right-brain communication, or more verbal, left-brain to left-brain communication is called for at any time. These studies also help us to think about the intensity of up-going (stimulating) or down-going (calming) emotional and physiological processes, the rhythms of interactions, levels of consciousness, and which sensory channels are under- or overdeveloped in our clients. However, this theoretical knowledge has to be underpinned by knowing how to be with clients. This is the subject of Chapter 3.

Chapter 3

BEING WITH THE SELF,
BEING WITH THE CLIENT

Tony came for psychotherapy and announced, "My wife thinks I would benefit from it." He had been diagnosed with a form of cancer—not immediately life threatening—and with treatment he could expect to live for several years. What Tony did not say was that he was frightened and did not know how he was going to live with cancer. Instead his eyes conveyed this with a mixture of fear and panic.

*Tony always talked easily, but his words did not convey his deeper feelings. Instead, his words hid his feelings. He was intelligent, had artistic flair and a way with words. Outwardly his life was successful. He ran his own business, had enough money, a second wife and family, who got along well enough, but deep inside himself he felt that it was all a sham. He derived little satisfaction from the way that he presented himself and entertained those around him with his camouflage of words. He would never say this. He came regularly to therapy, intrigued more than engaged by how he found himself experiencing new aspects of himself. I mostly listened to him without much comment. I learned **to be** with him, **to "listen" to what was going on underneath his words.** I did this by alternating between **turning my attention inwardly to my body sensations, thoughts, and feelings,** and then turning my attention **to unobtrusively observing his body in a "heartfelt" way.***

INTRODUCTION

This chapter is about learning how to be with ourselves first, and then turning towards being with our clients. The idea is to be with ourselves, and then our clients, before any doing. Practices for "being with" are the bedrock of non-verbal communication. The running assumption is that the practices and theory described in this chapter underpin all of the subsequent chapters, although they may not be discussed explicitly.

These practices are taken from meditation and awareness practices. They enable us to be aware of our own experiences and at the same time make heartfelt, unobtrusive observations of clients. Heartfelt observing is staying subjectively engaged, in a kind way, as we look at clients. Keeping ourselves close to our subjective experiences, as we glance at clients, keeps us away from cutting ourselves off emotionally from clients and objectifying them. The awareness practices enable us to keep a verbal dialogue going, but to be more focused on what is going on non-verbally. This was what I was doing with Tony, and indeed Caroline in the introduction.

Awareness of our *own body sensations*, for example, can, through the phenomenon of resonance, indicate to us something of what clients are experiencing beneath the surface of their words. While we are sensing our experiences, we assume that they have some connection both with our client and ourselves. Our experiences will also tell us about how we are jointly constellating new ways of relating for both of us. Our experiences can be confirmed and enhanced through observing our client's face, posture, breathing, and so on. We can also talk with clients about our experiences. Choosing what to do with our experiences is the craft of psychotherapy.

The skills of *self and self-other awareness* cultivate a *being-to-being relationship* (right brain to right brain). Awareness practices help us to track our unfolding experiences and to trust our intuitions. We use our personal curiosities, in the immediate moment, to navigate our way through interactions with clients. This keeps the therapy vibrant and novel. It almost goes without saying that this is, of course, combined with thorough training and theoretical knowledge.

THE AMBIENCE OF THE CONSULTING ROOM

Before we discuss how to be with ourselves and clients, we need to consider where we will be meeting with clients. Being with clients starts with being somewhere, usually the consulting room. Where we meet clients has much to say about us. The ambience of the consulting room constitutes a background non-verbal communication from us to our clients. It is necessary to be aware of the messages that we are communicating in our consulting rooms.

The Consulting Room as a Secure Haven

For many clients, psychotherapy begins to function as a secure haven as the therapeutic relationship develops. The consulting room is part of feeling safe enough. In the same way that a child who has a secure relationship with her mother can venture out into unknown territory and return to her if frightened, so the client can keep returning to the security of the therapist (see Chapter 2). The room, with its furnishings and ornaments, alongside the relationship with the psychotherapist, take on meanings that may not be conscious. The reliability of psychotherapy with regular meetings at predictable intervals is part of building a secure base in which to explore and discover. Especially for clients with insecure early attachments, the whole setup of therapy can have a calming effect in itself with its accumulated experiences. As clients come to trust the security of the relationship, therapy becomes a place of surprise and fun. Gradually this basic security enables clients to create new relationships with new patterns of neural organization (the neural plasticity discussed in Chapter 1).

At the beginning of psychotherapy, all clients will have some anxiety simply from being in a novel situation with someone unknown. Early insecure attachments will compound this. We, too, will have our own anxieties about meeting someone new based on our early attachment patterns. Anxiety is reduced by the release of small amounts of the hormone oxytocin, and curiosity is increased. As we learned in Chapter 1 in the discussion of neuroplasticity and the window of tolerance, the better the balance between more aroused and calmer states, the more learning is enhanced. "When peace and calm prevail, we let our defenses down and instead become sensitive, open and interested in others around us" (Uvnäs Moberg, 2003, p. x).

We want to bring clients into the window of tolerance by inter-acting to reduce their anxiety. We want to nurture their openness and interest and we want clients to feel curious, safe to explore and to take risks. If they are highly anxious, it is impossible to make discoveries and stay with new experiences. As we have noted, the therapeutic situation in and of itself will have enough unfamil-iarity to increase anxiety. The way that we set up our consulting room will make it more or less conducive to learning. Our working environment has to be stimulating enough, but not too stimulat-ing. Overall we should set it up in such a way as to reduce clients' anxiety.

The Atmosphere of the Consulting Room

Our working environment creates an atmosphere that begins to constellate (form) the therapeutic relationship. It gives clients a sense of welcome and communicates our receptivity to them (or not). As clients come into the consulting room, their right brains will register instantly their overall impression. Chögyam Trungpa, the Tibetan meditation teacher, tells us that apparently unimport-ant details can "affect the atmosphere a great deal" (1985, p. 129). Many clients will have grown up in chaotic surroundings, and we can present "a contrast to that chaos." He advises, "It is important for the therapist to create an atmosphere that makes people feel welcome. That attitude should infuse the whole environment" (Trungpa, 1985, p. 130). Our attitude toward ourselves and our clients is expressed in the physical environment. Keeping our work environment clean and ordered sends the message that we regard ourselves and clients with respect. Even the simple inclusion of a well-tended plant, within a drab institutional setting, can lift the spirits and bring hope to those with profound suffering.

It is worth taking time to reflect on whether the consulting room supports or hinders our work. What sort of atmosphere do we want to create for clients? The furnishings for a non-verbally focused psychotherapy are intended to invite sensory experience. They will be different if we want to invite a thinking space. Books will suggest thinking and stimulate more verbal left-brain activity; plants and a few unusual objects will create impressions and stimulate imagery—non-verbal right-brain activity.

Room Size, Colors, Objects, Positioning of Furniture

The size of a room has an impact on a client. For some a smaller room is containing and not overwhelming; for others it feels restrictive. Usually we have to work within the limitations of the room that we have. A discussion with clients about the room at least gives them the opportunity to make their feelings about it known. Consulting room color schemes are best kept simple without clashing patterns. Soft and warm color tones are suitable for most clients. For a more right-brain-dominant approach, we want to include plants, paintings, and interesting objects to stimulate the senses. This could include smelling and touching objects as well as feasting the eyes. Our personalities are best not stamped so strongly on the room that it leaves little space for the clients' worlds to come in.

It is a given that consulting rooms should be clean, private, light, warm, and quiet. Rooms are best uncluttered with a sense of order and of where things belong. Furniture and objects can be moved around in the service of therapeutic explorations, but at the end of a session, it is best if everything is put back in its place. This maintains the reliability of the secure haven.

Even minor variations in the physical arrangement of the room seem to affect babies' behavior (Ainsworth et al., 1978), and these observations apply to adult clients with insecure attachment histories. The absence of an object such as a cushion or plant in the consulting room registers just as much as something there regularly. Before September 11, 2001, the twin towers of the World Trade Center in New York were not necessarily admired or particularly noticed, but after their collapse, when people looked at where the two towers, "significant skyline markers," should have been, they experienced "profound disorientation." Prior to their demise they were taken for granted, but as people looked in the aftermath of their collapse, they imagined the towers were still there and were shocked again to see that they were no longer there (McNeur, 2008, p. 24).

Ideally, if the consulting room is at home, it is a dedicated space and does not double up as a family room. Perceptive clients such as those with the heightened sensitivity that comes with disorganized early attachment will know intuitively that something has been disturbed in the aftermath of a family event. This is not necessarily a problem in itself, if it can be spoken about, but may put some clients off altogether.

The furniture in the consulting room also gives out messages. Straight-backed chairs suggest rationality; arm supports give physical and emotional support and containment; upholstered chairs invite relaxation (Rowan, 1988). The type of furniture and its positioning are significant for traumatized clients, but are pertinent for all clients (Rothschild, 2000; Ogden et al., 2006). Time spent exploring the positioning of furniture with clients gives us information about how close or far away they need to be to feel safer.

Chairs placed head-on can feel threatening and oppositional (van Deurzen-Smith, 2010). Chairs at an angle of 45 degrees give us space in front of the body to orient to the rest of the room or to each other. This enables clients and therapists to look, and look away, easily. This enables choice about making eye contact with each other or lets us take a break from the intensity of the encounter. This is beneficial for us and our clients as we emotionally and physiologically modulate our interactions. It is important for all clients whose signals in babyhood that they had had enough contact were overridden by caregivers. In the therapy setup, clients can indicate that they have had enough, and this can be respected. In this process they learn new ways of regulating themselves with others.

Being able to easily look and look away is more relevant for some clients than others. You will recall from Chapter 2 that sensitive-withdrawn clients (early insecure-avoidant attachment) protect themselves by withdrawing, when stressed. They find comfort in objects rather than people.

A final consideration is where the furniture is placed in the room. Some clients prefer to be close to the door to have the sense of being able to get away if necessary. Others like to be able to look out of a window to see a garden or the sky, or perhaps a building that is always there to get a break from the intensity of relating to another human being. For those who are traumatized and those with insecure-disorganized attachment histories, this is particularly relevant.

AWARENESS AND MINDFULNESS
FOR THE THERAPIST

Once we have prepared the physical space for being with clients, we can prepare ourselves to be with clients. Awareness and mindfulness practices are central to this. *Each time before I met with Tony, I prepared the room by airing it out, adjusting the cushions, and putting everything back in its usual start position. Next I prepared myself.*

A Brief History of Awareness and Mindfulness Practices in Psychotherapy

Awareness and mindfulness practices, taken from meditation practices, have seeped into psychotherapy through the dialogue between Eastern psychology and philosophy and Western psychology over the last 40 years. The terms *mindfulness* and *awareness* are often used interchangeably. Some writers offer some differentiation: "mindfulness directs us to the details of our experience; awareness refers to the larger context, the space within which experience arises" (Wegela, 2009, p. 58). In a later book, Wegela writes, "mindfulness is paying precise attention in the present moment to whatever object we have chosen to observe" (2014, p. 17). Meditation has different forms and usually practices to develop concentration are learned first. Then as our ability to concentrate develops, mindfulness can be expanded into awareness, a "more open state of presence, with less fixed attention than pure mindfulness" (Aposhyan, 2004, p. 54).

Mindfulness meditation is a central part of Buddhism, which is 2,500 years old and has been incorporated, one way or another, into all of the major psychotherapies. Humanistic psychotherapies came into contact with meditation practices from the 1960s onwards. Gestalt psychotherapy, for example, incorporated meditation practices from Zen Buddhism from its inception (Gilbert & Orlans, 2011).

Mindfulness is a basic tenet of the body psychotherapy Hakomi (Kurtz, 1990; Weiss, 2009) and of sensorimotor psychotherapy (Ogden et al., 2006). Contemplative psychotherapies steeped in meditation practices emerged in the 1970s and 1980s (for example, Donington, 1994; Wegela, 1996). Core process psychotherapy, for example, is a depth, relational mindfulness-based psychotherapy working at the interface between Eastern and Western psychologies (Sills, 2009; Sills & Lown, 1999). Psychodynamic psychotherapists became interested in meditation practices through writers such as Epstein (1995). The dialogue between psychoanalysis and Buddhist psychology continues with writers such as Fulton (2005), Mace (2007), Safran (2006), Hick and Bien (2008), and Siegel (2010). Mindfulness is also part of couples therapy (Germer & Siegel, 2012) and family therapy (Borofsky & Borofsky, 2012).

Mindfulness-based stress reduction was developed in the 1970s to treat chronic conditions such as pain, which medicine found difficult to treat (for example, Kabat-Zinn, 2001). Mindfulness-based cognitive-behavioral therapy for depression was developed from the recognition of the limitations of cognitive-behavioral therapy for the treatment of depression (Segal et al., 2002). Professionally and in the general public, there is more acceptance that meditation can be practiced by non-Buddhists.

Being Present

We have discussed the importance of simply being with clients for non-verbal communication, yet being with the raw suffering of others is the most difficult part of psychotherapy. We tend to have agendas, want to find solutions, make interpretations, and offer advice. Information giving and education can be part of psychotherapy, but when we get into this too speedily, we are probably closing down some of our experiences, rather than getting to know them in detail.

Mostly, people who are distressed want us to *be* with them. They want to feel that we "understand" because we feel our version of it too. We communicate this to them in our way of being with them (right brain to right brain). Giving a bereaved friend an affectionate embrace communicates far more than any words. What is most important "when we are trying to be helpful, is to *be present*. . . . It sounds so simple, yet it is one of the most difficult things to do" (Wegela, 1996, p. 20, emphasis added). Meditation practices build our capacity to be present. They enhance our experience of ourselves, fine-tune our capacities to be with clients, and develop our awareness of the environment.

An Exercise for Building the Capacity to Be Present

You might like to read the following exercise first and then try it out. Sometimes, if our eyes are shut, it helps us focus on ourselves. Open or shut is fine.

The first step in building the capacity to be present is choosing—using the left brain—to direct our attention inward. We ground ourselves by noticing points of contact between ourselves and what is outside: noticing our feet on the ground, sensing the bones that we are sitting on, being aware of the back of the chair against our back.

Then we ask ourselves, What am I experiencing right now? What am I sensing in my body—aches, pains, nothing much? Am I hot, cold? Am I comfortable or uncomfortable in the way that I am sitting right now? What am I thinking? What am I feeling?

This exercise was the next part of my preparation for seeing Tony. Then, throughout the session with him, from time to time, I chose (left brain) to place my attention inward, to keep track of my inner experience (right brain).

In meditation practices we learn to be aware of ourselves without the internal verbal chatter that so often occupies our thoughts. We learn to listen to the silence. In escaping from the distraction of internal verbal chatter, we become aware of sensations, emotions, and thoughts. When we practice this way of listening, we become more acutely aware of clients' non-verbal messages. We learn to listen to the gaps in speech, the silences between the words. The meditation teacher Eckhart Tolle observes, "To listen to the silence, wherever you are, is an easy and direct way of becoming present" (1999, p. 103).

Awareness happens in the present, often expressed as being in the "now." "Nowness is with us, of us but yet always elusively evading our grasp" (Brandon, 1990, p. 62). We cannot force ourselves to be present. It is more a question of softening into the present moment. I can decide to turn my attention inward, but then I have to let what I am experiencing just happen. Generally speaking, the more we apply effort to be present, the less present we will be. However, we can support ourselves by *lightly holding the intention* to be present, to be aware of our stream of experiences. We can also *intend to attend* to the whole person, rather than a part of him or her. If we hold an intention, it is likely to be realized (Bugental, 1987). Volition, another name for intention, "is the ground of all our actions" (Hanh, 1998, p. 34).

One way to help us stay present is by sensing the body and asking ourselves what we are experiencing (as in the exercise above). The body acts as a constant reference point for interoception and exteroception (see Chapter 1).

> When we are willing to be present, we tap into direct experience: that is experience that is not filtered through our thoughts, expectations, hopes and fears. Instead, we see, hear, taste, touch phenomena, and recognize thoughts and images in the mind without adding judgments or preferences. Things are just what they are. Putting nowness and direct experience together means being awake in the present moment. (Wegela, 2009, p. 26)

Being present opens us to "Presence." Presence is universal and always there. "Presence is not just an attribute of a particular person; it is a universal expression of interconnection and interbeing" (Sills, 2009, p. 260). Terms such as "inherent health," "essential self," "brilliant sanity," "essence," "God," "core," or "Buddha nature" attempt to describe Presence, but do not capture what is indescribable. The words are only representations of the ineffable.

Interconnection, or "interbeing," is assumed to be the normal state in Buddhist psychology. We "inter-be" and are not separate beings. We are connected with all human beings, all living creatures, and the environment including forests, rivers, mountains, and minerals (Hanh, 1998). Being aware of Presence puts psychotherapy in a wider context and reminds us of our humanity. It also builds humility, which makes it more likely that we shall be able to maintain a being-to-being relationship with clients.

Presence and Healing

Working in a process-oriented way, as we do, with a non-verbal focus (see introduction), we have lots of opportunities to practice being present. This can be supported by regular meditation practices outside our clinical work. Meditation develops our awareness of our subjective experience, and we learn to stay in these states of awareness longer, getting to know the contours of our experience. This capacity to stay more present transfers to our ways of being with clients and, indeed, to relationships generally. As we become more aware of ourselves, we tune more acutely into our clients; we become more non-verbally interconnected. Clients will then experience us (non-verbally) as receptive to them. This in turn non-verbally invites our client's experiences to come into the room. Indeed, awareness itself is transformative (Maslow, 1973; Bugental, 1978; Siegel, 2010).

Training to Be Present

Training to be present comes not only from meditation but also from having had depth individual psychotherapy. As well as having psychotherapy, bottom-up psychotherapies train their students how to stay aware with clients through experiential explorations. These explorations are always followed by reflections on them, a reflecting on reflected experience. This is not the same as thinking about the experience. It is reexperiencing the past experience in the present. As a student recounts the experience of perhaps a practice session, he or she experiences physical sensations, feelings, thoughts, and imaginings (embodied reflecting). This recasts the session in the immediate moment and deepens "understanding" of it through embodied reflecting.

Reflecting and Mentalizing

Reflecting is different from "mentalizing" (Fonagy et al., 2002). Mentalizing is having an internal observer and thinking about what is in our own minds and infering the likely mental processes of others (Wallin, 2007; Ogden, 2009). Sletvold (2014) sees the mindful stance and the mentalizing stance corresponding respectively to embodied-affective and verbal-reflective forms of self-experience. Both activities are complementary in psychotherapy (Wallin, 2007; Sletvold, 2014). Ogden (2009) reminds us that our mentalizing will be affected by factors such as body postures, sensations, and movements. "Directed mindfulness" can bring awareness to our mentalizing and make it more known and explicit. Mindfulness, therefore, can include mentalizing.

Reconnecting With Presence

Staying in present experience, with acceptance of unfolding experiences, is the essence of mindfulness. Mindfulness lets us attend to the stream of our body sensations, feelings, ideas, and imaginings with the possibility of reconnecting us to Presence. "When we are rooted in mindfulness, we can see clearly what is unfolding within us. We don't grasp it and we don't push it away; we simply recognize it" (Hanh, 2001, p. 219). The "four fields of mindfulness" or areas on which to rest our attention are body, feelings, mind, and objects of mind. Each field contains the others. We are always mindful of something and so when we dwell in mindfulness, we are always in contact with something.

A basic mindfulness practice is mindfulness of breathing. We choose to turn our attention inward and then notice our breathing—as it is. See Chapter 5 for some breath-based awareness practices. The discipline of these practices increases our capacity for sustained concentration on a particular object of awareness. The object of our focus can be internal or external, involving heightened interoception or exteroception (see Chapter 1). So we can focus on what we are hearing internally, such as the sound of the breath, or externally, such as the look in the client's eyes. With both Caroline in the introduction and Tony, the clients introduced to you so far, looking at their eyes gave me information about what they were feeling, but not saying. When focusing inwardly, I gained more information about what they might be feeling through resonance.

Awareness and Bodily Experiences

All awareness practices are anchored in body experiences collectively known as somatic awareness or, as Fogel (2009) calls it, "embodied self-awareness." Awareness practices and the focus of their attention can be grouped in different ways, such as these:

- Inner awareness of subjective experiences: physical sensations such as itches, tension, tingling, pressure, and movement.
- Outer awareness: sense impressions from the environment through seeing, hearing, smelling, touching, and tasting.
- Awareness of fantasy: processes that take us out of the present moment of sensory experiencing into imagining, explaining, planning, and thinking.

Awareness practices in this book are intended mostly for therapists, but some of them can be used with clients. When used with clients they are presented less formally, as and when it seems pertinent to draw the client's attention to something. Wegela (2014) discusses the pros and cons of teaching clients to meditate and does not have a hard and fast view but does include some simple practices for clients. My own view is that there is a difference between teaching clients some basic awareness practices to become more self-aware and the formal teaching of meditation. I think that teaching meditation is best kept separate from psychotherapy, and many clients seem to find their own way to meditation teachers, tai chi, yoga classes, and so on, which often enhances their lives.

The following awareness practices are used to train body psychotherapists in Cambridge, England. They include the three aspects of awareness: inner, outer, and fantasy. You might like to try the practices yourself. I suggest you read this section through first and then try it out. The first part is intended to make contact with the feet and the ground. Grounding brings us in touch with our bodies, and especially our legs and feet (in this exercise), and our connection with our physical boundaries—what is me and not me. It anchors our experience downward in the body.

> The first part of the practice is to wander around a sizeable room wearing socks, or with bare feet. Walk in whatever style is preferred. Focus your attention on the feet and their contact (or otherwise) with the floor. If you walk more slowly, you may be able to sense (be aware of) your feet more. If you do not sense your feet, rub them on the floor—top, bottom, sides—to get the blood circulation moving and to bring sensation to the feet.
>
> What do you notice about your feet? Are they hot or cold? Maybe they are sore. Perhaps they are tingling. Maybe they feel numb. Whatever you experience is just fine. This basic grounding and walking practice can be done for about 10 minutes.
>
> The second part is to go outside, preferably into a garden. Let yourself meander around the garden with no particular aim (aimless walking), and notice your experiences. Notice what you are curious about: What do you want to touch? What do you see, feel, hear, smell? What are you imagining? Thinking? This can be for 10 minutes. You may want to stay outside or move back indoors.
>
> After Parts 1 and 2, sit and notice how you are feeling, and reflect on your experiences of both parts.

Below, Susan, a student body psychotherapist, writes of her first experiences of awareness practices over a training year:

Reflecting on the first training weekend, I note that for both of the body awareness exercises, walking around the room, and the aimless walking outside in the garden, I was totally in fantasy. My thoughts were full of my house move and I felt ungrounded and disembodied. However, this changed when I reached the silver birch trees at the back of the garden. Without "thinking" about it I just reached out to feel the smooth white bark which looked so appealing. I put both my hands around the trunk and felt the whole tree move in the breeze. I looked up at the tracery of the leaves against the very blue sky and heard them rustle in the wind. I noticed this shift in my awareness at the time, but only now as I write this I appreciate its significance fully. . . .

Over the year I have continued to practice being in the now and come to know hurtful thoughts colouring my present experience. . . . I was able to track an incident with my partner which had evoked a jealous reaction. . . . I feel a cold shot of adrenalin in my stomach which feels panicky and cold. I am shaking and it feels as if my blood is being drawn away from my feet and hands. They feel cold. I go still and stop breathing. My heart is beating faster. I feel a hot feeling rising up from my guts—it is anger come to save me. By really engaging with the bodily sensations my mind was diverted and unable to bring up past experiences to fuel the pain.

Effectiveness of Mindfulness

A plethora of studies have demonstrated the benefits of training patients in mindfulness, for various conditions and Germer, Siegel, and Fulton (2005) and Khoury et al. (2013) provide an overview. As I've already stated, this is not the focus of this book. However, for therapists, bringing awareness practices into our work increases our capacities to remain present to strong emotions, traumatic experiences, and moments of hostility from clients. A therapist participant, Rebecca, in a research study reflected:

It's kind of noticing and being aware of it so that in the awareness of it I'm not acting out from that place, I'm aware it has become part of my field of experience, oh, all right, right now I'm feeling attacked and as part of that I want to defend myself and in that I notice the sensation of tightness in my chest or I notice the sensations . . . so it's the ability to know kind of what's happening moment to moment in myself and also with the client. (Cigolla & Brown, 2011, 709–721)

The "warrior stance" cultivated in martial arts is invaluable for psychotherapists. Marks-Tarlow (2013) describes it as a quiet, kind steeliness, which comes from the sustained practice of meditation. From this practice the warrior can maintain inner quiet and outer stillness in the heat of the moment, enabling alertness and readiness for whatever may come.

PREPARATION FOR BEING PRESENT WITH CLIENTS: ESTABLISHING A RECEPTIVE FIELD

Having prepared the consulting room and brought some awareness of myself in the present moment before clients arrive, another practice we can cultivate is one that establishes "horizontal and vertical holding fields" (Sills & Lown, 2008). This builds a receptive field into which clients arrive. The practice can also be used silently, when actually with clients, to enhance our receptivity when we notice that it is slipping.

I used this practice as a third step of preparing for Tony. I also made use of it when with him. The more solidly I felt in my own experience, the more I could accept Tony and be with him.

First of all, you might want to read the practice through, and then take yourself through it, or you may want to ask a colleague to talk you through it. After each full stop, give yourself about 10 seconds or so before you move on to the next sentence. Take your time.

Establishing the Horizontal and Vertical Fields

Phase 1: Positioning

Find a position that is comfortable and invites alert relaxedness and can become, with practice, second nature. You can stand, sit on a chair, sit on the floor cross-legged, or sit on your haunches. Take time to establish the position. Close your eyes, or keep them open, but with a soft gaze—seeing, but not looking—directly in front of you.

Gently straighten the back. It should be straight, but not stiff. Sense the neck and head resting on the top of the spine. Gently tuck the chin in, keeping the head upright. Softly pull the shoulders back, imagine the chest widening out slightly. Begin to have a sense of coming home. Let the arms rest by your side, the hands resting in your lap, or on your leg, by your side, if standing. The palms can face up or down—whichever feels right to you.

Phase 2: Finding the Vertical

Sense your sitting bones—if they are not easy to feel, then try putting some pressure through each buttock in turn. Whatever you sense is all right—it is all information—notice how you react to your experience.

Let your awareness travel up your spine, taking your time—sensing into each vertebra. Sense into the vertebrae of the neck. Sense into your skull as it rests on your spine. Let your chin be tucked in and your head aligned with your spine. Extend your awareness through the top of your skull. You might sense or imagine a thread extending skyward from the top of your head. Sense the line connecting you to the ground through the sitting bones. Extend your awareness, as far as you wish into the ground, then up your spine, through your skull and skyward—as far as you wish.

Let yourself rest in the vertical connection between sky and earth. Feeling yourself gently held. Feel the solidity of it and how it fluctuates in your awareness.

Phase 3: Finding the Horizontal

Now slide your awareness to the rest of your body. Sense the edges of yourself from inside your skin. Imagine a liquid flowing into the whole body—going into the tips of your toes, your fingers, into all the nooks and crannies—letting yourself expand and fill your skin.

If you find yourself wandering in your thoughts, come back to finding the vertical, finding the sitting bones.

And now exploring space beyond your physical self—imagine or sense your energy field moving through your skin and just onto the outside of your skin. Sense clothing on skin, perhaps a current of air brushing your skin—sensing inside and outside.

Let yourself expand energetically further away from the physical body, just a short distance. Sense how far you would like to expand and let your-self explore that. Stay with what feels right for you. Your experience will change and you may want to expand further or come back in.

Dwell in the vertical and the horizontal holding fields.

Phase 4: Coming Back Into the Room

Now find a way to bring yourself back into the room. Give your-self time—and sense the journey back. Look around and notice your surroundings.

When your client arrives, enter into relating from the vertical and hori-zontal holding fields. When your client leaves, prepare for your next client.

Infusing the Therapeutic Field With the Qualities of the Core State

Referring to clients, Wegela observes, "Knowing directly what it feels like to be in their world leads to compassion" (1996, p. 131). Compassion opens to loving-kindness, joy, and equanimity. These are the embodied qualities of the core state. They are described in Buddhist psychology as the Brahmaviharas, the four Illimitables or Immeasurables. If we are open to these qualities, they become a source of nourishment. They "lighten the burden" of psychotherapy and open up the possibility of resonating with these qualities in cli-ents without being overidentified with clients or indifferent to their distress (Bien, 2008, p. 48).

> Psychotherapy is an expression of love—love as compassion, joy, equanimity, and kindness. It gives us a chance to renew and reclaim the deepest elements of our own practice, and the deepest elements of connection and healing. It reminds us that not only compassion, but also joy, equanimity, and basic kindness are within us and within our patients at all times, however hidden. (Surrey, 2005, pp. 98–99)

Compassion is heartfelt empathy and is not to be confused with sentimentality. Loving-kindness is open-hearted and loving. It is often described as friendliness. Sympathetic joy lets us enjoy our own and our clients' pleasure, well-being, and success. It counter-acts all the negative experiences of early relating. It is valuable in the ending of psychotherapy and helps us to genuinely rejoice in a client's independence and strength (Sills & Lown, 2006). Equanim-ity is having space for everything to come into the room, no matter how significant or trivial. It has wide perspective. If we can invite these qualities into psychotherapy, they are healing in themselves.

There are specific meditation practices for cultivating these qualities that go beyond the scope of this book. Usually cultivating loving-kindness is the place to begin.

> A simple way to start cultivating loving-kindness is to go into a relaxed, awake state, sitting upright and with the eyes closed. Notice points of contact between your own body and the chair that you are sitting on (ground yourself). Take time to establish this state as best you can.
>
> Let yourself become aware of your body sensations. Give yourself time to do this.
>
> Bring to mind people that have been kind to you in your life.
>
> Let yourself become aware of your bodily sensations as you recall someone.
>
> Gently put that person to one side and let the next kindness come to you. Take your time.
>
> After some minutes, bring to mind people that you have been kind to in your life. Let each kindness come to you and then gently move it to one side, making way for the next kindness. Let yourself be aware of physical sensations and feelings.
>
> After a few minutes, bring your awareness back into the room. Let yourself become aware of how you are now. What are you experiencing?

With Tony, my heart stayed tender toward him by letting myself imagine what it might have been like to be him as a little boy. I assumed that the lack of authenticity in his words came from not having his true feelings accepted in childhood. It helped me not to become frustrated and then critical of his camouflage of words.

AWARENESS AND MINDFULNESS WITH CLIENTS

Let's return to Tony now, and how the practices discussed so far were part of the therapy. As Tony talked, I turned my attention inward every so often. When I did so, I was often drawn to my chest area. Often, it felt tight and aching. I had little sense of my abdominal area, which felt hollow and empty. I took all of this as mostly being about Tony. These are not usual body sensations for me. I assumed that I was resonating with him. (See mirror neurons in Chapter 1, and attunement in Chapter 2.) Week after week, when I turned my attention inward, it was drawn to my chest and abdomen. When I looked at Tony, I might see the flicker of fear in his eyes, when he told me the test results were not so good, but our conversation continued without Tony speaking of his fear.

Generally, after about 45 minutes or so, Tony would be "performing" less. His body would look more open; his chest would expanded slightly. He would look less rigidly held up. He would "drop down" into himself more. When this happened, he would speak in metaphors, referring to landscapes, art, and poetry. I would feel whispers of emotional connection with him, authentic relating without pretense. He would be easier to listen to and to be with. During these moments, if I turned my attention inward, I would sense the edges of sadness and longing in the middle of my chest. My chest would be less tight. Week after week my chest felt less tight and I felt more uncertainty and vulnerability when I tuned into myself. I was making more emotional connection with Tony non-verbally.

Sometimes I would attempt to bring these feelings into words. When I did that, mostly it interfered with Tony sharing his feelings non-verbally. Tony would feel attacked by me and jump into performing. It was as if he has been caught out and had been reminded that he had to maintain his false but protective self-image. Occasionally he would "let me in" and for a few brief seconds there would be two of us relating together, rather than one (Tony) talking in safe but lonely isolation. Our deepest levels of relating came when I just tuned into him non-verbally, listened to whatever he was saying, and accepted him as he was.

Tony was not unaware of his predicament, namely that he was emotionally like a child in a man's body, and that he role-played being a man rather than feeling grown up. His cancer had shaken his self-image. At times when he felt ill, he had less energy to preserve his image. He did not state this explicitly. The vulnerable look in his eyes told me, and he seemed to know that I had caught the look (or received it). If I tried more firmly to put the non-verbal aspect of our relationship into words, he felt humiliated and defeated. We lost our deeper non-verbal connection with each other.

In the beginning of therapy, his only recourse was to protect himself with entertaining words. If I pushed verbally on his way of protecting himself by wanting to be part of the conversation, rather than the audience, he felt deeply hurt and lashed out with well-aimed, bullying verbal barbs. Tony was not open to verbal engagement for a very long time, but, by being with him in a non-verbal way, as best I could, he slowly, but surely, showed me the wounded little boy inside, and the two of us came into dialogue. I gradually learned what it was like to be him.

I assumed that Tony's habitual way of relating with a false image, with his words hiding his true feelings, came from having to defend himself from someone hostile to him, someone who wanted him to be other than he was authentically as a child. This is the nature of a narcissistic defense. People with these defenses are part of Nolan's fragile group (see introduction and Chapter 2). So although Tony was outwardly a strong and capable man, inwardly he was quite fragile. I learned much later on that his fear was that he would be overwhelmed by his feelings. I was particularly welcoming of his metaphors. You will recall that metaphor is understood by the right brain (Chapter 1). When Tony talked in images and metaphors, he was entering a more authentic form of self-expression, edging toward emotional expressiveness.

Adapting Presence

Expanding or Pulling in Our Presence

Attention (awareness) can intentionally slide, shift, and shuttle from one point of awareness to another and also take in the transitions between the points of awareness. Notice how the use of these different words suggests different ways of moving to different points of awareness. We can choose to share, explicitly or not, what we are experiencing with our clients. With Tony my choice was not to share explicitly with him. He was not receptive to it.

Earlier in this chapter, the actual physical distance between therapist and client was discussed, but there are less obvious ways to explore space and distance. We can take up more or less "energetic space" with our clients by drawing ourselves in or expanding outward. Rustin (2013, p. 41), for example, writes of deliberately "shrinking" her presence and dampening her arousal to make a better fit with her client Jack, who visibly shrank in her presence.

Taking Up Less Energetic Space

Lily, who had a traumatic childhood, is an example of a client who needed me to take up less energetic space. We had been meeting for about 18 months. Although her bodily signals (pulling back her upper body slightly) indicated that she wanted to get away, I knew that she liked me and wanted to stay. It was just difficult for her to be in the room with me.

Lily sat on the edge of her chair, not looking at me. Her eyes darted around the room furtively. She looked ready to spring up and run away at any moment. In response, I focused on myself and pressed my bottom firmly into my chair to create a strong sense of being present (grounding myself). I sensed my arms resting heavily on the chair arms and felt my feet firmly planted on the floor. I softened my breathing and pulled my awareness inward, placing it into the back of my spine. I kept my hands still. I reduced the amplitude of movements in my whole body. I anchored myself and became a less stimulating person for Lily.

Lily remained on the edge of her chair, but she was now able to tell me that she felt too close to me. I suggested that I could move or she could move. She abruptly stood up and deftly moved her chair further away. She found a better place for her chair. I noticed that Lily then breathed out more fully. Her breathing deepened slightly. The atmosphere in the room felt less restricted. I thought that her sudden movement came from being near to panic. She leaped at the chance to move.

Taking Up More Energetic Space

With Pauline I needed to expand myself to meet her powerful energy, which filled the room. On first meeting Pauline, I felt pushed into the corner of the room as if there was no space for me. My breathing was shallow, as if I was not getting enough air. I did not know how I was going to survive the hour. I told myself that this is what Pauline does when she meets a stranger. It must link with her early relationships. Understanding that did not help much.

I let myself breathe in and out more fully. I inwardly puffed myself up to three times my usual energetic size—like filling a balloon up with air. I breathed in and out from this expanded place. I had claimed more space for myself. There was now space for both of us in the room. I did not speak about this, but our sessions became easier for me as I regularly prepared for Pauline by adjusting my size.

Several sessions into getting to know Pauline, she told me that the supervisor of her counseling practice had pointed out that she did not give the client enough space to speak or reflect. Pauline thought that her mother may have been the same. She had no memory of it and did not really know. I felt that I was getting a glimpse of what it was like for her as a child with her mother.

Focused or Panoramic Awareness and Short and Long Rein Holding

We can make our focus of attention panoramic, like taking a wide-angled overview picture of a scene, taking a metaperspective of everything in a generalized way to get the overall feel of things. This might mean taking an overview of our relationship with the client, the room, and perhaps sounds outside the room. In contrast, we can be very finely focused on the sensory contours of a sensation, such as an aching wrist.

We can also energetically hold clients in different ways, keeping them either on a short rein or a long rein or something in between. We do this by imagining a reel of fine but very strong silken thread connecting us with our client. We hold the end of the thread in one hand and the other is firmly linked to the client. We can let the reel unwind or keep it more tightly held, but all the while keep hold of the reel of thread.

Short rein holding keeps the dialogue and sensory experiences close and tightly grasped so that the client does not drift off into loosing themselves (dissociate). This short rein holding is a particularly useful way for relating with more traumatized clients. For these clients, we do not want fantasy space to open up. We want to keep up-going emotional and physiological arousal down. This means not allowing silences and keeping close track of what clients are experiencing and asking them to put words to it. Putting words to experiences will keep the left part of the brain active and reduce subcortical arousal.

In contrast, *long rein holding* allows silence and opens up psychic space. Emotions have room to emerge, along with wandering reflections. Generally clients are given a wider arena in which to roam around with their experiences. Long rein holding is suitable for more robust clients. Usually over the course of a session the thread of connection will tighten and loosen as required and feels like a dance. For example, a client may go toward being flooded with feelings and moving in the direction of being outside the window of tolerance (Chapter 1). We respond by moving into short rein holding by asking a left-brain question starting with when or why. Then as the client stabilizes himself or herself, the rein holding can lengthen a bit. This allows more feelings to emerge. These forms of holding clients are non-verbal and fast, and can be left unspoken. They "speak" to clients subliminally (non-verbally).

RESONANCE

The word *resonance* comes from the Latin verb *resonare*, meaning to echo, resound, or sound out together. Receiving clients, or "getting them," is about resonating with them implicitly, or non-verbally. Biologically we resonate or attune with others through the mirror neuron system (described in Chapter 1). The fact is that people are social creatures and are very sensitive to the feelings and experiences of the people around them. This sensitivity is essential to social processes, and it is no surprise that we have evolved the ability to understand much more than what words can convey. In due course, neuroscientists will probably be able to tell us more about this.

Another perspective on resonance comes from some spiritual traditions, in which resonating with the world is regarded as our normal state. In contemplative psychotherapy, resonance is called exchange. Wegela explains:

> Since we're not solid, when we meet someone else there is an intermingling of energy. If we sit with a friend who's very sad, we might find ourselves feeling sad. Our sadness is not merely a response to hearing about what is happening to our friend. It is as though we catch their sadness. (1996, p. 128)

In physics and music, when one object vibrates at the same natural frequency as a second object, it forces the second object into vibrational motion, called resonance. Musical usage of the term *resonance* gives the sense of the movement in a sound and the impact that one vibrating object has on another. Meditation teacher and psychologist Jack Kornfield captures both the interconnected aspect of resonance and its biological mechanism:

> Each time we meet another human being and honor their dignity, we help those around us. Their hearts resonate with ours in exactly the same way the strings of an unplucked violin vibrate with the sounds of a violin played nearby.

> Western psychology has documented this phenomenon of 'mood contagion' or limbic resonance. If a person filled with panic or hatred walks into a room, we feel it immediately, and unless we are very mindful, that person's negative state will begin to overtake our own. When a joyfully expressive person walks into a room, we can feel that state as well. (2008, p. 17)

Resonance is called somatic resonance in body psychotherapies in recognition of its physical nature. It is part of embodied relating. The bodymind of the therapist receives and impacts on the bodymind of the client and vice versa in a joint process. Somatic resonance is the direct experience of the client's feelings, bodily sensations, and thinking. It is more than empathy (see comments on empathy in Chapter 2). The physical body can be thought of as a receiver of information about what is happening in any moment energetically, physically, emotionally, and imaginatively.

We can deliberately cultivate somatic resonance and use it as a vehicle to set the tone for how therapeutic relationships unfold non-verbally. We can turn our attention inward to gather information about the unfolding relationship with our clients. We can respond to this silently or more overtly and adjust the relationship with a client. For example, with Pauline, I noticed my shallow breathing and struggle to breathe. I adjusted my breathing and found a way of coming into relationship with Pauline. This enabled Pauline to find her own energetic size with me without speaking about it at the time.

Resonance and Reaction

Although we are wired to resonate with others, we develop ingrained patterns of *resonating and reacting*. Patterns of reaction, or interference, are laid down in our attachment patterns in babyhood. They come from how caregivers related to us either resonantly (attuned) or dissonantly (misattuned; see Chapter 2). Repeated patterns of misattunement, without repairing, become habitual interference patterns. We bring patterns of resonating and reacting to therapeutic relationships. Interference patterns obscure our capacity to resonate with others. In any therapeutic interaction, there is a mixture of the client's and the therapist's resonant and reactive patterns of relating going on simultaneously (Boadella, 1982). Resonant and reactive patterns are inevitable in psychotherapy. They can be explored by slowing down our experiences and getting to know them in detail using awareness practices.

Tony's reaction pattern was his defensive way of speaking and his false presentation. For a long time in his psychotherapy, we were only able to be non-verbally resonant with each other for brief moments. I would feel hurt by his bullying words, when I lost contact (misattuned) with him non-verbally and commented on him, instead of being with him. Being aware of my hurt, feeling it more fully and reflecting on how our interactions touched on my own history, helped me not to react. Then silently tracking how I had provoked Tony's attack also enabled me not to lash out at him. I think Tony probably saw that I was hurt and had mixed feelings about that.

Body psychotherapies speak of somatic reactions and somatic resonances. For ease of dialogue with other forms of psychotherapy, the term *somatic reaction* is used interchangeably with the more familiar analytical terms *somatic transference* and *somatic countertransference*. However, there is different theoretical understanding behind the terms. Somatic transference and somatic countertransference are both reactions and interfere with resonating. In top-down psychotherapies, somatic transferences and countertransferences are generally thought about. Then they are interpreted rather than staying with them experientially and deepening into the subjective experience of them. Conversely, bottom-up therapies can lose sight of naming and understanding experiences.

Recognizing Reactions

Over- or Underinvolved Presence

Two kinds of reaction are underinvolvement and overinvolvement. The underinvolved psychotherapist is aloof, cool, and insufficiently responsive. The overinvolved psychotherapist has lost touch with boundaries and become submerged in the client's world, with his or her own needs being subsumed in those of the client. Therapists can fluctuate between being over- or underinvolved. Particular therapeutic relationships will draw out these different responses at different times. Clients with early disorganized attachments provoke both extremes. Those with early avoidant attachments can stimulate underinvolvement.

Exploring Under- and Overinvolvement

An awareness exercise often used in the training of body psychotherapists is for one student to be the client and another the therapist. The client lies down on a mattress and is asked to shut her eyes. The client speaks about whatever comes to mind or says nothing, whatever she is at ease with. The therapist sits to the right-hand side of the client on the floor in view of the client. She explores adopting three different sorts of therapeutic presence without speaking. She tells the client when she is about to change her presence, but not the sort of presence that she will be holding. The positions are:

- Neutral: just intending to be present
- Overinvolved: energetically reaching into the client or, if the client has his eyes closed, leaning into the client's personal space
- Underinvolved: perhaps looking out of the window, thinking about getting the groceries

Student therapists are usually surprised by how much their non-verbal communications are picked up by the student clients.

Developing Resonance

Somatic resonance can be cultivated to deepen our non-verbal experience of our clients. The following exercise is used widely in body psychotherapy (see, for example, Sletvold, 2014). The assumption is that the information gathered in the exercise is about both the client and the therapist. You might want to read the exercise first and then try it out, or find a colleague to read the instructions out to you.

An Awareness Practice to Cultivate Resonance

Allow pauses between each instruction and go slowly.

You can choose to sit, stand, or walk.

Let yourself feel your feet on the ground and your points of contact with the external environment—perhaps your back against a chair or seeing a picture on the wall. Sense the qualities of your breathing.

Bring a client to mind. Perhaps close your eyes to help to see this client. . . . Gradually move from your usual way of sitting, standing, or walking into the manner in which your client sits, stands, or walks. . . . Take time to feel the transition from your style to that of your client. . . . Recall the overall posture—let yourself focus on the detail. . . . Catch the nuances of the detail—how exactly are the fingers intertwined? . . . how far does the neck poke forward? . . . where do the eyes gaze? . . . how is the mouth? . . . how does the client breathe? . . . Stay in the posture for a few minutes, whatever you feel comfortable with. . . . Loosely gather up your physical sensations, thoughts, feelings, and imaginings. Put them into a list—like making a shopping list. Explore being with more uncomfortable experiences, but let yourself dwell in more easy experiences too. As you stay in the posture, you might want to speak about your experiences in the present tense to a colleague or just to yourself: "Now, I'm feeling tight in my chest. My neck aches, and so on."

When you want to move out of the posture, do so very slowly and come back to your own posture. Notice how that is.

This practice deepens our experience of clients. It can be used in actual sessions with clients, as well as in supervision. Times to consider using the practice are when we are feeling lost or have gone into reacting. It can also be done overtly with clients. This will depend on the client being able to tolerate us going more into our own experiences and the client not being the obvious focus of attention. Some clients will like the pause this creates, as it can give them a break from the explicit dimensions of relating. Others, such as those on the borderline personality disorder spectrum, may not be able to tolerate the apparent lack of attention. Adaptations can be made for specific clients and circumstances.

The exercise might be introduced along the following lines: "I'm feeling lost at the moment, or I think that we are missing each other. I want to take a pause to gather up my experience of what is going on." Sitting alongside clients makes it easier to sense them. For those psychotherapists who work routinely with changing physical positioning during sessions, it is relatively easy to get out of one's chair and to sit alongside. This can be explained to clients: "I want to come and sit beside you to get a sense of things from your perspective." For those psychotherapists used to dialogue happening in fixed places in the room, it is a much bigger step to change the usual form of sessions. Introducing something novel into therapy has to be negotiated carefully, and psychotherapists also have to be comfortable with it.

PERSONAL QUALITIES

Awareness practices develop the personal qualities of therapists, and these qualities are more important than techniques and theory (see introduction). Qualities such as intuition, spontaneity, creativity, humor, and playfulness are particularly valuable and are right-brain functions (Marks-Tarlow, 2013). Allan Schore observes, "Much of the therapist's knowledge that accumulates with clinical experience is implicit, operates at rapid, unconscious levels beneath levels of awareness, and is spontaneously expressed as clinical intuition" (2012, p. 7).

Intuitions are what make us ask or do something out of the blue without knowing why. Sometimes we just have a gut feeling and work it out conceptually later on. We can check out gut feelings and intuitions by turning our attention inward. Then we can deepen into the intuitions and check out what else is going on inside us. Mindfulness training also increases insight, which in this context is nonconceptual problem solving. Mindfulness meditation does this by focusing on nonconceptual awareness, which reduces the influence of habitual conceptual and verbal processes, and the interpretation of experience (Ostafin & Kassman, 2012).

An illustration of an intuitive leap comes from my work with Tony. *Tony had had about 3 years of therapy at this time. By then Tony trusted me more and was less defensive. One day, as he was talking about his daughter, I had the urge to ask about his father. He had spoken of his father before, but I felt a particular urgency to know more. I let my question crystallize into some words to say to him. As I did that, I silently asked myself what I was sensing in my body. I noticed an excited curiosity in my abdomen. I was aware of my feet touching the ground and I felt the back of the chair that I was sitting on. I was in my body and aware of my bodily sensations. I was present and grounded. I had deepened into experiencing the impulse. I had not said anything to Tony. The impulse was still there.*

I did not know why I wanted to say something about Tony's father, but there was an imperative to do so. I had paused to know my impulse experientially and more fully. This is not the same as pausing to understand by thinking about why an intuition might be followed. When Tony had finished his sentences about his daughter, I told him that I found myself interested in asking about his father. He looked taken aback and went quiet. Then he said, "It's funny you say that. It would have been his birthday today. . . . I regret being so rebellious when I was young." He paused and then said, "I think that I could have got to know him now I'm older. It's too late now—he died a long time ago." And then after a longer pause, "I think that he loved me. He was just so bottled up that he could not show it." These words were very moving and I was hearing about a father that Tony wanted to know. Previously, Tony had been reluctant to speak of his bullying father.

Attending to experiences is a process of reflecting on them experientially and nonconceptually. We make the decision to pay attention to our experience and then attend to it. This is the left and right hemispheres of our brain working together. The skill for therapists is to pick up the non-verbal signals in their relationship with clients and to sense what is going on at any moment. This can be done by remembering to silently ask questions such as:

- What is the atmosphere like?
- What is happening in me?
- And then, when focusing on the client, what am I noticing about the client?
- What is happening in me in response to that?
- What else am I aware of right now? This could be something outside the consulting room, noises, smells, thoughts, and so on.

All this supplies information about how to proceed. The more experiential knowledge fleshes out the relationship.

CLARITY, COMPASSION, AND SPACIOUSNESS INQUIRY

A final practice to introduce in this chapter for reflecting on interactions and helping us to be aware of resonances and reactions is the clarity, compassion, and spaciousness inquiry. It was developed by Maura Sills, director of the Karuna Institute. The intention is to reveal the wisdom of the psychotherapist and to connect with intuition. In Buddhist psychology, Buddha nature is characterized by spaciousness, clarity, and warmth. By inviting the qualities of intrinsic health to the psychotherapy process, an atmosphere is created in which client and psychotherapist can flourish. The inquiry supports us with "not knowing" and not having to know intellectually. It gives us a way of monitoring the nature of the qualities and their balance with each other. When our connection with one of the qualities is disappearing, these are moments to heed more closely and to inquire further. It is also a way of reflecting in supervision on clients.

Spaciousness

The hope is to bring space to open up contraction, soften solidity, widen narrowness, and still to give containment where there is a lack of boundaries. Is there space to accommodate whatever experience arises? Questions to consider include: How much space is there? Is there room for everything? Is everything held lightly? What is not there or not allowed? What have I become identified with? Spaciousness includes space, time, content, right distance in relationship, relationship to experience. How is the contact reflected? How is the client held? Where is the boundary? What is communicated in the silence?

Clarity

Clarity is the antithesis of confusion, chaos, and excessive sharpness. Lack of clarity will come when perceptions are distorted by our habitual responses to events. What is going on? What is there? How do I clarify what is going on? What level is clarified?

Compassion

Compassion is in contrast to meanness and hatred. How much is tolerated? What is defended against? What is the quality of warmth, safety? How do I respond to suffering? Am I warm in my whole experience?

Sometimes when working with Tony, I noticed that what had provoked his bullying responses to me was that I was less open-hearted (compassionate) with him. My idea of what he should be like created a lack of space in me (spaciousness). I wanted to have my say and felt left out. This made me mean to him (from excessive clarity). When I noticed that and breathed to create more space inside (by expanding my breathing, both in and out), I felt more spacious, less mean, and more open-hearted. In these moments Tony usually became more authentic in his relating.

CONCLUSION

Our first task, as psychotherapists, is to set up our consulting room so that it supports us and our work. The next task is to become aware of ourselves through awareness practices. From there, we can move into contact with clients. We can use any of the practices described so far to broaden or focus our attention, to be aware of reactions and resonances, and stay present to ourselves and the client. Resonances in the relational field will come into awareness and deep interpersonal contact emerges. Old patterns of defensive strategies loosen in the expanded awareness (Sills & Lown, 2006). This is the foundation of the healing process.

Chapter 4

VERBAL AND NON-VERBAL COMMUNICATION

TWO COMMUNICATION STREAMS INTERACTING TOGETHER

Eliza sought psychotherapy because she was "stressed." On our first meet-ing she told me that she enjoyed her work in customer care, but "There are too many people every day—and there's no time to do it as well as I would like." She also lacked confidence in relating with colleagues. She was okay with customers because there were procedures to follow. Colleagues were different: "There is no rule book to follow." She was "mostly too busy" to feel her stress, but whenever she stopped, she felt "anxious" and exhausted. She had been anxious for as long as she could remember—probably going back into childhood, but, although willing to do so, she could not elaborate on her anxiety.

In this chapter we explore the two streams of communication, the verbal and the non-verbal, and reflect on how they interact. Central to this chapter is my work with Eliza. Understanding and using non-verbal communication was an essential part of the thera-peutic process for Eliza.

From Eliza's introductory sentences, we can see that her "stress" had different aspects. One factor was her demanding work, but this was exacerbated by her difficulties with relating "without a rule book," that is, spontaneously with colleagues. She had been anxious from childhood without really knowing why. The anxiety and her relational difficulties suggested that patterns of interaction with her childhood caregivers were misattuned and were encoded in her implicitly. She could not elaborate on her anxiety, as it was more implicit and not available to her explicitly in narrative form. It looked like she had early insecure attachment (see introduction on memory, and Chapters 1 and 2). Before Eliza arrived, I had done my usual preparations of the room and myself (see Chapter 3). As with Caroline in the introduction, I intended to make contact with her non-verbally at the same time as I gained factual information about her.

I did gain factual information about Eliza, but instead of "listening" to the sensory-emotional non-verbal communication of our conversation as I had intended, I noticed that I was trying to figure out what in her past was causing Eliza's anxiety. Why was Eliza so anxious? What had happened to her? Maybe it was this or that. I asked Eliza questions, almost to prove my speculations, such as, "Why did that happen?" "When did you do that?" "Who else was there?" Eliza responded with thoughts about her anxiety, but our conversation was stilted.

Eliza's conscious-thinking, left-brain activity was stimulated by my questions, and my speculations were increasing my own left-brain activity. We were in a more left-brain-dominant dialogue and it was not really going anywhere. Eliza could not find the answers there about her anxiety.

I looked at Eliza and silently noticed that she neither looked anxious nor spoke with any trace of anxiety in her voice. When I turned my attention inward, I felt no physical discomfort, such as my breathing becoming shallow or held, which can happen when one is with someone who is anxious. I was baffled. I kept my awareness on my bafflement and reflected that I had become overfocused on clarity, had lost connection with spaciousness, and I was a bit less compassionate toward Eliza (the clarity, compassion, and spaciousness inquiry from Chapter 3 in action). I decided (left brain) to move my attention away from my preoccupation with factual information and thinking. I let myself become more receptive to Eliza's non-verbal communication by noticing my body sensations. The shift in my focus of attention entailed sensing my back resting against my chair, feeling my feet on the ground, and silently asking myself about my body sensations (for example, what is happening in my chest?). All this grounded me and I became more present.

I became curious and asked Eliza to tell me more about her childhood.

Our relationship began to change as it became more spacious and less cognitively driven. Eliza was an only child, brought up by her "single, young Mom". Her childhood home was always full of her friends "making mess." Her mother never minded that and "let them do what they liked." Eliza spoke with genuine affection for her mother, and her face was warm and open. I turned my attention inward again, noticing that my thinking had lessened considerably, and that I had an odd sensation in my forehead. I was beginning to resonate and relate non-verbally with Eliza.

Eliza remembered making a fairy costume for a school play with her mom. The odd sensation in my forehead became more pronounced. My forehead and then my eyes felt blurred, like looking through a camera lens out of focus, but my vision was not actually blurred and I was thinking clearly. It made no rational sense to me, but I stayed with the odd sensation. I encouraged Eliza to continue by saying, "Tell me more about your mom." I spoke with a tone of voice intended to stir Eliza's feelings. Eliza's mom was a healer, "a bit of a hippy." She could "know things" about people, "but as a child, it was confusing." Her mother had told her things about people that she could neither see nor understand. Her mother had treated her as a friend and told Eliza her worries, but often she did not understand what her mother was telling her. Eliza spoke more slowly. She told me that her mother would ask her to talk about herself, but then she did not listen. She reflected, "It was like she was trying to be a mom—doing what she thought she should do, instead of just being a mom." After this part of our meeting, my forehead had cleared completely.

I had resonated with and received Eliza's non-verbal communication—the odd, blurred sensation in my forehead and eyes—through my body non-verbally. Eliza had put her childhood experiences with her mother into words and I had listened, unlike her mother. I surmised that my odd forehead sensations were something like the confused state that she lived in as a child, which was encoded implicitly in her and had been brought into the present.

LISTENING TO THE NON-VERBAL

As already noted, placing non-verbal communication at the heart of psychotherapy involves moving back and forth between focusing on the client and then ourselves. *We observe how clients speak* and what their bodies are telling us non-verbally. *We keep the conversation going and notice our internal experiences.* Being able to keep two levels of interacting going on simultaneously comes from the skills developed by the awareness practices in Chapter 3. The different experiences, those observed and those experienced, build a picture of the therapeutic relationship. With Eliza, what I was internally aware of (interoception) told me more than what I observed about her.

As we become proficient with awareness practices, we can observe gestures, postures, and movements of clients, and concurrently put our awareness inward and get the feel of clients, as we resonate with them. As our awareness develops, through practice, we notice less obvious bodily changes in clients and ourselves. We do this by slowing ourselves down by breathing more slowly and fully. This calms the sympathetic nervous system down and enables us to sense more of what we are experiencing. We can also speak more slowly and allow more pauses between our words. As we slow down, we come to see more subtle phenomena in clients. We might catch a glimpse of a minute increase of moisture in an eye, a ripple over the skin, the hairs standing up on a bare arm, a smile starting to break out around the mouth and then gone, or a twinkling of the eye—briefly there and then gone. We also come to resonate more with these observations. In Eliza's case, it was not what I saw, except maybe the absence of visible anxiety, but my inner experience that was more significant.

THE SPOKEN WORD AND EMOTIONAL STATES

Let us turn now to thinking some more about words and emotions. Words are sounds. They carry energy and are suffused with vitality or rendered flat when energy is withdrawn from them. Words are carried on the "energy of breath" (Watson, 2002, p. 205). Speech emerges from musical rhythms (Bunt, 1994; Cross & Morley, 2009; McGilchrist, 2009a) and babies make sounds with the intonation and rhythmic phrasing of words and short sentences before they acquire verbal language. As we saw in Chapter 2, the "music" of speech (prosody) carries emotional messages back and forth between the parent and little one. They carry the emotional meanings between them implicitly, right brain to right brain.

Clients with insecure early attachments have impairments in communicating their feelings in their speech. Their parents may not have permitted them to babble freely, telling them as little children to be quiet. Or their parents may have frightened them with angry, loud words, or just not appreciated the joy in their child's communications. Babies are startled by parents speaking in angry, loud tones. They react with a sharp intake of breath as they startle, and where angry interactions are frequently repeated, they do not breathe out fully because they learn to anticipate the next bout of shouting. The startle becomes encoded in their bodies (Boyesen, 1980; Keleman, 1989) and they develop disturbances in their breathing. Breathing disturbances restrict movements, vocal expression, and general physical mobility (Reich, 1970). Children's voices become constricted, perhaps dry, flat, and mechanical, or limited in emotional range (Pierrakos, 1969). Braatøy observes, "Restricted breathing is the preverbal equivalent of the incomplete sentence. In psychotherapy, the important aspect is incomplete emotional expression. It is not an accident that 'to be inspired' means to participate with the whole person" (1954, p. 176).

As baby babbling gives way to words, the music of babbling goes into the background and speech becomes the foreground. Even in secure development, words become split off from the emotional meaning behind them (see Chapter 2). This splitting is more pronounced in clients with insecure early attachments. Normally there is interplay between words and our physical state. Reich writes, "It is clear that language, in the process of word formation, depends on the perception of inner movements and organ sensations, and that words which describe emotional states render, in an *immediate way*, the corresponding expressive movements of living matter" (1970, p. 361, emphasis in original).

These "movements of living matter" are experienced as the "felt sense" (Gendlin, 1981, 1996) or "somatic markers" (Damasio, 1994). The felt sense is the collection of physical sensations, both kinesthetic and emotionally "tonal," occurring in the body, which are the precursor of a named emotion. Thinking exists alongside "somatic markers," which provide vital information for decision making and are essential in social communication (Damasio, 1994). *With Eliza there were already hints that she had difficulties connecting her non-verbal and verbal processes. She could think, but her feelings, apart from "anxious," "stressed," or "tired," were limited.*

RECOGNIZING DIFFERENT KINDS OF SPEECH

Clients have different ways of talking, and we can learn more about the non-verbal communications expressed or missing in their speech by listening in a low-key way to the content of their words. This frees us up to listen more intently to the way that clients are speaking. It is a question of getting used to listening not so much to content as to form. Listening to the form of the client's words will tell us about the non-verbal level of our relating in the present. It also hints at what communication the client may have initiated (non-verbally) that was not fully expressed in babyhood because of lack of attunement, or frightening or abusive interactions.

A Practice for Listening to the Form of Words

You might try practicing listening to the form of words by asking a group of colleagues to read out some brief information, something like instructions for how to prepare pasta. Ask each colleague to read the same information in turn, but choosing to read anxiously, in a depressed way, angrily, and so on. Do not let your colleagues tell you how they plan to read the instructions.

Use the first exercise on turning your attention inward in Chapter 3. Keep your eyes open. Then *look and listen to what is in the words*. Listen to the melody of the words, and the tone of the speaker's voice. Notice any changes in your colleague's body as she speaks. From your receptive, sensory-emotional perspective, what do you notice internally as you look at your colleague and listen to the feeling tones of the words? What are you seeing? Try to put the feeling and any body sensations into words. Did you know what each person was conveying? Please treat this lightheartedly, rather than as a test.

Rooted or Dead Talking

At the start of psychotherapy, clients may lack emotional expression as they speak. In the first meeting we can start to observe how "rooted" or how "dead" a client's speech is. We then continue over time to get to know the client's style of relating through words. We observe talking by looking at how clients move and breathe, and their loudness and so on as they talk. We do this in tandem with inner sensing of the impact of the talking on us.

Rooted Talking

Clients are described as "rooted" in their words when their words have a direct and immediate *connection* with what is moving them emotionally, energetically, and physiologically. Their speech is alive as they talk from the "movement of body sensations." The connection between the internal movements and the words being spoken is the bedrock of rooted talking. The client's *words resonate with and are directly expressive of their movements of life.* We can describe this as embodied talking. Rooted talking feels authentic because the words literally and emotionally move the client. When clients are unrestricted in their breathing and movements, their talk will be rooted. We sense this in our own bodies by turning our attention inwardly. Both of us will be moved. Neither Tony in Chapter 3 nor Eliza were rooted their words, although this showed differently in each of them.

Being moved by clients comes about non-verbally through mirror neuron resonances and also because the body acts as a sounding board. Words carry energy and make vibrations, and we sense the impact of this through our body vibrating as the energy reaches us. The body "vibrates in sympathy" and adds "changes to the quality, loudness, pitch and duration of the sound" (Bunt, 1994, p. 47). The specific quality of "rooted aliveness," with the expressiveness of the spoken word, creates contact with others; we feel more intimacy with the other person. Moments of rooted talking come and go. When they come, they are firmly rooted in the body. The words come on the out-breath emanating from below the diaphragm, the main muscle of breathing, which bisects the trunk. In contrast, words may be spoken from a tight throat, or from a restricted upper chest, and not be rooted. This is what happens when our breathing is restricted. Speaking from a restricted throat muffles the communication of feelings.

When clients enter into phases of rooted talking, their attention goes inward. They may look down or "inward" and are unlikely to look at therapists. Clients need time to catch their feelings and thoughts without interruption. Often their speech slows down as they search for the words closest to their immediate experiences (Southwell, 2000). Rooted talking is unrehearsed and is like live streaming of present experience. The words may come in fits and starts, with long pauses. Sometimes the words may come in fragments of sentences or sounds as clients attempt to find the right word, a word or phrase that is resonant with their experience (Southwell, 2000). When clients do find the right words and phrases, their words feel truthful. "Rooted words" are not rehearsed and are formed as they are being spoken. Sometimes clients might try out a word or phrase for its fit. As they speak the words and hear their sounds, they may say, "No, that's not quite it. . . . It's more . . . more . . ." as they seek something more accurate for their self-expression. Often they start over again in their quest to find the right words. Clients need ample time to play with this process of finding their own words. This is a time for the long rein holding and quality of spaciousness discussed in Chapter 3. This helps clients to focus inwardly rather than outwardly as it gives them more space.

Dead Language

In contrast to rooted words, there are dead words. We have observed already that words may be used as a defense, perhaps to distract or fill silences. Sometimes clients are "drowning in verbiage"; the "meaningless activity of muscles" (Reich, 1970, p. 362). We can "talk about" something rather than talking expressively. "Talking about" something, rather than being expressive, is dead talk. The delivery of dead words is without aliveness and expression of "living process" (Andersen, 1991b). When we work with a non-verbal focus, dead talk can be hard to listen to as it is divorced from the client's direct experience. We become distracted and unengaged because we are not moved by the words. The content may feel as if it ought to be interesting because of the topic of conversation, but we have no curiosity to know more. Ironically, something banal can be highly engaging, when a client speaks in a rooted, lively manner. Another way of describing Tony's talk, his entertaining tales (Chapter 3), is "talking about talk."

Dead talk develops when children learn to limit their breathing, through specific patterns of interactions with early caregivers, but its origins can be more diffuse, such as the pervading atmosphere of the family home. The atmosphere comes from how various family members interact and the context of the home. A client once told me (in a rooted manner) that her family was loving, but the urban neighborhood that she grew up in was "harsh and you could never take your safety for granted." She did not know how terrifying this was until she had left and experienced other towns. I believed that this accounted to some extent for her dead talking. As we saw (see Chapters 1 and 2), these experiences of insecurity get encoded sub-cortically in implicit memory. Where the atmosphere of the home creates "security and trust," the baby can recover from startling and frightening moments, but without it, "the child stays on the alert" (Southwell, 1988). "One could literally say that the rather tense circumstances make the person reduce his/her inspiration from the surroundings" (Andersen, 1991a, p. 18). Dead talk comes from above a restricted diaphragm. Dead talk is also described as "talking above the diaphragm" or "talking on top of oneself." Working with clients who characteristically speak in this manner, with its lack of resonance, is exhausting and can lead to burnout, if it is not addressed (Boadella, 1982; Westland, 1997). *Eliza's words were dead and not rooted for the first part of the session described so far. Her words were more rooted from the time when I had the odd sensation in my forehead and she began to talk frankly about her mother.*

Patterns of Speech

Dead talk comes in different ways of speaking in which the words do not resonate with and express feelings. Deceptively, clients can talk in an apparently expressive manner but not be authentic. The test is whether they move us (emotionally) and engage us. As we observe clients, we notice whether the client's body and breathing is synchronized with their words. With Tony, I was entertained, but unmoved. Different patterns of speech correlate with character strategies mentioned in the discussion of attachment theory in Chapter 2 (see also Pierrakos, 1969; Boadella, 1987). These are characteristic forms of protective defense that babies develop with their caregivers to cope with the stresses of unrepaired misattunements or to fend off hostile interactions. Clients often have a dominant style of talking but are likely to have combinations of protective speech styles. When clients talk in a dead way and in any of the following styles, it tells us that they do not feel safe. They are showing us what they do when unsafe. This relates to both past and present interactions. Clients are unlikely to know this explicitly and consciously.

As you read the next section, let yourself read with a tender heart and sense physically what it is like to be each client. What does the speech show you about what the client was protecting himself or herself from in childhood?

Talking on One Note

The client speaks in a monotone, which could be depicted as a flat line. The speech lacks musicality and any emphasis on key words. The speech has a dry quality and lacks warmth. The emotional range is very limited. This way of speaking belongs to what Kurtz (1990) calls the sensitive-analytic person, with an early insecure-avoidant attachment history. Peter, whom you will meet in Chapter 6, spoke in this way at the start of therapy. Eliza, when she was figuring out the cause of her anxiety, spoke in this way too.

Talking on the Horizontal

Close to "talking on one note" are clients with a bit more expressive range. Eliza fitted this description too, and Tony had elements of this. As with clients who talk on one note, their words are monotonous. There is a lot of "talking about" to fill the space up. There is no sense of depth, and of their "dropping down" below the diaphragm to feel what they want to express. However, there is more resonance and contact with such clients than with those who talk on one note. Outwardly such clients appear friendly and may chatter, but the therapist feels empty inside listening to it. This way of speaking belongs to what Kurtz (1990) calls the dependent-endearing character style.

Enticing and Enthralling

This client has a bewitching quality while telling engaging stories. The stories are entertaining and perhaps humorous. The engagement is with the good yarn, but afterward the listener realizes that she does not know much about the person telling the yarn. The story has substituted for personal connection and has kept the listener at bay. This is Kurtz's (1990) seductive-charming character style. It does not correlate easily with an early attachment style.

This was Tony's predominant way of speaking when he first came for psychotherapy.

Circumlocutory and Oblique

This client talks convivially but never gets to the point. If asked a direct question, the client appears to be coming toward the answer but never gets there. After a while it can feel frustrating to be with someone like this, especially if the therapist is invested in wanting some direct answers. This is Kurtz's (1990) burdened-enduring character style. Again, it does not correlate easily with an early attachment style.

Runaway Train

The client's words are pressured and the client cannot seem to get them out quickly enough. There are no pauses for reflection and sentences all run together with no commas or periods. Becky, whom we will meet in Chapter 5, is such a client. The more the client talks, the more the speech speeds up. The speed of the speech pushes the momentum on. It is as if the client is not in charge of herself and cannot catch up. Content is everything. Often the speech is high-pitched. This way of speaking belongs to the "clinging-expressive" character style (Kurtz, 1990) and correlates with early insecure ambivalent-resistant attachment histories.

Talking Without Resolution

This client talks, maybe with some apparent expression, but there is never a sense of resolution. It is as if the music has to keep playing with no sense of a movement toward the finale. It leaves the therapist expecting the final musical cadence, waiting for what should be coming. There can be a relentless feeling of being stuffed and overfed when sitting with such clients. This is characteristic of borderline clients, those with disorganized insecure attachment histories. In Chapter 6, you will meet Suzy, who spoke like this.

Eliza's speech patterns were a mixture of talking on one note and talking on the horizontal. It transpired that her mother had been depressed after her birth. Apparently her mother had been able to look after her, but Eliza mentioned in passing that she was not a "cuddly mom." We can surmise that Eliza's (non-verbal) baby communications were not resonated with sufficiently for her thoughts and internal sense of her baby self to link up. Her right brain did not develop optimally and link up with her left brain. Although her mother seemed loving, she seemed unable to resonate with Eliza as she grew into childhood (inferred from Eliza's descriptions of her mother and how Eliza was with me). Tuning into Eliza non-verbally and helping her to link her thoughts with her feelings and actions became our therapeutic intention. Eliza accepted this idea and could see how being unable to do this contributed to her stress. For example, she could not express her feelings with colleagues.

BEYOND WORDS

So far we have looked at the actual words of clients, but words emerge out of silence. We can observe the way that silences are broken perhaps elegantly, roughly, or as a bursting forth. However, we should not forget that the most profound moments are silent. Not all experiences can be put into words, although music, poetry, dance, and art can point us toward them. Describing the beauty of a setting sun loses something when it is reduced to, "It was a beautiful red, with hues of gold and yellow. It took my breath away." Instead, touching someone's arm and saying, "Look at that!" is much more direct. Reich was of the view that experience "not only functions before and beyond word language; more than that, it has *its own specific forms of expression which cannot be put into words at all*" (1970, p. 361, emphasis in original). Reich also asserts, "What is described as the 'spirituality' of great music, then, is an appropriate description of the simple fact that seriousness of feeling is identical with contact with the living beyond the confine of words" (1970, p. 361). For our purposes we can take "living" as experience.

Similarly, Sills writes about the "relational field." When it embodies qualities of stillness, warmth, and empathic resonance, "implicate information is subliminally conveyed and known silently with clear comprehension. Within this kind of relational field, a client might truly hold their suffering in balance, and open to an *experience of their human being-ness that is beyond words*" (Sills & Lown, 2006, p. 211, emphasis added). Implicate information is non-verbal information.

Winnicott too writes of a crucial aspect of mothering in which the mother dwells in silence alongside the infant to foster the development of the true self: "it is the experience of being alone while someone else is present" (Winnicott, 1990a, p. 30). The baby has the experience of the mother being present and aware of her while being free to be alone and with herself. The mother is neither impinging nor depriving. The baby is freed from the need to be alert and closely watching the mother's moods to feel safe. The child can trust the mother's love and can just be with his or her experiences. In a similar way, moments of silence with clients can be profound. They are there simply to be experienced together.

OBSERVING NON-VERBAL COMMUNICATION

Before we learn more about Eliza's psychotherapy, I want to introduce a model that develops and builds on our observational skills and our capacity to stay with our internal sensations, known as body-speech-mind inquiry.

This is an awareness practice drawing on Tibetan Buddhism (Rabin & Walker, 1987; Wegela, 1996, 1999, 2009, 2014). It is a way of "deep listening" to clients. It is invaluable for catching implicit information and deepens our experiences of ourselves and clients. In its original form, body-speech-mind inquiry, in the context of psychotherapy, is used mostly in group supervision. Additionally, the model is particularly useful after an initial assessment consultation to reflect on a new client. Later in psychotherapy it can guide personal reflections after sessions with clients. The practice is descriptive, rather than diagnostic.

A client is described using simple, direct language, in the present tense. This helps us to get close to what it is like to be the client. Direct language is closer to our internal experience. For example, the description "the client is depressed" does not tell us much. However, "the client's shoulders are dropped forward," "he shuffles his feet," "he speaks slowly in a croaky whisper," "he sighs a lot" is closer to the direct experience of being with this client and his internal non-verbal state, which we want to communicate with. Clients are not static, but our choice of language can give the impression that they are. So if we think and describe the client diagnostically as "depressed," we fix and limit our thinking and may overlook a fuller understanding of the experience of depression. We may not capture the particular experience of depression of this client and the nuances of his moods.

As a client is described as directly as possible using the model, we begin to (intentionally) identify with the client. Often this practice is enough to deepen experiential knowledge of a client, without necessarily having more cognitive understanding. Body, speech, and mind are not separate parts of a person, but by grouping themes in this way, it helps to organize the material. You might like to read through the next section to familiarize yourself with it and then go through the practice. After each category of description, pause, give yourself plenty of time, and ask yourself:

- What am I sensing in my body?
- What am I feeling?
- What am I imagining?
- What am I thinking?

Simply note your feelings, thoughts, sensations, and imaginings that arise in you without trying to make rational sense of them. They are information about your client. We are capturing information from right-brain processes rather than conceptual understanding.

Body, Speech, Mind Inquiry

From the *Courage to be Present*, by Karen Kissel Wegela, © 2009 by Karen Kissel Wegela. Adapted from the original and reprinted by arrangement with the Permissions Company, Inc., on behalf of Shambhala Publications Inc., Boston, M.A. www.shambhala.com

Start by finding somewhere quiet and becoming more present to yourself using the above questions or any of the other methods from Chapter 3. Then bring a client to mind. Describe your client, speaking out loud, starting with body.

Body

Body includes a person's age, general body shape, height, and size. What clothes does he wear? What colors are favored? Are the clothes fitted? Baggy? Are the clothes coordinated? Is he groomed? Casually dressed? Dirty? Dishevelled? Is the clothing contemporary? What footwear does he have? Does he wear jewellery or accessories? Has he any visible piercing or tattoos? Does he have any scratches or grazes? Any bandages or band aids? Walking aid? Does the client carry a handbag? Briefcase? Rucksack? Grocery bag? Bag from a conference? Does he bring a shopping cart? iPad? Laptop? How is his posture? How does he move, sit, walk—in reception and in the consulting room? What mannerisms and gestures does he make? Is he aware of his appearance and body?

Next the detail of the body can be reflected upon—a description of how it is, for example, "He has short brown hair. His nose is small and his face is round." How is his hair? How is it styled? How are his eyes, nose, mouth, ears, teeth, hands, fingernails? How is his complexion? Is his skin clear? Are his muscles toned? How do his body parts move together? Do they seem coordinated? Flowing, jerky, random? How does he breathe—fast, slow, irregularly? How does his skin tone change with movement, speech, silence? Are parts of his body still and others active? How much space physically and energetically does he take up (spatial dimension)? Does he mention his body and his relationship to it? Does he describe physical experiences?

Reflections on the body also include the physical environment. Where does he live? With whom? Who else is important? Are they friends, family, neighbors? For this part, just name the people in his life. How does he travel around? Bike, car, subway, bus? Walks? What does he like to eat? Does he cook, eat out, eat irregularly?

How someone spends time is also included in the body category. Does he work? Do voluntary work? How does he spend leisure time? What is his daily life like? Busy? Too much time?

You might like to pause here. How present and embodied do you feel right now?

Speech

The speech category includes how someone communicates in speech, and also information about relationships and how someone experiences and expresses emotions. Again, description is used. How does the client speak? Softly, quietly, in a whisper, booming? Does he have an accent or occasional word with a different inflection? Where does his voice come from in his body—throat, chest, belly? Does he modulate his voice? How quickly or slowly does he speak? Does his voice sound dry, tight, juicy, gushy? How does he phrase his words? Does he pause? What is his rhythm of speaking? Is it melodious, staccato? If his speech were a song, could you hum it? What is the style of his communication? Does he tell a story, diagnose himself, give a detailed diary of his week, speak concretely, metaphorically, with visual imagery? What vocabulary does he use—extensive, sparse, technical, colloquial? Does he search for words or speak fluently? What cultural references does he make? Does he speak directly, circuitously, obliquely? Are his sentences completed? Do they trail away, or become emphatic? Does the client carry conviction that he can mean what he says, and say what he means? Is the talk rooted or core connected?

Borrowed from meditation, the metaphor for speech is breath. It indicates a sense of aliveness and connection with it. How does the client's breath move or not move through the body? Does he listen to himself, talk at you, with you, through you, beyond you?

What facial expressions and gestures does he make? What emotions does he describe and express? How does his mood change in different situations? Is he prone to depression? Confident? Angry? Does he hold his feelings back, or let them flow freely? What conditions elicit emotional states? What is missing emotionally, avoided? Where is the client most alive, least alive? What does it feel like to be with him? What is invited? Are you curious, bored, impatient? Is it possible to feel compassion for him with a speech focus? How is it to be describing him now?

Who is important in his life? Friends, family, neighbors, family pets? Stay descriptive. Does he spend time with them? Does he have a partner(s) or spouse? Other relationships? Previous partners? How does he relate to groups, individuals, animals, money, dreams, images? How does he describe his sexual orientation? Does he enjoy his sexuality? Is sexuality never mentioned?

What other forms of expression does he have apart from speech in his life? For example, writing poetry, cake decorating, singing in a choir, gardening, sewing?

You might like to pause here. How present and embodied do you feel right now?

Mind

Mind is reflected and revealed through body and speech and is inferred. What is the sense of the client's mind? Playful, sharp, tight, detailed, quick, intelligent, dull? How does he think? In repetitive thoughts? Hopping about? Rambling? Analytically? Either/or thinking? Concretely, metaphorically? With gaps and assumed understanding by the other? Focused, dispersed? What does he think about? What relationship does he have to his mind? Confident, inadequate, highly prized? How does he work with gaps in thought? How much range is there? Narrow, tight, broad, inclusive? What situations expand or contract the mind view? What are his spiritual and religious beliefs and practices? If his mind were a landscape, what sort of landscape would it be? A jungle, a desert, a snowy wasteland? What happens to your mind with the client?

You might like to pause here to catch feelings about mind.

Let yourself reflect on the whole experience of your client. How present and embodied do you feel right now? Let yourself slowly let go of the reflections on the client and come back to yourself. What are you sensing in your body? How are you feeling now? What are you thinking?

A Sample Inquiry

If we apply this inquiry, in an abbreviated form, to Eliza, here are some observations.

Body
Eliza dresses in smart clothes, often a navy short skirt, matching jacket, and white blouse. She carries a slim briefcase. She walks briskly with coordinated movements. Her hair is styled in a short bob and frames her face. Her complexion is fresh, pinkish-white in tone. She wears light makeup. She smiles a lot in an appealing way. She has no extraneous movements, and the overall impression is of order and neatness. She lives in a rented apartment with her boyfriend of 3 years. She is busy at work and in her leisure time. She tries to get to the gym three times a week. She does not cook much and eats out a lot with her partner. As I tune into myself, I feel frightened.

Speech
Eliza speaks fluently in an audible tone. She has an extensive vocabulary. Her voice is mostly a bit flat without much melody. She tends to speak concretely and tries to diagnose herself. She directs her speech toward me and invites me to provide the solution to her stress and anxiety. Her words come from her upper chest and lack emotional conviction. Her gestures are sparing. She has two cats and a small group of friends.

Mind

My sense of her mind is that it is analytical, tight, intelligent, focused. Eliza thinks about her difficulties and tries to find strategies to resolve them. As a landscape, I imagine Eliza's mind as a well-ordered garden with neatly clipped hedges, with plants evenly spaced and color coordinated in straight rows. She has no religious affiliations, but leans toward Buddhism. As we have already seen, my thoughts are activated with her, if I do not pay particular attention to this. I feel afraid of anything without order as I reflect.

BUILDING A COLLABORATIVE RELATIONSHIP WITH CLIENTS

To work well enough with Eliza, I needed to establish a collaborative relationship with her. In the introduction, I briefly noted the importance of a collaborative relationship when working non-verbally. A collaborative relationship communicates with the non-verbal, emotional parts of clients carried mostly by the right brain. Collaborative relating is pertinent for all clients with early insecure attachments. It is required especially for those with histories of insecure disorganized attachment and fragile clients generally. In collaborative relationships, we place ourselves metaphorically (and sometimes literally) "alongside the client."

We put ourselves close to the client's experiences. When this is achieved, clients experience us as being with them. We choose our words carefully to resonate with the client's non-verbal, emotional state (see comments on words in the introduction). As therapists we put more of ourselves to one side in the service of the client's inner experiences. We maintain as best we can our own integrity, as we resonate with clients and how they are influencing us. This is akin to the task of a caregiver with a baby, who puts her own feelings on hold as she puts helping the baby deal with his feelings first. As clients develop "independent well-being" from becoming more proficient at self-regulation, our inevitable reactions, rather than resonances, will feel less threatening to clients. As clients become emotionally stronger, we can afford to be more ourselves; clients can be with our perceptions and rhythms, which may be different from their own.

Nevertheless, at the start of psychotherapy, fragile clients can find words attacking, or feel that there are too many words for them to understand. This is especially so if the words are not connecting with their implicit, unspoken experiences. It leaves them feeling that the therapist is not with them. This is especially pronounced when they are distressed. An example of this is "Jack," described by Rustin (2013). Jack grew up in a chaotic family, was traumatized, and survived by withdrawing into himself and taking refuge in books. Although Rustin softened her voice, "questions seemed to terrorise Jack" and he shrank "more into his shell by tucking his chin down even further" (2013, p. 19).

Wright (2009) bravely describes, early in his career, making a "catastrophic interpretation" with a "psychotic man." He had asked his patient to stand back and look at the possibility of ending psychotherapy because he thought that the man was not benefiting. Much later he realized that for this man, the psychotherapy sessions "were the only times in his life when he felt in any degree safe, if not alive." The "standing back" proposed by Wright was experienced as a "murderous attack":

> Interpretation leads to a relatively distanced kind of knowledge which codifies experience and places it in a larger context. It involves a person seeing himself as an object in relation to others and offers an explanatory account of his feelings and behaviour. It uses a form of language that is poorly suited to capturing the uniqueness of individual experience and in this sense can be felt as diminishing. Some patients react to this interpretative process badly, feeling observed and dislocated from themselves in a way that transforms them into objects or specimens: they feel scrutinized and looked at, and robbed of their subjective individuality. In such cases the observer/analyst is at best experienced as un-empathic, at worst as a mortal threat to the self. (2009, p. 127)

Using the Client's Words and Ordinary Language

We build a collaborative relationship with clients by using ordinary, straightforward, and unambiguous language. Professional jargon is to be avoided. As far as possible, we want to use the language that the client uses. We build collaboration by speaking in the same register (within reason and common sense) as the client. Perhaps the client says, "I'm feeling low today. It was hard to get here today." We respond using the same word "low" to describe the client's state. We do not want to substitute a synonym (our word) such as "flat." This creates emotional distance between us.

We can the use the client's own words to connect more strongly with her background feelings conveyed in the words. We do this by repeating "low," and "it was hard to get here," the most evocative words and phrases that the client has uttered. We repeat the words, letting our words carry the feeling tones of "low" and "it was hard to get here" as conveyed to us by our client. We repeat the words, putting their melody into our voice. We emphasize, "You're feeling *low* today. *It was hard to get here today.*" As we repeat the words using the client's intonation, we let our words go a whisker deeper into the feelings that our client was conveying and that we are resonating with non-verbally. We slow our words down and let ourselves resonate with the client, feeling the word "low" as fully as we can. We stay present and grounded and adopt long rein holding. We shift from hearing about the client's experiences to resonating with them and giving the non-verbal communication back to her in the rhythm and intonation of our words. This is how we make a body-mind, more right-brained response to the client using our words. Initially, in this way of working, clients are usually unaware of their non-verbal communication.

In the collaborative approach, we do not want to paraphrase the client's words. Paraphrasing would be something like, "You are telling me that you are more depressed today and it was an effort to get here." It shifts the level of the discourse to one with more distance between client and therapist. This might be an appropriate response later in psychotherapy, when clients might require a relatively more separate relationship. This was certainly true for Eliza after the first 2 years.

In speaking in this way, the client's non-verbal, emotional experiences are received in the present moment.

> The listener understands that the word carries a meaning that makes the person relive what she has experienced before, without the listener understanding what that was. The conversation has brought the person back to the movements of

the moments, when what she now relives was experienced. Frequently the listener is drawn into the feelings of experience and gets moved by seeing the person moved by her own expressions. These moments, when both are moved, are good moments to investigate what was said that moved the other. (Andersen, 2007b, p. 36)

Bringing implicit information to the present, reexperiencing past childhood interactions, and having them received differently happens frequently in a non-verbal approach. It is what makes a difference to the repetition of old patterns of relating.

Staying Embodied, Present, and Receptive

Staying collaborative demands an actively receptive presence. This approach has been called the "midwife approach" (Southwell, 2000). A competent midwife is there to assist and keep things safe. She intervenes if the birthing process is going off track; she is not there to interfere. She stays receptive but attentive to any risk, when she may have to act fast. The assumption is that birth is a natural process and that the birthing woman innately knows how to do it. The job of those around a birthing woman is to trust her and the process, and to provide a calm, protective environment so that the woman can be inner focused. Similarly with clients, we focus on the client's internal process, what is impinging from within (mentioned in the introduction). The working assumption is that the client has the capacity to be moved and to find her way to express her inner movement in words, and in her own way. We enable the client to give birth to her inner experience.

We use awareness practices to enable us to be present. We take the experience of the relationship through our body and let ourselves be aware of what is happening in our body, when observing and listening to the client. The shifting focus of our attention backward and forward, between the client and ourselves, should now feel familiar. The practices help us to slow down and create an atmosphere of endless time. We listen deeply from expanded awareness. This capacity for expanded awareness comes from the repeated discipline of being mindful and aware with clients and in daily life. We might have the support of the practice of vertical and horizontal holding, but perhaps focus especially on the horizontal (see Chapter 3). We widen our perceptual field and expand into horizontal holding. We expand what we can resonate with non-verbally by speaking sparingly. We leave gaps between our words and hold the client with a long rein (see Chapter 3).

Practice Example

An illustration of staying with an experience, deepening into and exploring the fine details of its contours, starts by noticing tightness in my chest. *My chest aches and my first impulse is to move away from it and to find something more pleasant. I resist this . . . the tightness and ache radiate from the center of my chest . . . the tightness is strongest in the center of my chest . . . there it feels like a hard ball of pain . . . toward the edges of the ache, there is an impression of it having irregular edges . . . the edges are moving toward the hardness . . . then back to the periphery of the ache . . . the ache is black at its center . . . grayer at the periphery . . . now the center is less hard . . . less painful. And so the awareness continues.*

As well as focusing on the detail of what we are noticing about clients, we can notice how the atmosphere of the room is changing. We all know how atmospheres can be felt in our daily life. We walk into a room and we feel we could "cut the tension with a knife." Or we walk into a room and we sense that we have interrupted something. What we are doing in therapy is just giving these aspects of communication more attention than usual.

Supporting Clients in Their Flow

When a client is rooted in their talking, we want them to say more and to continue to put words to their experiences. The collaborative relationship encourages this with its both/and perspective, in contrast to an either/or one (Andersen, 2012). It conveys an attitude of "in addition to" rather than "instead of" or "my view is better than yours." So another response to the client describing herself as "low" in a both/and way of relating would be, "low and?" (I've not used a capital "L" in "low" here to try to convey the gentleness and delicacy of the word as it is spoken). The question and form of the word is quietly slipped in with the intention of addressing the right brain. Our voice tone suggests to the client that we are interested. We want her to elaborate. Of course, we have to be genuinely interested, otherwise our words will not address the non-verbal parts of a client. If the inflection in our voice resonates with the client's implicit state, then the client might respond with "low . . . and . . . lonely." In doing this, she deepens the expression of her feelings.

Yes, And . . .

The "stepping stones" way of interacting was developed by Boyesen (Southwell, 1988). It extends the both/and collaborative style of relating. It sends a message, "Yes, go on, I'm interested," to clients. Again, this form of interaction occurs when a client is rooted in the flow of his words. We convey encouragement to the client to continue. This is often unspoken and communicated tacitly by listening to the client's non-verbal communication. We combine this with encouraging head nods and welcoming facial expressions. We may make positive sounds such as "umms" and "ahs" in the rhythms of the words tipping out of the client.

This style of communicating cannot be faked. If it is treated as the stepping stones technique, it will inhibit or stop the client's expressive flow altogether. If it is a technique rather than genuinely resonating with the expressive flow, the subcortical structures and the right brain will no longer be addressed. As the client speaks, *we listen for key words and phrases* and notice their impact on us. We can set the scene for this at the start of early sessions with clients by telling them to speak about whatever comes up, no matter how irrational it may seem. Gradually this becomes part of our history together in the therapeutic process. When the client is rooted in his words, we can invite elaboration by saying "and" and "like" when the client takes a pause. We wait a second or two and then gently say, "and." The message conveyed by our intonation and demeanor is, "say some more, it's interesting." We want the client to be barely aware of us speaking. The words should not have the imperative of a command. The words "say some more" suggest that there might be more to say (if you would like that). (Again I've not used capitals to suggest the subtlety of these ways of speaking).

The form of the words spoken is significant. The word "I," as in "I want you to say some more" is not used. Using "I" would emphasize the interpersonal relationship, an "I" talking to a "You". Such a sentence would lift clients out of their inner experience. When clients are in their flow, and rooted in their words, they may not have a sense of themselves speaking. Their words are moving them with their own momentum. This is similar to when a dancer is moved by the dance, rather than being conscious of performing a dance.

Threading Rooted Phrases and Words Together

Rooted words and phrases can be found in the midst of "talking about" dead talk as clients speak. When this situation arises, we can gather up the rooted phrases and give them back to the client, talking to the non-verbal communication in the words. We leave out all the "talking about" talk, only selecting words rooted, or beginning to root. We talk in the ways already outlined, in the first person, as if we are our client. We let our words convey our identification with clients and lead them more deeply into the feeling of what they have said.

An example of this occurred when Eliza mentioned her father. It was rare for her to speak about him. She had not known him and was a teenager when he connected with her and her mother. Interspersed with comments about him one day, she said the following sentences over a few minutes. I gave them back to her by repeating them slowly in an evocative tone of voice and leaving pauses between my words. "I had a letter from my father . . . he rarely writes. . . . I wish I'd known him. . . . I like him. . . . I'm not supposed to like him." Her words conveyed a wistfulness, longing, and regret, which was obscured by her remark, "Well, you don't miss what you've never had." As I repeated her phrases conveying the non-verbal feelings, I deliberately repeated them with feeling, so that Eliza would feel her words more fully. Eliza became quiet and quietly cried. Then she said, "I never knew that I longed for a dad and to be like everyone else."

HELPING CLIENTS TO BE AWARE OF THEIR IMPLICIT COMMUNICATIONS

Central to helping clients make sense of their implicit communications is guiding them toward a relationship with their bodily experiences. It is all too easy to forget that thinking and talking have accompanying physical sensations (see introduction). Nick Totton reminds us, "thought and language are not 'mental' qualities which exist over and against the body. On the contrary, in line with the holistic bodymind concept, *thought and language are qualities of the body itself*" (2003, p. 133, emphasis in original).

To help clients develop an awareness of their bodily experiences, we introduce them to the "how" of their communications. We guide them toward being aware of how they are speaking and how their bodies move as they speak. "How" questions to both our clients and ourselves keep us in touch with ourselves. "If we feel our bodies, the process of how we have learned to do things, what is lived, then we can change it, reorganize ourselves, and teach ourselves anew" (Keleman, 1979, p. 43).

As a first step toward Eliza linking her thinking with her feelings, I wanted Eliza to become aware of her body sensations as she was talking (or soon after). A question that I frequently asked Eliza was, "As you are speaking, how are you feeling in your body?" Sometimes my questions were more focused on a part of her body: "As you are speaking, how are you feeling in your chest?" Often she would be surprised by the question. For her, the content, the narrative was what was important. She would want to get on with the story but would respond, "Tight, anxious." I would then ask her to say more. Often she wanted to understand why I wanted to know more about "tight", or "anxious." At these moments I reminded her why I was asking the question, namely to link her words with her body sensations (a left-brain-biased response).

Eliza began to "listen" increasingly to her body as she talked. Her anxiety was much reduced and she came to see that her anxiety was connected to her feelings. "When I notice my anxiety, I feel sad and cry and then I feel better—the crying seems to help, but I'm scared of it." Slowly in our sessions, she became curious about how her shoulders got tighter or looser as she talked. She came to recognize that the way she spoke and what she talked about seemed connected with her tense shoulders. She noticed that when she spoke, albeit hesitantly, in our first year about her feelings toward colleagues, often the pain in her shoulders lessened. Frequently she was critical of them for not following procedures well, but she also struggled with feeling disloyal to the company by telling me something about the company, which was not as it should have been, that is some employees were not diligently following the procedures.

Interrupting the Client

Another way of relating to what clients say is to carefully interrupt their stream of unrooted words. With Tony (Chapter 3), this was less appropriate for a long time, as it tended to shame him, and he "lashed back." Explicitly interrupting a client's words is a more challenging way of interacting than implicitly receiving non-verbal communications. This is necessary when a client is getting lost and overwhelmed. It is possible with more stalwart clients such as Eliza.

The interruption is along the lines of, "Let's pause a moment. . . ." "How is it to pause?" Then, in Eliza's case, I asked specific questions about her bodily experiences. It often interrupts the client's protective defense system and habitual ways of relating that do not convey her feelings.

Grading Questions

Questions about the client's body sensations can vary in their degrees of complexity and challenge. The following list goes from easier to more complex and challenging questions:

1. "As you are speaking, how are you feeling in your shoulders?" This is focused and directed toward inner experiences. The choice of body part by the therapist is based on noticing a movement, perhaps some stiffening, or simply something that catches the attention of the therapist.
2. "As you are speaking, how are you feeling in your body?" This is an open and more general question, again directed toward inner experiences.
3. "As you tell me that, how do you feel in your body?" This brings in the interpersonal aspects of relating. The question links the interpersonal relationship with the client's inner experiences.

With our questions, at first, we are looking for the naming of sensations by clients. Body sensation words include *stiff, tight, aching, tingling, warm, cold, pressure, numb,* and so on. When clients are proficient at this, naming feelings can be a progression.

Sometimes Eliza required help to find the right words to express what she was feeling. She could describe her bodily sensations, but could not put this collection of sensations into a named feeling. She would be in touch with her physical state and search for a word, but be at a loss. This was probably a manifestation of her mother's inability to attune with Eliza sufficiently as a baby. This was possibly her inability to perceive others compounded by her depression. At those times when Eliza searched for a word, I tentatively offered her some possible words to describe her feelings. I found the words by closely observing her and letting myself resonate with her. I would sense that she might be "sad." I would ask if it was okay for me to suggest some words for how she might be feeling. She would nod her head and I would say "sad." I would say it in such a way as to resonate with my felt sense of it and hope to resonate with her. This was reparative work with Eliza.

I would drop my voice down and speak in the rhythm and intonation of the emotion of the word. "Sad." She would respond, "No, that's not it." "Miserable." "No." "Melancholy." She would move her head, indicating no. "Lonely." Her face would begin to light up. "Yes, l-ow-ne-ly,_l--ow-ne-ly, l-Owne-ly. That's it, lOwne_ly." It was as if she was trying the word out for the right fit and playing with the sounds of the words as she found it and repeated the word in different ways. When she found the right word, its resonance felt right for both of us. I felt in contact with her. Eliza was learning how to name her feelings.

Supporting the Expression of Feelings in Words

Once clients can name feelings, we can support the intensity of their feelings.

Over our first year, Eliza increased her connection with her feelings. She often spoke of a particular colleague with irritation in her voice. The colleague was "sloppy" and "messy." These were key words, which I would repeat and encourage her to say more by providing stepping stone words to encourage the expression of her irritation.

As clients come more in contact with their feelings, we can adjust our responses so that clients deepen into their feelings or are pulled away from their intensity. We keep in mind the require-ment for some arousal for learning, but want to keep clients within the "window of tolerance" (see Chapter 1). We want some clients to put their feelings into words rather than going into a direct expression of their feelings such as weeping or sobbing. Naming the feelings helps to reduce the arousal in clients, and links the right side and subcortical structures of the brain with the left brain. Suzy (Chapter 6) is an example of this. A model that helps us with modulating the emotional arousal levels of clients is called levels of interaction.

Levels of Interaction

We can choose what level of interaction, what level of consciousness we want to reach in our clients. In Chapter 2 I discussed Brazelton's levels of consciousness observed in babies. Babies require sensitive ways of relating to the different levels of their consciousness. Although adult clients have more complex levels of consciousness, we can choose which level we want to address.

At one end of a spectrum is the *matter-of-fact level*, which is closest to the everyday. It is mundane and relatively neutral in terms of emotional expression. This is the level of choice when clear instruction with no emotion is required by a situation. For example, "The fire alarm has just gone off. Please file quietly out of the back of the room and assemble by the reception desk." We want no alarm or dramatic voice tone in this sort of situation. When clients are beginning to get flooded with feelings, we can use a matter-of-fact tone to pull them away from their feelings. In contrast, at the other end of the spectrum is the *deep emotional level*, which pours with feelings. Poignant music or tragic news reaches this level and is what makes us cry. In Chapter 7, we discuss this level in more detail.

In our interactions with clients, we can move up and down the scale of emotional arousal, fine tuning and calibrating the range (Figure 4.1). It helps to think of this as a dance. The matter-of-fact level of relating comes from what feels more "up" in the body and with less bodily spaciousness (without disconnecting from oneself). The deep emotional level comes from deeper "down" in the body. To relate in this way, we focus internally, ground ourselves, and keep ourselves in present experience. We can bring our awareness up closer to everyday consciousness or down our bodies toward more expanded levels of consciousness, depending on which level of consciousness we wish to respond with. Often the matter-of-fact level is coupled with short rein holding, and the deep emotional with long rein holding (see Chapter 3). A further

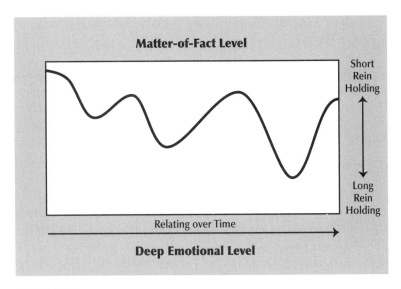

FIGURE 4.1 LEVELS OF CONSCIOUSNESS WITH SHORT AND LONG REIN HOLDING OVER A BRIEF PERIOD OF TIME SHOWING HOW THESE CHANGE IN INTERACTIONS.

dimension is noticing the autonomic nervous system and responding to relax or stimulate clients (see Chapter 5). In a way similar to an attuned mother responding to different aspects of her baby, exciting or calming interactions down, we can increase the feelings or lower them.

With Eliza I mostly had a deep emotional style of relating. Eliza increasingly voiced criticisms about her colleagues. Speaking about her colleagues was the route for her feelings to emerge. She was fiercely loyal to her mother and it was only in the second and third years of therapy that she began to voice her feelings about her mother's self-interested way of relating, her lack of parental boundaries, and the chaos (mess) that she ignored. Eliza came to feel how frightening this had been. I also became someone to criticize—my focus on her feelings neglected, as she saw it, the positives about her skill at thinking analytically. What was projected onto me from her past childhood relationship with her mother came more strongly into our relationship. Eliza's work became easier and less stressful. She became less critical of colleagues and she spoke of attending work social events and enjoying them.

Using Living Words and Being Aware of the Metaphors That We Use

Earlier, the discussion of body-speech-mind inquiry explained descriptive rather than fixed language. This attention to language is an ongoing theme in a non-verbal approach. The language that we use creates a field of implicit meaning. Much professional language implies that structures are fixed and static. Language also conveys how we think about things. A common example from body psychotherapy is clients demanding "bodywork" and therapists doing "bodywork." This implies fixing an objectified body, suggestive of a medical model. It can preclude exploring physical processes using awareness practices, which is more in keeping with a non-verbal approach. So, for example, noticing that our language has become static is important. We can get curious about that and perhaps move into using living words instead. We can also guide clients into recognizing that a fixed way of speaking about themselves, as for example, "I am a personality disorder," limits their explorations.

The metaphors that we use also create meaning. The metaphors of psychotherapy can be mechanical, humans as machines, or technological, e.g. humans as computers. With words such as *resistance*, *defense*, and *conflict*, psychotherapy metaphors also imply struggle and difficulty. When defense is described as protection, it has quite a different ring to it. Watson writes that the feminine voice is concerned with being, receptivity, play, and context rather than just doing. In contrast, the masculine voice is "logical, hierarchic and masterly" (Watson, 2002, p. 218). Words themselves can be feminine or masculine. For example, fostering a capacity is more feminine and developing a capacity is more masculine. These are of course not linked with gender.

The feminine voice corresponds more with right-brain functions and the masculine voice with left-brain functions. The feminine voice has been the most neglected in society and has been a "subtext" within "a milieu embodying the masculine and patriarchal, against the background of which the feminine voice can only be seen as 'other'" (Watson, 2002, p. 218). So in psychotherapy, words such as *allowing, exploring, inviting,* and *interacting* are feminine words deliberately used to evoke sensing and feeling. In contrast, *intervening, interpreting,* and *probing* are masculine words. Both masculine and feminine ways of speaking with clients are necessary at different times in psychotherapy. They invite and strengthen different parts of clients. Our words have an impact on clients and have to be chosen carefully, depending on how we want to interact with clients.

CONCLUSION

In this chapter we have looked at how to observe the way clients talk. We have discussed how to use our words to interact with the non-verbal aspects of clients in a collaborative style of relating. We have learned how to use the skills from Chapter 3 to adjust our presence and the levels that we want to address in clients. In Chapter 5 we explore breathing and relating. Some of the subthemes of this chapter, such as helping the client to deepen emotional connection, are explored further in Chapters 6 and 7.

Chapter 5

BREATHING AND RELATING

Breathing plays a central role in non-verbal communication. Not only does our breathing change with our different physiological needs, but it also changes as our feelings change. Usually we do not pay much attention to our breathing, and it changes even if we don't want it to. When we are in the company of others, our breathing provides information about the exchanges going on between us non-verbally. We can become aware of our breathing and explore with clients what changes in breathing patterns might tell us about our relationship. Breathing is central in self- and interactive regulation. Therapists and clients regulate themselves (self- or autoregulation), but we also regulate each other (interactive regulation). In this chapter, the therapeutic relationship is described in terms of breathing cycles and how they can guide our interactions.

When we breathe, we move. We sense breathing movements in our bodies. Our breathing is an enduring reference point around which to orient in psychotherapy. Indeed, breathing is the foundation for many awareness practices. When we want to gather more information about the therapeutic process, we can bring our awareness to our breathing. For example, if we feel lost with clients, not knowing what to do or say next, we can ground ourselves by noticing the movements of our breathing. This brings ourselves into relationship with our bodily sensations, and we can explore the experience of being lost. Often this is enough to know how to continue. Later in this chapter we learn how to do this.

With training, we can observe breathing movements in our clients, especially when we are looking for them. We can use these observations to pace and shape our relating in a finely tuned manner from moment to moment. *Tony (Chapter 3) rarely took a breath all the way down into his abdomen. He breathed mostly from his chest. In those rare moments when he spoke authentically, he breathed down into his abdomen and felt his feelings. At these times, I encouraged his words as I wanted him to linger in these moments.*

Our breathing functions like a barometer, reflecting our immediate relationship with our clients. Being aware of our breathing keeps the body in mind. It sharpens our thinking about the therapeutic relationship as two bodyminds interacting moment by moment. This helps us to keep to the fore the non-verbal aspects of communicating, experienced by changes in the bodymind. "Breathing . . . can be a wonderful, stable backdrop to a sense of one's own, embodied self and for a vital sense of relatedness to others" (Knoblauch, 2000, p. 4). Breathing creates internal movements in the bodymind and are an aspect of how we have a sense of ourselves.

> The fact is that all of us experience ourselves and the world through our bodies. Filtered through our mental models, our initial impressions of events register by way of the five senses as they interact with the proprioceptive "internal sense" that informs us about goings on in the interior of our bodies— heart rate, *respiration*, muscular tension, visceral sensation and so on. *It is largely this internal sense that allows us to know how we feel.* (Wallin, 2007, p. 292, emphasis added)

Awareness of our breathing also supports our self-care, and we can adjust our breathing so that we are not drained by clients. *An illustration of this is with Pauline in Chapter 3. You will remember that I found it hard to breathe fully when I was with her. So I deliberately breathed out more fully. I could then take deeper breaths, which not only brought me into a better relationship with her but also boosted my energy.*

We can explore breathing with our clients, and they can discover how they experience themselves when breathing in different ways. To introduce this to a client who is not too self-conscious, the therapist might say something like, "How would it be for you to breathe out a tiny bit more and see how that feels?" or "How would it be to take the breath a bit further down into your belly?" Then, "How does that feel?"

The cue for this sort of exploration might be that the client has noticed that as he speaks about a difficult subject, he holds his breath and is curious about that. These explorations are part of creating new experiences, which build small but incremental changes in clients. Clients can take the learning (both implicit and explicit) from these explorations of breathing in psychotherapy sessions into relationships in daily life, as they gain awareness skills and see how their breathing is affected by different people. They can become more in charge of themselves by deliberately choosing to breathe differently. This is hugely empowering, creating a stronger sense of self.

BREATHING AS THE FOCUS OF ATTENTION IN INTERACTIONS

Breathing is like a wave, with different phases of surging, reaching a peak and subsiding. We can make breathing the object of our attention in psychotherapy, becoming aware of the detail of our own and our client's breathing. Furthermore, we can also regard the breathing wave literally and metaphorically as a perspective from which to view the therapeutic process. First of all, we can put our awareness into *sensing our own breathing*. As we do this, we may find our breathing adjusting itself. Second, we can *observe the client's breathing*, and then *guide the client toward sensing her own breathing*. Clients can explore whether they feel better, worse, or neutral by adjusting the way that they are breathing. Third, we can *become aware of the more interactive aspects of the relationship* that we are creating together. We can draw a client's attention to noticing their breathing, perhaps just after we have said something. We can also notice how the client is affecting us and make conscious changes in our breathing, sometimes overtly, sometimes less obviously, for both our own and the client's well-being. Often we do a mixture of both. *An illustration of implicit breathing regulation was given in the introduction, with Caroline. She had indicated to me non-verbally that she was frightened, so I responded by lengthening and slowing my breathing to communicate calmness to her non-verbally. I felt calmer and so did Caroline.* Breathing slowly and fully, especially on the out-breath, is calming.

A Caveat

There are some clients who experience being overtly aware of their breathing as "too close for comfort," that is, being aware of their breathing is disturbing. Caroline was such a client initially. For these clients, a breathing focus is too challenging as not being aware of their breathing has been their self protection. Making breathing a focus can take them away from themselves, making them more dissociated rather than more embodied. It is not always easy to predict who these clients will be. Often they are more fragile clients. However, observation in early sessions of how a client's breathing patterns change without any explicit reference to his or her breathing suffices as a guide. For these clients, it is possible to work more implicitly with their breathing patterns. We do this by adjusting our own breathing, which affects the client.

THE BREATHING CYCLE

As discussed in Chapter 1, breathing is controlled by the autonomic nervous system. Breathing is central in emotional, energetic, and physiological regulation, and maintaining equilibrium. Most of the time, our breathing happens automatically. However, we can also bring our breathing under voluntary control. We can choose, for example, to slow it down, perhaps because we want to feel less anxious. Breathing involves and links conscious and unconscious processes, leading Boyesen to regard the diaphragm, the main muscle of breathing, as "the gateway to the unconscious" (2006, p. 132). As we notice breathing, we become more aware of nonconscious processes within ourselves, and they gradually become more conscious. This is often a working edge in psychotherapy.

Our breathing constantly changes, stimulated from inside by our thoughts, feelings, sensations, and imaginings, and from outside by changes in the environment, such as hearing a sudden, loud noise, which makes us startle and take an in-breath. There is a constant interplay between internal and external events. When we are asleep, relaxed, or depressed, our breathing is slower. It is common, however, for those thinking that they are relaxing to be breathing more quickly than the situation actually demands. This happens, for example, when watching a TV program for relaxation, but the viewer is on the edge of the seat because it is a horror movie or violent news program. In exercise, our breathing gets faster to supply the need for more oxygen. During average breathing, when we are resting, we take about 12 to 15 breaths in a minute. It gets much faster during exercise and if we are very excited or stressed.

The very first breath at birth is an in-breath, and our final breath as we die is an out-breath. Another word for in-breath is *inspiration* (Latin, *spirare*, to breathe or coming into breath) and is associated with being filled up, inspired, and in spirit. Another word for the out-breath is *expiration* (Latin, moving out of breath) and coming to an end. Expiring is dying.

Breathing, Movement, and Rhythm

To repeat, breathing always involves movement. "The absence of movement is death" (Lowen, 1975, p. 224). All living matter not only moves but also pulsates in rhythmic patterns of expansion and contraction. Expansive movements extend the self toward the world, and contractions move the self inward and away from the world (Reich, 1983). Together clients and therapists form "living systems" influencing each other, especially non-verbally.

> Living systems are units of interactions; they exist in an ambience. From a purely biological view they cannot be understood independently of that part of the ambience with which they interact: the niche; nor can the niche be defined independently of the living system that specifies it. (Maturana & Varela, 1991, p. 9)

Clients influence therapists non-verbally, and therapists influence clients non-verbally. Breathing is a central and constant part of this communication.

The Phases of the Breathing Cycle

As already stated, but worth underscoring, is that therapists and clients each have their own cycles of breathing, but their cycles change as they interact. Each person's breathing cycle has two basic aspects: a breathing in phase, and a breathing out phase. Breathing in, we fill up and expand, and when breathing out we become smaller. This is something that we can observe in others. Breathing in is followed by breathing out; breathing out, by breathing in. There is a constant ebb and flow, with one phase of breathing always completing and another beginning. We are in a continual process of "creating ourselves" with the in-breath and letting ourselves "die away" with the out-breath. At the end of the in-breath there is a brief hovering and pausing movement. At the end of the out-breath there is another brief hovering and pausing movement. In these moments there are subtle changes of completing the previous phase and preparing for the next one. Psychologically speaking, hovering and pausing give time for fully feeling our experiences, reflecting on them, and digesting them. We also incubate and anticipate what is yet to come in pauses.

And so the breathing cycle has four phases: in-breath, pause, out-breath, pause, and so on (Figure 5.1). The in-breath is the more active phase of breathing. The main muscles of breathing, the diaphragm, the intercostals (muscles between each rib), and the ancillary muscles of breathing in the neck, move to draw air in. The in-breath may be experienced as a slight feeling of coldness around the nostrils. The incoming air fills and energizes us. It is controlled by the sympathetic nervous system. When we relate with others, our in-breath is affected first. Do we let the other person affect us by breathing in fully or keep him out by not breathing in as far as we might do otherwise? In contrast, the out-breath is a less muscularly active phase of breathing, and it can feel like letting go and deep surrendering. The out-breath is regulated by the parasympathetic nervous system and, as the air leaves our nostrils, it feels warm. The out-breath is the falling part of breathing and how we make our mark or "impress" ourselves on the world (Keleman, 1970, p. 19). If we do not breathe out fully, we are not only less expressive but less effective in our relationships.

The four phases of breathing are all equally important, but

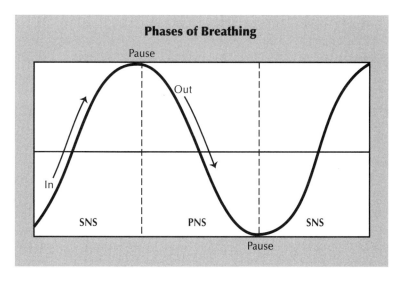

FIGURE 5.1 PHASES OF THE BREATHING CYCLE IN A FICTIONAL PERSON BREATHING IN A REGULAR MANNER. IN REALITY THIS SELDOM HAPPENS. SNS, SYMPATHETIC NERVOUS SYSTEM; PNS, PARASYMPATHETIC NERVOUS SYSTEM.

people tend to skip over bits of the cycle without realizing it. Colloquial phrases such as, "I'm so busy at work, I don't have time to breathe" or "I'd hardly caught my breath and then the next disaster happened" capture this sense of missing parts of the cycle and the emotional impact of events. Although breathing patterns form in childhood like a relational signature, being exposed to hostile situations and atmospheres without respite continues to reinforce and further restrict breathing styles. Andersen observes poignantly, "One could literally say that . . . rather tense circumstances make the person reduce his/her inspiration from the surroundings" (1991a, p. 18).

The Movements of Breathing

The movements of breathing are not located only in the apparatus of breathing. The breathing wave in normal circumstances creates movements throughout the whole body, just as throwing a stone into a lake sends ripples across the water. The movements of the in-breath go to the furthest parts of the body, to the tips of the fingers and toes. The movements of the out-breath flow out from these far parts of the body. Notwithstanding this, breathing movements are most easily visible in the chest, midtrunk (diaphragm), and abdomen, and in the smaller muscles of the face, around the mouth, the tongue, the jaw, and neck. However, with training, and especially using awareness practices, it is possible to see the breathing wave move down into the legs and feet, into the arms and hands, and indeed throughout the whole body.

Restricted breathing, which happens when someone feels threatened or frightened, tends to be created by tightening and reducing the mobility of the flexor muscles. These muscles contract our body parts inward and generally make those parts of the body smaller. By observing different parts of the body, muscle contractions may be recognized. Contracted parts of the body look shorter, denser, and restrained, without much visible movement. Less breath flows into them.

Most clients (and therapists) will have disruptions in their breathing. Some clients breathe only minimally (for example, those with early insecure avoidant attachments); some breathe mostly in their chest; some do not move the chest much, but breathe with movements mostly of the abdomen. Some clients reverse breathe, that is, sucking the abdomen in (instead of moving it out to make space for the in-breath) when they are breathing in. *Tony's chest, for example, looked quite large, blown up, and expanded. It moved as a whole rather than the individual muscles of the chest moving more separately, while his abdomen looked small compared with his chest and moved even less. Mostly he breathed into his chest, but not all the way down into his abdomen. This way of breathing helped to preserve his self-image and to keep his vulnerable feelings at bay.*

EXERCISES FOR CULTIVATING BREATHING AWARENESS IN PSYCHOTHERAPY

At this point, I would like to introduce some practices for developing awareness of breathing for use in the consulting room. They are intended primarily for therapists but may also be taught to clients. As you sit reading this, you might want to read the instructions below to yourself and then try out the exercises.

The first practice is to become aware of your own breathing style and to simultaneously make connections with different body sensations and feeling tones. The idea is to adopt a spirit of inquiry in the practice. After becoming more familiar with your usual breathing, the next step is to change the way that you are breathing, then to become aware of the changing sensations and feelings that can follow from making some small changes.

Practice: Breathing Awareness

This practice is to be done for about 3 minutes, in a sitting position.

First Phase: Preparation

There is no need to sit in any particular way, but if you sit more upright without any back support, with your legs uncrossed and both feet on the ground, you will find it easier not to get drowsy. You may want to close your eyes so that you are less distracted by your surroundings. Sense the connections that your body has with the chair or floor (basic grounding).

Second Phase

Take your attention to your breathing. Pause for a short time after each question to gather up your experiences. Without changing your breathing in any way, simply notice how it is.

- Where do you breathe—chest, abdomen, to the tips of your toes and fingers?
- How quickly or slowly do you breathe?
- How do you feel about that?

Third Phase

You might try exaggerating the out-breath slightly. How does that feel? You might try exaggerating the in-breath slightly. How does that feel?

- How does it feel to dwell in the pauses a bit longer (if they are discernible)?
- How does it feel to breathe in, to breathe out? Do you prefer breathing in to breathing out?
- How are the phases of the breathing cycle when viewed altogether?

Next we can relate our breathing to a client.

Breathing and Imagining Clients

First, let yourself bring to mind your most difficult client, who is about to come to see you. How does your breathing change? What feelings arise in you?

Let your client go from your imagination.

Observe as you let yourself find your own breathing style again.

Second, now imagine a client that you look forward to seeing and generally enjoy being with. How does your breathing change?

Let yourself bring the imagining to a close.

Let yourself find what ever it is your breathing wants to do as you let go of these imaginings and come back to you own breathing rhythm.

At the end of the 3 minutes, reflect on how this practice was for you. What feelings, thoughts, imaginings, and sensations were there? Let yourself move in any way that you want to so that you come back to yourself more fully.

Practice: Breathing Observations With a Colleague

The next part is to practice observing others and their breathing. Perhaps a friend or colleague would like to try this with you for 3 minutes.

Ask your colleague to sit in a chair. She may want to read a book or do an activity. It is better if her attention is on something else rather then you.

As your colleague sits in a chair, let yourself be openhearted and accepting. Let your gaze be soft, and observe your colleague.

How quickly or slowly is she breathing? How big or small is the breath?

There is nothing right or wrong with how someone breathes. The breathing is as it is.

Where does the breath go to in the body? Maybe it is not easy to know. Maybe the chest moves but little else is discernible. Let yourself be relaxed about what you observe. The less tense you are, the more you will notice.

At the end of the 3 minutes, discuss how this was for your colleague and yourself.

Try this practice with other colleagues so that you have different experiences.

Practice: Breathing and Observing a Colleague and Bringing Awareness to Your Own Breathing

When you feel more confident with the earlier practices, you can add in moving between being aware of a colleague's breathing and being aware of your own breathing. Let yourself move back and forth between awareness of your own breathing and that of your colleague. Do this without talking.

Go slowly and notice the transition between observing yourself and observing the colleague.

Is it easier to observe the colleague or yourself?

Is it harder to move away from observing the colleague? Are you more reluctant to observe the colleague? Do you get preoccupied with your own breathing?

Let yourself find different ways of adjusting your awareness. What happens if you shift, rather than elegantly glide, between the awareness of yourself and your colleague? Whatever you experience is fine.

At the end of 3 minutes, discuss your experiences with the colleague and listen to her experiences.

BABYHOOD, BREATHING, AND INTERACTIVE RHYTHMS

Breathing patterns and their associated movements are developed in babyhood in interactions with our caregivers. As we saw in Chapter 2, if we had sensitive, attuned caregivers who resonated with our non-verbal communications, we become securely attached. We feel safe to breathe in and out fully; we trust the world. Our caregivers will have read our non-verbal messages, such as turning our head away, or closing our eyes, our slower breathing, showing them that we wanted a rest. Our caregivers will also have responded to our wanting more action and excitement, signaled by our eager smiles and looks, and our breathing becoming quicker with our keenness. These sensitive caregivers will have helped us out when we were unable to regulate ourselves, perhaps when we became overtired or overstimulated. Finding balance and equilibrium together will have included adjustments in our breathing, encouraging us to quicken it or slow it down, to deepen the out-breath or the in-breath. They will also have adjusted their breathing to regulate us and themselves. All of this happened implicitly.

Insecure Attachments

The breathing and movements of securely attached babies are relatively smooth, predictable, and flowing. As circumstances change, their breathing and moving respond easily. However, repeated failures of caregivers to respond to moments of misattunement and contradictory or unpredictable responses from parents and other significant childhood figures leads to a loss of smooth movements, changes in breathing patterns, and difficulties in self- and interactive regulation.

Disrupted breathing may start from birth. "If the cord is cut early, and no other source of oxygen exists, the baby must inspire immediately or else it will be dead. But the inspiratory rush of air can be felt as invasive and traumatic. It can precondition a person towards reduced respiration" (Boadella, 1987, p. 188). The premature cord cutting may have been necessary, but then the baby requires time to breathe out and recover and adjust to his new circumstances.

Babies who are insecurely attached and children living in inhospitable environments develop inhibitions of breathing and movement. These children stifle their liveliness and interest in exploring the potential in situations, which inhibits development and learning at a higher level (see, for example, Marcher & Fich, 2010; Southwell, 1988). Movements are performed by muscles, and muscle movement is inhibited by holding the breath. Holding back breathing and movement stifles creative and emotional expression (Reich, 1983). This ability to function in difficult circumstances, but not thrive, has been described as the *somatic compromise* by Boyesen (1980). It is the physical aspect of the difficult circumstances or relationships.

Signature Breathing

Adult clients with early insecure attachments that have not been modified by life will bring their signature "insecure breathing" to therapy. "The breathing movements are as personal as finger prints" (Andersen, 2007a, p. 90). They are stable and endure over time (Christiansen, 1972). The signature patterns of reduced breathing and moving are the client's protective way of being, but they also hold the potential for change in the present (transformance; see introduction). The adult breathing patterns may not be exactly those of babyhood, perhaps having been modified by more secure relationships later on, but they guide us in how to interact thera- peutically with our clients. The idea is not to fix the breathing, not to make it right, but for clients to experience how it feels to breathe in their signature style. This is in the service of finding more equi- librium. As we have noted, becoming aware of something is often healing in itself.

We can think of signature breathing as baseline breathing. It is like the constant bass beat in music and is modified with changing circumstances. A person's signature breathing demonstrates her basic capacity for relating at that time. For example, if a client is habitually frightened, she may hold the in-breath, not daring to fully breathe out.

Any of the four phases of the breathing cycle can be disrupted, which correlates with the character styles mentioned in Chapter 2 (see, for example, Lowen, 1971; Boadella, 1987). Someone with a sensitive-withdrawn character style, which correlates with inse- cure-avoidant attachment, will have much reduced breathing and minimal body movements with each breath. We shall meet Peter in Chapter 6 with this style of breathing.

Often clients have mixed, irregular patterns of breathing, depending on how challenged someone was and is by their current circumstances, the therapeutic relationship included. The signature breathing can be drawn diagrammatically. Parts of the breathing cycle will be less pronounced (Figure 5.2).

Movements and Rhythms

Breathing is rhythmic. Other systems of the body are also rhyth- mic and occur simultaneously with breathing. The heart beats and blood pulses around the body and digestion occurs in peristaltic waves. "The process of relating to another person requires that each have more or less continuous feedback about the state of the other, and rhythms can provide this information" (Beebe & Lachmann, 2002, p. 99, paraphrasing Byers, 1975). In adult relationships we tend to like those who synchronize with our rhythms. When the

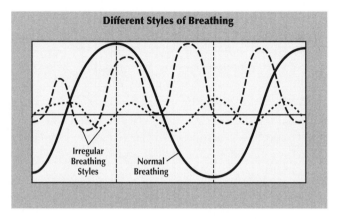

FIGURE 5.2 SCHEMATIC REPRESENTATION OF NORMAL AND IRREGULAR BREATHING STYLES.

rhythms of another person are out of harmony with ours, we tend to feel misunderstood, maybe frustrated, and we may tune out to avoid the discomfort of someone not quite getting us (Beebe & Lachmann, 2002). Again, this is picked up non-verbally.

In the therapeutic process, breathing movements and rhythms going on between us and our clients can be out of rhythm. As we speak on an out-breath, we may say something at the same moment the client starts to speak, and cut across his rhythm. The client can be anxious, not hear what we are saying, and butt in with a response before considering what he wants to say (turn-taking out of sync). The "communicative musicality" between us is disrupted and lacking in harmony. Becoming aware of breathing patterns in both of us shifts the focus of attention and takes us into exploration of interactions around breathing.

Cycles of Relating in Adults

When we make breathing the focus of psychotherapy, self- and interactive regulation also becomes the focus (Figures 5.3 and 5.4). Adults generally have more capacity and options for self- and inter-active regulation than babies. Carroll observes, "Self regulation is not a singular process, but occurs in a kaleidoscopic way because it is a function of a complex system with many layers (the bodymind)

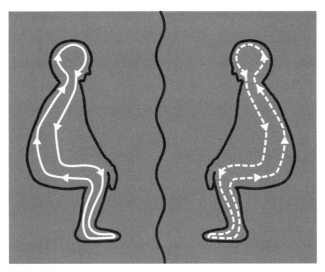

FIGURE 5.3 SCHEMATIC REPRESENTATION OF TWO PEOPLE REGULATING THEIR OWN BREATHING.

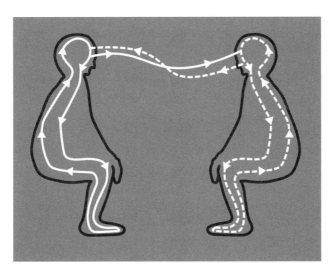

FIGURE 5.4 SCHEMATIC REPRESENTATION OF HOW THE TWO BREATHING STYLES OF CLIENT AND THERAPIST INTERACT NON-VERBALLY. IN PRACTICE, AS NOTED, BREATHING IS NOT THIS REGULAR. BOTH SELF- AND INTERAC-TIVE REGULATION THROUGH BREATHING HAPPENS CONCURRENTLY.

interrelating with a complex human environment" (2009, p. 102). Bringing awareness to these layers and using a breathing focus provides a way into exploration of this complexity.

PSYCHOTHERAPIST AND CLIENT: TWO BREATHING STYLES INTERACTING

We are now prepared to consider a client and a therapist with their two breathing styles interacting. I describe the movement back and forth—*the awareness of the therapist being aware of inner sensations and breathing* and *what the therapist is observing in the client.* First of all, I provide questions for the therapist to ask herself, which have a more self-regulatory focus. In reality, when with another, breathing does not move back and forth like this. Interacting and breathing are concurrent.

The Breathing of the Psychotherapist: Self-Regulatory Focus

Before the Client Arrives

We learned in Chapter 3 about preparing ourselves before clients arrive. Additionally, before the client arrives, our task is to become aware of our breathing. Some questions to ask are:

- How am I breathing? Is it just right, too fast, too slow?
- What moves as I breathe? Is my breathing deep or shallow, irregular?
- How is the in-breath, the out-breath?
- Do I prefer the in-breath or the out-breath?
- How does the breath sound?
- How is being aware of my breathing changing it?
- Do I want to explore breathing differently? How does my breathing change with exploratory modifications?

To illustrate this, if I notice that I'm tight in my chest, I can choose to breathe out more fully and move my shoulders around. Perhaps I realize that this tight chest feeling is related to the previous client.

Maybe having moved and breathed, I feel more like my usual self. I am ready for my next client.

Imagining My Next Client

The next part combines breathing awareness with focusing in the imagination on a client about to arrive. Let's call the client Gary. As I imagine Gary on his way, how does my breathing change? I notice I feel welcoming of him and my breathing gets a bit quicker, but also fuller. I can also decide to explore modifying my breathing. If I modify my breathing, how is that?

Imagining the next client coming to the session gives a general sense of how a client affects us. It guides us with how we might modify our breathing for our well-being. There may be differences between the imagined client and the actual client in the room when he or she arrives.

The Client Arrives

As Gary arrives, how does my breathing change? Do I want to change my breathing? As I modify it, how do I feel? Maybe I let out a longer, deeper out-breath. I notice that I feel welcoming of him still, but more at ease with myself. All of this is done silently.

Throughout the duration of the session, the idea is for us to notice our breathing every so often, and to adjust it accordingly for our well-being.

Breathing Cycles: Interactive Focus With a Client

Having described my imaginings and breathing when considering Gary, I now want to illustrate interactions between myself and Becky, a female a client. I will describe how awareness shifts back and forth between us with the focus on breathing. I also comment on the interactions. I will start more simply and build on the descriptions later in the chapter. This is like learning the basic steps of a dance first and then developing more complex moves as competence grows.

Becky came for psychotherapy because she had had a panic attack. She was unable to sleep and was perpetually anxious, without knowing why. She had been prescribed medication by her doctor and felt somewhat better, but could not stop thinking about things that she was ashamed of, and could not talk to anyone about.

Becky's mother had been unreliable, and her father had worked hard and was not at home much. Becky learned to look out for herself and grew up quickly. As a young teenager, she gave birth to a child. Becky grew up in a religious country where sex before marriage was strictly forbidden. Prior to the birth, she was sent away, "so that no one would know about it." She spent minimal time with her newborn son, and he was adopted. His father, another teenager at school, moved away, and she did not see him again. Her son would be well grown by now and Becky had constant thoughts about where he was and what he was doing. Becky was skeptical about psychotherapy, but she had no one to confide in. She had married in her late teens and had other children who were now teenagers themselves. Her husband knew of her first baby, but advised her not to think of her adopted baby. "It only upsets you."

The strong momentum of Becky's anxiety, particularly for the first 20 minutes of the session, pushed her to talk in the runaway train style mentioned in Chapter 4. Her words gushed, particularly at the beginnings of our sessions. She felt that she had to get out everything she had "bottled up for years." To me, it felt like she was emptying an overfull bucket of water. Every so often Becky gulped a breath and rushed on. She looked red in the face, hot and bothered. Becky breathed out more than she breathed in. Both the in-breath and the out-breath were shallow, and she skipped the hovering pauses between the in- and out-breaths.

As the session continued, usually some of Becky's momentum subsided with each gush of sentences. Her speech slowed down slightly. She took deeper breaths, and her spine elongated, her trunk widened, and her breath dropped down more into her body. Gradually she looked less like a balloon filled to its maximum expansion, about to burst. Eventually she felt better. "It's a relief to have got it out. I'm tired in a good way." With each subsequent session, Becky started from a less intense, less urgent place. Together we were regulating her emotionally, physiologically, and energetically.

The scene is now set for going into the detail of our interactions. I write in the first person to bring the interactions alive as you read. As you read, every so often let yourself become aware of your breathing.

Before Becky Arrives: Therapist Focus on Self

As I consider Becky, before she arrives, I notice pleasure. My breathing is smooth. I look forward to seeing her again. Then I remember how it is to be with her, especially at the beginnings of sessions. I hold my breath momentarily. I think of whether I will be able to stay present with her and not be flooded with her urgent story, stored up a long time. I think about her teenage children, who seem to be triggering explicit memories of her own teenage years. I also wonder about her babyhood and implicit memories. Then I remember that the runaway train style of talking slows quite quickly.

I think about Becky wanting my attention and yet finding it hard to trust that I will give her time. This reminds me of what she has said about her unreliable mother. As I am having these recollections, I notice that my breathing has subsided, particularly with the memory of how Becky quite quickly calms. I feel ready to welcome her.

Becky Arrives: Focus on Becky

Becky walks into the room and it is easy to welcome her. I convey my welcome non-verbally in my posture, general warmth, and the tone of my opening words: "Hello, come in." Becky comes in and sits down in her usual chair. I also take my seat and continue to be receptive to how she is.

This is a familiar beginning, which has become part of our starting—*the coming into relationship ritual.* It builds predictability and Becky, after about 26 sessions of weekly 1-hour sessions, now sits back more in her chair and finds a comfortable position (see Chapter 3). At a later date in our developing relationship, I may choose to start Becky's sessions differently. The ritual may have become constraining and deadening, rather than security building. As Becky becomes a more experienced client, she may enjoy being in silence, going inward, and finding what she wants to say or do. Maybe sometimes she will start, and sometimes I will.

Therapist Out-Breath Movement

I open the conversation by asking, "How are you?"

My words are slower than my ordinary speech, said in a matter-of-fact manner (see Chapter 4). I let the contours of my voice go down to speak to the non-verbal, emotional parts of her. I convey receptivity to these parts of Becky. This is my out-breath movement (literally and metaphorically). My question means, "How has the process been moving in you, since we last met? What is your subjective experience of yourself and how has it changed?"

Becky understands that I do not mean "How are you?" in the everyday sense. My open question leaves Becky free to answer in any way that she wants to. I initiate our conversation to give structure, and not to leave silence, which tends to agitate her. I want Becky to find a way of lowering her arousal, when we first meet, without drawing attention to it, which, in Becky's case, increases her arousal. My voice intonation, and the speed and rhythm of my words are speaking to what is emotionally sitting below the explicit and familiar social language (see Westland, 2009b). I invite a response with some emotion in it, but deliberately do not want to invite deep emotions, which could overwhelm her or threaten the relationship that we are building together (see Chapter 4).

In earlier meetings with Becky I have suggested being aware of what is "moving in her" as she goes about her life. What has she been thinking, imagining, dreaming about? What physical sensations, bodily movements, feelings has she been aware of?

Therapist Focus: Therapist In-Breath Movement and Pausing

Having asked Becky how she is, I bring my attention to myself, and I silently ask myself questions about my experience. This is my in-breath movement. How has asking the question changed me physically? How is my breathing now? What body sensations am I experiencing? What am I thinking, feeling, imagining? Did the tone of my voice and the modulation of it strike the intended note *in me*? How am I moving or not moving? Noticing spontaneous gestures and any paralanguage are all important in catching nuances of experience. As my attention turned more toward myself, what was the flavor of the experience? Getting away? Relieved? Reluctant? Elegantly timed?

I remain aware of Becky, but I am more with my inner experience. I remain looking at her and connecting with her non-verbally, but she has a bit more space for her own reflections as I am slightly more with myself than her. I am holding her somewhere in the short-to-middle range of long rein and short rein holding (see Chapter 3). My focus is on my responses and reactions to my own question to Becky. Responses to the previous out-breath movement come in split seconds. I notice that I am soft and warm inside, and my question "How are you" is consistent with how I feel about Becky. That is I'm interested to know how she is. While this is described as the in-breath of the psychotherapist, in reality there may be several cycles of in-breath focus within this cycle.

Therapist Focus on Becky: Therapist Pausing to Out-Breath

I now turn my awareness to Becky, look at her more intently, but kindly, and notice the impact of my question on her. How has Becky been "touched" and then "moved" by my words, my demeanor, and having my attention on her? I want to know if she has received it as an inviting comment, encouraging her to say more about how she is feeling, but with the feelings unfolding from less conscious parts of herself. The impact on Becky makes itself known to me in barely perceptible movements, subtle breathing changes, and larger physical movements such as shuffling around or moving forward in the chair. Becky's response may be a cough, a sigh, a shadow across her face, a shudder of her breath, a reddening of her cheeks, her feet moving around, or her hand stroking her hair. The overall impact of my question on Becky might be felt more intuitively as we gather information from the field of "subliminal mind," and have a direct knowing through resonance (Sills & Lown, 2008). I might just know that it made an impression on her. Jennifer Tantia (2014) offers us some research on this intuitive knowing without "gut feelings," where intuition is felt around the body in the "kinesphere", particularly to the right of the head. More research is needed on intuition and its forms, especially as it arises in auditory, kinaesthetic and imaginal ways.

My opening question will also have elicited a breathing response in Becky. Her breathing response will give some indication of how she has received my initial inquiry and whether she experienced it as strong enough to have experienced something new happening, or perhaps it was too strong, or too little; too "unusual," or "too usual" (Andersen, 1991a, p. 19).

> If our contributions in psychotherapy are too close to how our clients talk, little happens. If, however, they are "appropriately" unusual, life comes to the conversation. If our contributions are too unusual—, for instance, if they make people fearful or create pain—the flow of the conversation stops. We must, therefore, carefully watch the ways our clients participate in the conversation to see if it is of value or not, which means how they respond to what we are saying. (Andersen, 2007a, p. 87)

If my direct focus on Becky and my question are gently curious and with an intensity that Becky welcomes, Becky is likely to receive my question, take it in, stay or sit with it, and be able to watch her own reactions. Her breathing will be deep and regular: "Yes, how am I?" Then probably she will put words to her non-verbal response to me. I just have to give her time to go more inwardly to discover what is happening for her. If my question, in its tone and my body movements, was "too strong" or "too little," Becky will probably increase what she has a tendency to do—talk more like a runaway train. Her talk will get faster, with more vigor and few pauses in which to gulp air. This signals to me that Becky has received a "No" from me rather than, "Yes, I want to hear what you have to say."

At the end of my speaking, there is a natural pause. In the pause, I am noticing what I am experiencing, and what I am observing in Becky. I am also considering timing. Does Becky require more or less space and time from me? If Becky could not find her words, and goes into her signature breathing with its disrupted phases, I might come in again with a comment. If her reaction to me has been receptive and her breathing has indicated "Yes" to me, I might give her more time to be with her experience.

Becky's Out-Breath Movement

I have barely invited Becky to speak about how she is and she launches into words. This tells me that she does not really take me in, on her in breath. She speaks with a rapid out-breath emphasis. As she speaks, I notice what is happening in her body and every so often check what I am thinking, feeling, and sensing by referencing what is happening in my body. I ask myself, what am I thinking? What happens in my body as I think that? Am I relaxed and breathing easy, or do I feel breathless and tight chested? Is my breathing shallow, or full and deep? I see my own internal experiences as resonating with Becky's, and I keep using awareness practices to explore them.

She speaks fast, "I could hardly wait to get here, yesterday was when the official papers were signed for the adoption, many years ago now, where is he now, he could be anywhere, his baby clothes are in a box, at the back of the wardrobe, it's not been looked at, I was not supposed to have them, Freddie thinks he's my first child, Sarah thinks she's my second, Frank knows, he married me, knowing about me, I didn't hide it from him." She ran out of steam, took a small pause, and came down a bit.

Notice how you feel after reading the previous paragraph. Give yourself a moment to do whatever you need to do—perhaps breathing out more fully, or moving around.

Therapist's Concurrent Response to Becky's Out-Breath Movement

As I listen to Becky, I slip my attention toward my experience, and I notice that I am beginning to feel breathless and my chest is tightening. There is a brewing sense of something hard in my chest. It feels tight, dark, constrained. I realize that I do not have some details in Becky's narrative and I do not know either explictly or implicitly how she feels about the topics that she speaks about at this moment—the adoption, her later family and life. As I glance at Becky I see that her face is reddening, her shoulders look tight, and her fingers are tightening around her thumbs and enclosing them. Her eyes look frightened, a bit panicky rather than terrified.

At the mention of Frank, her right hand opens out and her fingers stroke the arm of the chair. Silently I breathe out more fully and deliberately drop my shoulders and slowly stretch my chest open. From the outside this is not exaggerated and barely noticeable, but Becky is probably picking it up non-verbally via her right-brain awareness that takes in the whole. I am curious about the hard feeling in my chest and notice that it is still there, but easier to be with. I decide to interrupt Becky's speech. She has been coming to therapy long enough to be familiar with the situation, and previous interruptions of her speech have enabled her to slow down and bring her arousal down.

Therapist Out-Breath Movement

I ask her, "As you are talking, what are you noticing in your body?" This prompts Becky to notice what is physically happening for her. It stops the runaway train style of talking and invites her in-breath to come more. This is what she is least able to do in the breathing cycle. As she breathes in more, taking a pause, she may reflect on our exchange, reexperience it, and feel the effects of it in her own body. Her physiological arousal is likely to come down as she pauses to reflect. Reflection, you will recall from Chapter 3, is not just thinking about it, but reexperiencing the interactions and becoming aware of physical sensations and feelings.

As Becky takes the opportunity to observe inwardly the impact of her words on herself, she may digest her expressions and perhaps make acquaintance with less familiar parts of herself. She may clarify something and add to what she has said, perhaps elaborate in some way, change a word or phrase. She may catch more feeling tones and claim more of herself. She may also find a sense of satisfaction in finding her own way of expressing herself. Of course, she may also non-verbally decline my "invitation" and carry on. I can stop her again and insist, depending on the state of my relationship with her. Or I may let her continue. This is an individual clinical judgment.

Becky's In-Breath Movement

Becky receives my invitation and I see her pause for a few seconds as her attention goes inward. I notice her out-breath is then slightly fuller and comes from further down in her trunk, rather than her more usual breathing in and out from the chest, which keeps her arousal going.

Becky's Out-Breath Movement

Becky replies quickly, "It's a relief when you ask me that. I can't stop once I start. I want to get it out, but it all runs away from me." I notice that Becky's words come from lower down in her trunk. *She is speaking from her experience rather than about it.* She has slowed down considerably. As I turn my attention to myself, I notice that I feel less pressured and that we have more time and space for our conversation. My shoulders feel less taut.

Misattuning With Becky and Reattuning

As our conversation unfolds, it is happening in different dimensions, creating a tapestry of communication—through breathing, movements, sounds, words, and gestures—verbally and non-verbally. There will be moments of meeting (resonance), moments of disharmony (reaction), and a return to harmony.

An illustration of this comes in another session, later in Becky's psychotherapy. She perceives my facial expression and the way I speak as critical. Perhaps I have commented a bit abruptly or said too much for her to hear. Maybe she does not like the content of what I've said. In other words, my contribution to the conversation has been heard by her as a "No." We have become misattuned. I pick this up by noticing a slight holding of Becky's breath. Her body stiffens, and the stiffening does not release itself; her eyes glaze over. This sort of misattunement in psychotherapy is inevitable as the past and present of therapists and clients converge in the present moment. This is where new relating can begin for both.

As I notice Becky's reaction, I ask her, "What happened just then?" (What were you feeling when I asked that question/said that just now?) If, as I am assuming, our relationship is good enough and we have a good working alliance, Becky will be able to use my question to discover more about herself and tell me. *As she goes into in-breath mode, she discovers and then says, "I think that you do not approve of me quitting my job." As she says that, her stiffened body releases some of its stiffness; her out-breath is longer and her words ring true. My next question is, "If I do not approve of you quitting your job, what do you imagine that I was feeling?"*

As we become more attuned, Becky continues, "You think that I should have stayed in my job. It's a secure job and you think that I'm being impulsive, but I've always had to look out for myself." As Becky has been able to say what was implicitly encoded hitherto in the stiffening of her body and her slight breath holding, it strengthens our relationship. If Becky were less secure in our relationship, she might respond in polite words. So a different response from me would be to give her time to release the stiffening and let her breathing adjust. I could do this without comment and at the same time let my own breathing and posture become more in balance.

In the introduction, I emphasized the importance of techniques not being used to impose something on clients. With a breathing focus, this is particularly relevant. This way of relating to clients can only come from tuning into the client subcortically, below the verbal and analytical levels. If I had asked Becky to do these things as a technique, I would not have been with her; rather I would have been objectifying her. For a client who is more fragile than Becky, it may not be possible to interrupt or ask so directly what happened between the psychotherapist and client.

CONCLUSION

In this chapter we have looked at breathing as a continuous form of feedback on the therapeutic relationship and how it can be used to pace interactions and regulate ourselves and clients. Breathing guides us about where to place the emphasis in psychotherapy, on interactive regulation or self-regulation. We have also learned some breathing awareness practices for keeping a continuous sense of how the relationship is unfolding. In Chapter 6, breathing and relating become an integral part of working with emotions.

Chapter 6

BEING WITH EMOTIONS

Emotions and their regulation are center stage in a non-verbally focused psychotherapy. In this chapter, we explore working with clients who are emotionally overwhelmed and those lacking emotional expression. We continue to build on the discussion from previous chapters.

Working with Clients: Flooded with Feelings and with Limited Feelings

Broadly speaking, clients may be flooded with feelings, lurching from one feeling to another, one moment angry, then crying and afraid, that is, overwhelmed with their feelings. On the other hand, some clients have a limited emotional repertoire. They may have difficulty recognizing their feelings, and if they do experience their feelings, recognition of the changing contours and rhythms of their feelings may be stilted. They may find it difficult to withstand the intensity of their emotional experience. Emotionally overwhelmed clients are left without really knowing what they want as the torrent of their feelings leaves them unable to think and reflect (the amygdala is active, stopping higher cortical processes—see Chapter 2).

At the other end of the spectrum, clients may not know what they are feeling, let alone be able to put feelings into words. Clients who are overwhelmed with feelings benefit from discovering ways of dampening the intensity of their emotions, being able to contain them so that they can be experienced more slowly, reflected on, and thought about. This enables discrimination between different feelings, gaining some perspective on them, and being able to make choices about tactful ways of expressing them in words in different relationships, or keeping them (relatively) private. Psychotherapy may end when emotionally overwhelmed clients have taken charge of their emotions rather than being at their mercy. For some clients in this emotionally overwhelmed grouping, once they are more in command of their feelings, they are equipped to continue and deepen into the therapeutic relationship.

In contrast, clients with a limited emotional life, perhaps not able to recognize emotions, not able to put thinking, feeling, and acting together and express themselves to others, require an approach that underscores emotions and amplifies them, and links their feeling, acting, and thinking. This increases the capacity of these clients for recognizing and naming emotions, and expressing a wider repertoire of feelings and with varying intensity.

As we have noted before, because it can alter structures within their brain-body systems that were laid down in early attachment patterns, long-term psychotherapy focused on feelings offers hope for both sorts of clients (Schore, 2003b, 2003c). However, for change to occur, it "must involve unconscious, right brain limbic learning" (Schore, 2003b, p. 53). This means contacting a client's emotions non-verbally and tuning into her poorly developed right-brain processes with our own right-brain processes. This is where the emphasis is. It does not, of course, mean neglecting left-brain processes.

The non-verbal regulation of emotions requires:

- Tuning into oneself, then contacting clients
- Tuning into clients from an embodied stance
- Keeping clients within the window of tolerance (see introduction) and being with clients when they are outside this window

- Using breathing and autonomic nervous system signs to continuously resonate with and adjust the intensity of the non-verbal level of interaction
- Adjusting presence for short or long rein holding (see Chapter 3)
- "Talking" in words and non-verbally to different levels of consciousness in clients from the matter-of-fact to the deep emotional level (see Chapter 4, levels of interaction)
- Linking non-verbal and verbal relating to link left- and right-brain processes more densely and to link subcortical and cortical brain structures
- Linking thinking, feeling, and acting

Generally, clients who are overwhelmed by their feelings require firm and kind short rein holding, the reduction of our gestures to reduce stimulation, addressing the matter-of-fact level of consciousness, and a focus on body sensation and naming experiences. Those devoid of much feeling require looser long rein holding, addressing the deep emotional level of consciousness, and focusing on feelings about experiences.

Before we discuss further, let's pause and backtrack to remind ourselves of how emotions are regulated in babyhood. You might also want to refer to Chapters 1 and 2. From birth we learn non-verbally about our feelings from the way our caregivers respond to us. We learn to experience the fullness of our feelings without being overwhelmed as long as our parents are on hand to give us help when they see that we need it. They help us to adjust the intensity of feelings or they stimulate us when we are bored (emotional regulation). They tune into our feelings and put words to what we are experiencing. In this way they provide us with our first words for our emotions as they recognize what we are expressing. Their interactions with us help the development between the left and right brain, and between cortical and subcortical structures. We learn that what we are feeling and expressing is welcomed and understood. This encourages us to continue relating and, in the process, our brain develops. Those of us, however, growing up without secure early relationships will not have developed such emotional mastery.

Without the interactions necessary for brain growth at critical times, our brains will not have developed in optimal ways. This was the case with both Peter and Suzy. They each came to psychotherapy because they had relationship difficulties. Resolving their emotional difficulties was the way for them to resolve their relationship difficulties. They each needed, however, a different approach.

Peter and Suzy

Peter's partner of some years was pressing him for marriage. He was not confident about making the right decision. **He had little connection with his feelings** *but was a strong thinker, who had a successful career in software development. He enjoyed his work and life, and liked the way it was with his girlfriend. They did not live together and Peter enjoyed the companionship of his girlfriend, Jackie, when they met up two or three times a week. Peter was not against marriage but could not make a decision. He had made lists of pros and cons about marrying, but this left him frustrated and still not knowing what he wanted to do. Peter was used to complex problem solving in his work, but he could not solve this problem.*

Suzy had had a series of relationships, but told me, "I always choose the wrong men." **Suzy was easily overwhelmed by her feelings**, *and so kept them away by living in a frozen body. Her frozen state was not obvious on first meeting her. She seemed in possession of herself and spoke with a lively, animated face. She lived alone and enjoyed her work as a nursery school teacher. She was prompted to call because she had met a man that she was attracted to, but did not trust herself to know if he would be abusive, "like the others." How could she tell if this man was different?*

On the face of it, Peter and Suzy had similar problems, but how did I know that they had different emotional difficulties and would require different approaches? The first consideration, which should be familiar by now, was gentle observation of them, coupled with sensing my bodily experience of being with them. I used the body-speech-mind practice (Chapter 4) to get a descriptive sense of them. In the interests of brevity, I have selected elements of this in the descriptions of Peter and Suzy.

As Peter spoke, I saw that his face was lively and his eyes looked sensitive and kind. What was striking was that the rest of his body was inert. He hardly seemed to breathe. His arms hung by his sides and he did not use them to make gestures or emphasize his words. His head tilted to one side and slightly backward and his eyes seemed to pull away and try to find something to focus on in the room rather than me. This gave me the impression that he was trying to get away from me. He spoke with little lyricism in his voice, in a monotone. When I asked him about his feelings for his girlfriend, he said, "I suppose I love her. I've been with her a long time." In other words, length of time correlated in his mind with love, rather than feeling love in warm bodily sensations. His well-developed left brain seemed to think his feelings—like working out some sort of mathematical puzzle. His right brain seemed on vacation and he had little basis for making decisions that involved his feelings. When I tuned into my non-verbal sense of the relationship with Peter through directing my attention inwardly, my thoughts were active and I found myself thinking about love in an abstract way. I was not very aware of any sensations in my body below my neck, although my face felt warm and mobile. I took my inner sense of our relationship as clues about Peter.

Taking into account all of these features, Peter seemed to have had early insecure-avoidant attachment; he was also ambivalent about relationships. In body psychotherapy character strategy terms, he seemed to have sensitive-withdrawn and dependent-endearing protective patterns. I kept these thoughts loosely in the back of my mind, rather than using them as a formula for his therapy. If I got too hung up on theory about him to satisfy my certainty-craving left brain, I could miss out on relating to Peter more intuitively from my right brain. I was already being drawn by Peter toward more left-brain relating (i.e., thinking abstractly) because that was where he was accomplished.

With Suzy, my non-verbal sense of things was relating to a likeable, but too perfect mannequin—something felt quite unreal about her. I was not aware of much going on anywhere in my body. When I looked at Suzy, my impression was of meeting a replica Suzy. I wondered where the real Suzy was, buried behind this replica, which I took as a protective facade for the world. As I got to know Suzy and asked her about her experience of her body, she told me that she knew that she "drifted in and out" of having any physical connection with herself. Mostly she did not pay her body much heed, but when she did, she felt frozen.

Her memory of her childhood mother was that "she was volatile and critical, but could also be nice." Her father was an alcoholic, "fun when sober, but a nasty drunk." All of her relationships had involved men who were abusive to her. Some were alcoholics; some lived off her; usually they "put her down" and denigrated her, although "usually they were fun to start

165

with." When Suzy got anywhere near a bodily experience of herself, she left her body to protect herself from unbearable feelings. Suzy knew consciously that her childhood was troubled, but had no idea how it had impacted on her body non-verbally.

My general sense of Suzy as unreal, coupled with her childhood parenting, suggested early insecure-disorganized attachment with developmental trauma. As with Peter, I kept these diagnostic thoughts loosely in mind. What was more important was getting to know Suzy week by week. Both Suzy and Peter had difficulties with getting close to others. Peter wanted to be close, but feared that if he let himself get closer to Jackie, he would be taken over, so he kept himself distant. Suzy had been close before, but as she had little sense of herself, she became merged with her partners, who then treated her badly. Neither Peter nor Suzy could voice what they wanted, when close with another.

NEUROSCIENCE AND EMOTIONS

We shall come back to Peter and Suzy throughout this chapter, but first let us remind ourselves about terms. Emotions are observed, and feelings are felt inside (Damasio, 2000). Emotions are differentiated from "sensory and homeostatic affects," which are not true emotions (Panksepp, 2009). This is an important difference in clinical practice, which I discuss later.

Emotions form first in the body, and you will recall from Chapter 1 that emotional processing is at first a subcortical activity involving the autonomic nervous system, the limbic system, and in particular the right brain. It is nonconscious. As emotions move into becoming known, the cortex mediates and makes judgments about how the emotions are expressed (Rustin, 2013). Emotions organize perception, thought, memory, physiology, behavior, and social interaction, and coordinate mind and body, thus enhancing survival (Pally, 2000). We are at a considerable disadvantage, therefore, if we are not in touch with our feelings or we are not able to contain them. Since emotions emerge subcortically, they are responsive to non-verbal ways of exploration "through their physical dynamics" rather than "cognitive inputs" (Panksepp, 2009). In the therapeutic process, this means working through awareness of our own embodied experiences to contact directly the non-verbal, implicitly encoded developmental patterns, expressed in the habitual breathing and movement patterns of our clients. These patterns are formed in interactions in babyhood. They may have been somewhat modified by later experiences and relationships, but they form the template for a client's adult relating.

The Basic Emotions

Although neuroscientists have different ideas about what the basic emotions are, they recognize six universal, innate, primary emotions: happiness, sadness, fear, anger, disgust, and shame (Darwin, 1892/1998). Social emotions can be added to these basic emotions, including sympathy, embarrassment, guilt, pride, jealousy, envy, gratitude, admiration, indignation, and contempt (Damasio, 2000).

Panksepp (1998, 2009) describes seven basic emotional systems, which are concentrated in the medial and subcortical parts of the brain. The systems are identifiable in human and other mammalian brains. The seven basic emotional systems interact with higher and lower brain processes, and each emotion has its own neurological circuitry. They are not just output systems or discrete information modules. The systems indicate that we are active in the world and not just passively responsive to it. Panksepp, in his writing, uses capital letters for the systems to denote that they are specific systems. He sees them as "primes" but not "sufficient" for all of our interactions with others. The systems are SEEKING, FEAR, RAGE, LUST, CARE, PANIC, and PLAYfulness. The FEAR system has received particular attention in psychotherapy (for example, Rustin, 2013), as it is implicated in anxiety disorders and post-traumatic stress disorder. It generates the sort of free-floating anxiety that Eliza described (Chapter 4). Panksepp advocates mobilizing the SEEKING system, the "well-being" system in psychotherapy, as it underpins other emotional processes. It is involved in social bonding and seeking safety, when in danger. We have already discussed in Chapter 3 the importance of establishing safety in psychotherapy from the ambience of the consulting room and adapting our presence. Play and fun (the PLAYfulness system) can be neglected in psychotherapy, but "any therapist who can capture the therapeutic moment in mutually shared play episodes will have brought the client to the gateway of happy living" (Panksepp, 2009, p. 17). Play often brings laughter and humor, and gives pleasure. These ingredients in psychotherapy encourage us to go on with psychotherapy. Play also lets us try things out and experience new possibilities in relationships.

Interestingly, Panksepp tells us that "primary-process, *prepositional emotional energies* have a mind of their own—an ancient form of phenomenal consciousness that preceded language and sophisticated thought by hundreds of millions of years of evolutionary time" (2009, p. 2, emphasis in original). He goes on to explain that these primary-process emotional affects are not conditioned and are "objectless" affect-laden tendencies. In contrast, human cognitions are conditioned by life. He observes that for the researcher, it is important to distinguish "cortical cognitions" from "subcortical emotional arousals" and how they blend into "interactive mental wholes" (Panksepp, 2009, p. 2). This is relevant for clinicians too. Both Peter and Suzy had difficulties at the start of therapy with blending their thinking and feeling into an integrated sense of themselves.

The Face and the Body in Emotional Communication

Darwin perceived that "when our minds are affected, so are the movements of our bodies" (1892/1998, p. 37). He noted that when emotions are expressed, they appear at first in the facial and respiratory muscles, then the upper extremities, and finally in the muscles of the whole body. Emotions are also expressed in the voice. Darwin also observed that universal expressions of emotion could be overlaid by "artificial gestures" that could be confused with "true expressions" (Darwin, 1892/1998, p. 55). This is in accordance with Reich's view that our protective defenses show physically as "muscular armoring," and altered breathing patterns, which serve to obscure the original (unacceptable) expression (Reich, 1970).

Darwin's work has been built upon by Paul Ekman (2004), who sees emotions as arising physiologically, but also being influenced by culture and learning. He has codified specific facial muscle movements and correlated them with the expression of different emotions. However, Heller has observed the fluidity of facial activity, which *"only sometimes* gives the impression that the face constructs an expression that sends a particular message" (2012, p. 261, emphasis added). Ekman has also found that when groups of muscles belonging to an emotional expression are deliberately contracted, the individual feels the emotion connected with that muscle contraction pattern. While this may not always hold true so precisely, asking clients to explore different postures does give them new experiences of themselves. Suggesting to depressed clients that they might gradually open out their chest and pull their shoulders back to see what that feels like often does change their mood somewhat, partly because they breathe more deeply while making these adjustments.

We often pick up the significance of facial expression without being aware of it consciously. While facial expression is especially important in emotional communications, and this is universal, there are differences across cultures (McGilchrist, 2009a). I observed in the introduction the importance of arranging the seating for ourselves and our clients to be able to see each other to capture the messages going on non-verbally between us in facial expressions. We pick up lots of information subliminally through the facial expressions of clients, which we may be unaware of. A fascinating example of this is an experiment that closely observed a psychiatrist's face, when she was interviewing depressed, suicidal patients. Her observed facial expressions predicted which patients would make further suicide attempts. It seems that the psychiatrist was tuning in nonconsciously to the non-verbal communications of the patients (Heller & Haynal-Redmond, 1997).

However, facial expression is not the only way that we nonverbally communicate feelings backward and forward with clients. We also register them non-verbally through voice intonation, bodily posture, and movements (McGilchrist, 2009a). Indeed, there is some evidence that body cues, not facial expressions, are more significant in discriminating intense positive and negative emotions (for example, Aviezer, Trope, & Todorov, 2012).

Emotions and the Body: Autonomic Nervous System Reactions

Emotions are experienced in, and expressed through, the body. Emotions lead to action and our physical shape changes with the contours of our feelings, getting bigger or smaller. There are numerous colloquial ways of speaking about this embodiment of emotion. When we are emotionally moved, we "well up," "swell with pride," "shrivel up in shame," "shrink in fear," and "burst with joy." Our e-motions are energy movements, flowing out of us to connect with others.

Emotions are accompanied by physiological and energetic changes, movement patterns, and thoughts. Emotional expression is part of self- and interactive regulation. If we are to connect non-verbally with our clients, we have to tune into and tolerate the basic emotional energies coursing through our bodies. This is the starting point for helping clients to link their feeling, thinking, and action. Physiological changes in the autonomic nervous system accompanying emotions are observable, especially in the face. We go pale with fear, red with hot fiery anger, white with cold rage, and glow with excitement. With some practice, we can observe these physical changes in our clients and we can keep track of our own autonomic nervous system and emotional responses. This is part of a collaborative, intersubjective approach. The awareness practices mentioned in earlier chapters enable us to shift our attention between softly observing clients, sensing the atmosphere of the room, and then coming back to inner reflection on our experience. This continually changing focus of our attention from moment to moment serves to bring us into conscious awareness of our resonances with clients.

We can learn to notice changes in the autonomic nervous system to guide the regulation of the therapeutic process in ourselves and in our clients. For example, we can turn our attention inward and notice our breathing, and we can look at clients and ask them about their experiences. Observable changes in the sympathetic nervous system, the arousing, charging-up aspect of the autonomic nervous system, include faster breathing, quicker heart rate (pulse racing and palpitations), increase in blood pressure (sometimes experienced as pressure in the head and involving facial reddening), the pupils of the eyes getting bigger (dilation), dry eyes, the skin going pale, cold, having goose bumps (visible on the arms), increased sweating, cold and clammy hands (and other body parts), tension in muscles (stiffening of the body), and feeling alert or "wired." There is, of course, a gradation here from mildly to extremely aroused.

Discernible changes belonging to the parasympathetic nervous system, the energy-conserving, calming aspect of the autonomic nervous system, include slower breathing, slower heart rate, the pupils getting smaller, the eyes glowing, the skin pinking or reddening, the skin looking fresh, smooth, warm, flushed, and being dry, the muscles being toned for their task, feeling less alert, hearing peristalsis (gut rumblings), and having the need to urinate.

As we saw in Chapter 1, sometimes both aspects of the autonomic nervous system are activated, causing freezing. This happens in situations that are perceived as life threatening. The function of freezing is to numb the person against impending death. It explains why sometimes people being attacked can do nothing to defend themselves and feel shame about this (see, for example, Rothschild, 2000). In freezing, the limbs may become limp (tonic immobility) or rigid. With either manifestation, people in this state cannot move. Thinking is also disrupted, and there is no capacity to think about what to do, or indeed to order the subjective experience of one's feelings.

A brief example of regulating arousal is feeling sleepy with a client. This is parasympathetic nervous system activity. I am assuming that I am not tired and it is specific to the interactions with this client. There are several options here. I might mention it to the client and we might discuss it. If I want to work with it non-verbally, I can straighten my back, speak more quickly, and put more force into my voice to lift my energy to activate my own sympathetic nervous system, and then see what happens. Lifting my energy will have an impact on the client. I might mention my experience to the client; we can discuss it and try this option together. A different possibility is to discuss the sleepiness and go with the parasympathetic activation. Maybe I am feeling sleepy because the client is indicating that she needs a break from our contact. I can mention this and then we both close our eyes and focus inward on ourselves. We stay together in the knowledge that we are doing something together without the intensity of such direct contact. This latter possibility is appropriate for clients with whom there is a strong working relationship and who can tolerate silences.

Suzy had no control over her freezing and splitting off from herself (dissociation). As a child, Suzy could neither flee nor fight her parents, so her subcortical nervous system structures had automatically protected her by freezing. Her choice of abusive men helped to sustain these bodily defenses. Often Suzy froze at the beginning of a session. She felt trapped with me without any means of getting away. When she was not in this frozen state, she knew that it made no sense. She liked me, liked my soft voice, but could not stop herself from going cold and numb. Her early childhood attachments were activated subcortically and were outside her conscious control. At other times, when Suzy spoke of her work, which she genuinely enjoyed, she could sense the warmth and tingling of some pleasure in her body. We would build on this positive bodily experience—not all of Suzy's experiences of her body were terrifying. Our work would also involve Suzy becoming more conscious of her freezing, learning about what triggered it and building a relationship with her body through a combination of connecting with her body sensations and naming her experiences.

REGULATION OF EMOTIONS AND EMOTIONAL STATES

Regulation of physiological states goes hand in hand with the regulation of emotional states (for example, Darwin, 1892/1998; Reich, 1983; Porges, 2011). Certain feelings go with aroused, excited states (sympathetic nervous system) and others with more calm states (parasympathetic nervous system). Rage, hatred, frustration, irritation, touchiness, jealousy, excitement, exuberant joy, envy, fear, terror, spite, and desire, for example, are more arousing emotions. Pleasure, the joy of satisfaction, feeling the calm of being at one with oneself, love, sadness, peacefulness, grief, shame, and despair are more "calming" emotions (see, for example, Carroll, 2009; Reich, 1983). More arousing emotions are often (but not always) experienced as "up-going" and calming emotions as "down-going". In our work with clients this conceptualisation of emotions provides an easy reference. Does the therapeutic process call for more "livening up" or "calming down"?

Emotions and Rhythmic Cycles

Emotions are expressed in a series of rhythmic cycles. Breathing, discussed in Chapter 5, plays a part in these cycles. Let me illustrate this with Becky (Chapter 5). *One day she spoke of missing her son, who had been adopted. Her runaway train style of speaking slowed down and her feelings welled up. Her upper lip trembled and tears began to trickle—* **the opening emotional cycle.** *I stayed in tune with her.*

Becky deepened her out-breath, and then internally gathered herself up, as she took an in-breath. She was quiet and it seemed like something was gestating inside her. I observed tiny movements in Becky's torso, and she had an inward look in her eyes. On her next out-breath she sobbed. More of her body moved. Her shoulders shuddered and her hands moved. Her breathing deepened some more and I saw tension leaving her body. Her shoulders became bigger, more dropped down, and her spine lengthened— **the second emotional cycle.**

Again Becky gathered herself and on **the third emotional cycle** *her sobbing came from her abdomen and wracked her whole body. Eventually her grief was spent. Her peristalsis was audible and she felt sad, but at peace. She spoke of the adoption as "for the best." Her shame and "the need to carry on" as a teenager had meant that she had never let herself feel how much she wished she could have kept her baby.* **This is the final (completing) cycle.**

Vasomotoric Cycle

Let us unpack this cycle of emotional expression further by looking at the vasomotoric cycle as described by Boyesen (1980; Southwell, 1988). The cycle is widely used in biodynamic (body) psychotherapy to guide self- and interactive regulation in clinical work. It has its roots in Reich's (1983) four-beat cycle, although Boyesen is said to have come to her theory independently. Variants of the four-beat cycle have also found their way into Gestalt therapy.

The cycle is a physiological, energetic, emotional, movement cycle. I describe it for a person who functions well in life and is able to regulate his feelings and physiology, when alone or with others. The cycle begins with a stimulus either from inside us (a thought, a body sensation, a feeling), or externally (something we see, or smell, or hear)—a noise or a conversation, the room. The stimulus leads to some arousal (1). The arousal gets stronger and stimulates an action or expression (2). Having expressed the stimulus, the body moves toward relaxation (3) and recuperation (4). These are the four phases of the cycle (Figure 6.1). They are linked with the autonomic nervous system.

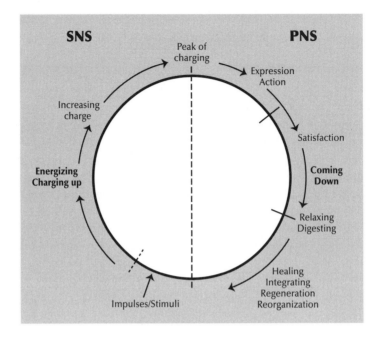

FIGURE 6.1 THE PHASES OF THE VASOMOTORIC CYCLE. SNS,
SYMPATHETIC NERVOUS SYSTEM; PNS, PARASYMPATHETIC NERVOUS SYSTEM.

The first phase of the cycle (stimulus and arousing phase),
related to the sympathetic nervous system, is the charging up and
energizing phase. The sympathetic nervous system is well known in
its role of preparing for flight or fight in threatening situations. The
other three phases, related to the parasympathetic nervous system,
are connected with states of calm, energy conservation, recuperation, and healing.

Phase 1: Charging Up and Arousal

In the first phase of the cycle there is a stimulus or impulse.
This first phase is related to the in-breath. Energy builds up ready
for action or expression. At the peak of the aroused state there is a
sense of being poised for action. The atmosphere can feel charged,
as if something is about to happen. The intensity and duration of the
arousal phase will depend on the individual and the circumstances.

Phase 2: Action and Expression

At the peak of arousal, the person moves into expression and action. The expression of arousal might simply be an out-breath. It might be a gesture, a movement, a look, or a combination of these. It might be a sigh or an exclamation or actions with accompanying expressive words. Expression and action go outward toward others or simply to the natural environment, but there is always something or someone that the expression is directed toward. It is an out-breath movement.

Phase 3: Calming, Relaxing, Sense of Satisfaction

The out-breath emphasis continues, and after the expression or action comes a sense of satisfaction, then an inward digestion of the expression followed by quiet reflection. Physically the body is in a process of returning to balance or homeostasis.

Phase 4: Recuperation, Repair, and Healing

The final phase is deep relaxation and rest, more inner reflection, and, during this phase, recuperation, regeneration, repair, and the deepest levels of healing occur. Davis (1984) refers to this as the in stroke, a flowing inward movement. At its most profound it feels like a delicious "melting," and clients will often report afterward (not while in this state) feeling "pleasurable tingles pulsing through them." Sometimes they also speak of profound feelings of universal love and "feeling at one" with the world. It is a silent, inner process and is not directed by thinking. It is automatic and no conscious action or direction is necessary. It is about being with the experience. Audible peristalsis often accompanies this phase. The meaning of an experience emerges later on from not interfering with the body processes. Meaning here is perceptual awareness rather than conceptual understanding (Gendlin, 1996), although conceptual understanding may emerge later too.

In any day, individuals go through many of these cycles. Indeed, within this schematic presentation of the vasomotoric cycle there will be several cycles. Cycles can be fleeting or extended over lengthy periods of time. We might think of the overall therapeutic process over some years as phases of the cycle with an opening cycle, deepening into the process (middle phase), integrating experiences, and completing (final phase). Regulatory cycles can be

175

observed in the life of groups and organizations (see, for example, Randall & Southgate, 1983). It can guide us in knowing the optimum time for beginning a new project, that is, after a slack time with sufficient organizational rest. It could explain why a new process has not taken off, as it was introduced at a time when the organization needed a break from a period of frenetic activity.

Variable Intensity of the Cycle

Depending on the stimulus and the way it is perceived, the arousal and the calming down will vary in intensity. If the stimulus and the reaction are strong, as in a fright of some sort, there will be a more intense process. An illustration of the cycle, taken from a commonplace situation, is driving to work. Driving requires a fair amount of arousal and alertness anyway. Then a pedestrian steps off the pavement (stimulus). The driver goes into higher arousal and slams the brakes on (action). The driver misses the person and breathes out with relief (release of tension and relaxation). At this point, the parasympathetic system begins to be more dominant. On getting to work, the driver tells colleagues about the near miss and calms down more. Fuller completion of the cycle does not happen until winding down at home in the evening and sleeping.

During therapeutic interactions, there are individual self-regulating cycles of the therapist and the client, and joint interactive regulatory cycles in which client and therapist are regulating each other. As with breathing and relating in Chapter 5, both the intrapsychic (self-regulating) and interpersonal (interactive regulating) aspects have to be kept in mind. Is relatively more horizontal (interpersonal) or more vertical (intrapsychic) relating required (Southwell, 1988)? Is a more individual or more interactive regulatory focus required? Should it be more explicit or more implicit?

Specific Emotions and the Vasomotoric Cycle

As we have already noted emotions are felt as a wave up or down the body. Anger can be felt as an upward and outward force. Subjectively it can feel exuberant, hot, pleasurable, and strengthening in its intensity. Other emotions feel like a movement downward in the body and a more inner experience. Sometimes excited emotional responses can quickly change into more downward-moving ones. Excited laughter, for example, can crescendo, peak, and tip rapidly into sobbing. Calm states are generally experienced as expansive and freeing, but can tip into sluggishness and resignation. More aroused states are experienced as contracting and stiffening, and they can be felt as strengthening rather than inhibiting.

Few of us, including our clients, express ourselves so freely and smoothly in emotional and physiological cycles. We swallow back feelings, bottle them up, or pour them out in torrents with no sense of completing something. As a rule of thumb, restricted breathing and bodily movements indicate inhibited emotional capacity (Reich, 1983). Our ability to move smoothly through the phases of the vasomotoric cycle depends on our early attachment history. Much of the cycle is nonconscious. *Peter, for example, could not feel the stimulus of the first phase of the cycle in his body, and so what he expressed in his flat voice and inert body was unconvincing. Presumably his mother had not attuned with his inner signals in her communications with him.*

Culturally, Western society reinforces and tends to overvalue activity and doing (sympathetic nervous system activity) in contrast to being (parasympathetic nervous system activity). Depending on our childhood, lifestyle, and cultural context, all of us have a tendency to function better at different phases of the cycle. The restricted patterns, however, also contain the seeds of different patterns of relating. They are ready to be "heard" (non-verbally) and to change (see, for example, Reich, 1983; Boadella, 1987; Keleman, 1979).

Domains of Experience

Another model, domains of experience, fleshes out in more detail the vasomotoric cycle. The model helps us to think about different areas of our experience, how feelings go from being nonconscious to conscious, and how to relate therapeutically in each domain. The model maps how experiences arise and comes from Buddhist psychology (see, for example, Donington, 1994; Sills, 2009). It provides a handy reference for conceptualizing client process. The model highlights where clients have the most capacity for relating. This guides us in where to place the emphasis in psychotherapy, especially in the early stages, and where therapist and client are likely to miss each other in communications. The idea is to cultivate the capacities of clients in parts of the cycle where they struggle, and to build on the parts that are working well. *Peter, for example, was strong on thinking, one of the domains, and I gained his cooperation by explaining why I was taking a particular approach with him; namely, that his thinking was very well developed, but his felt experience of his body sensations and his feelings had some catching up to do.*

Movements Arising From the Core State or Presence

Domains of experience have five layers: the core state, tonal sensations, emotions, named emotions, and expressed emotions. Energetic movements arise from Presence or the Core, characterized by joy, equanimity, loving-kindness, and compassion (discussed in Chapter 3). These movements arise nonconsciously, unless one is paying particular attention to this layer of awareness, perhaps in meditation practices. In any moment, millions of impulses are arising. As the impulses gather momentum and strength, a collection of physical sensations develops and they manifest in miniscule breathing changes, muscle stirrings, and visceral sensations. They are background experiences, often not consciously known, but can become known when attention is placed on them. As the impulses gain in strength, they manifest in collections of sensations with a tonal quality to them, rather than anything that can be specifically named. There is a vague sensing that something is stirring, more like smelling in the air that a storm is coming, or faintly hearing a far-off sound without knowing what it is.

Physical Sensations

As these tonal qualities grow, they become more distinct physical sensations. Some of these sensations soon fade away. Others become more intense and more sharply experienced. It is hard to find words for these physical sensations, which are "sensory and homeostatic affects" (Panksepp, 2009). Sounds, gestures, movements, and sometimes metaphors are the language of these physical sensations. Questions and invitations to elicit further information from clients about this layer of experience are:

- if it were a sound, how would that be?
- let a sound come (that puts the experience into sound).
- let a movement come (to express the experience).
- tap out the sensation in a rhythm?

Please note that the questions are phrased in specific words directed to the subcortical structures and the right brain. They are not "why questions" or questions such as "can you make, for example, a sound"? that the cortex and left brain understand. These sorts of questions suggest to the client that they think about the question. Movements and sounds for self-expression are discussed further in Chapter 9. Making connections with physical sensations *before* connecting with emotions is a safe way to proceed with most clients. It makes it less likely that clients will be overwhelmed emotionally and retraumatized in psychotherapy (see Rothschild, 2000).

With Peter, I wanted to guide him by "taking him by the hand," without him knowing it, into his subjective experience. I wanted him to be less aware of me, as he often felt awkward just being with me. Once he understood why we were exploring through movement and asking about his experiences, which had seemed at first tangential to him, he often felt the relief of not having to talk directly to me. He began to enjoy coming to sessions and letting his body movements communicate. Indeed, the sessions began to take on a playful quality.

Once I had Peter's cooperation, he responded surprisingly well to these sorts of questions. By shutting his eyes, he let go of his embarrassment and self-consciousness and showed me in a posture or movement how he felt that day. He let his body "speak" spontaneously, rather than figuring out (thinking) what movement to do. He would stand up and move farther away from me. As he shut his eyes, he would let his awareness go more inwardly and "find a posture." I would encourage him to exaggerate it, do it less, and play with it. I would take a lighthearted, matter-of-fact, encouraging, and permissive approach to him.

During one session, he bent his torso forward, keeping his head up. I suggested letting his head join in the movement, but doing it slowly so that he could experience the movement more fully. At intervals I asked him about his experience. At first Peter's movements looked mechanical, as if doing an exercise, but then they took on a life of their own and became expressive. He spoke of the weight of the responsibility (felt in his head and shoulders) of deciding whether to marry or not. He was frightened of making the wrong decision. It was a relief to just let his head go and feel less responsible. It had felt like his head was a "very heavy weight" on his neck.

We continued to work with these movements, and 6 months into psychotherapy, one day he bent his head and then his whole body forward. He kept bending forward and let himself drop to the floor. He curled up into a tight ball on the carpet. He did not want to move and just "wanted it all to go away." He felt safe in this position and I told him that he did not have to move—he could stay as he was. I suggested that he find a position that was really comfortable and as safe as he could make it. I would keep close by, but he did not have to talk to me. I spoke with a slow voice with dropped-down contours, and gave him long rein holding, which suggested that he had all the time in the world for his experience. I would be with him, but not interfering. The tightness in his body lessened and he turned on his front with his arms, legs, and head tucked in. He stayed like this for most of the session.

The sounds of his peristalsis were like a gently bubbling stream, and his breathing softened. He seemed soothed and looked less tense in his body. (His parasympathetic nervous system was activated.) He was communicating with me without words. As I watched him and let myself resonate with him, I felt warm and peaceful. He looked to me like a sleeping baby in his crib, and I felt very protective of him. At the end of the session, he spoke of feeling deeply rested. He looked pink and glowing. At the next session, he told me that he felt too young to make a decision about marriage. He had realized that he did want to marry his girlfriend but he did not feel old enough to make such an important life decision and commitment. Previously he had felt cornered by his girlfriend and pressured to decide and give her what she wanted. He had been able to tell Jackie about his feelings, and she under-stood. He had not been able to tell anyone before what he actually felt about anything, and they were getting on better. (The phases of the vasomotoric cycle are evident here too.)

Another direction in which to take explorations in this domain of physical sensations is to ask clients to find words, perhaps non-sense words, for their bodily sensations. It often helps to give some examples, such as, could it be thudding, thwacking, pulsing, throb-bing, tingling, muffled, dull, singing, sparkly, or a dry feeling, and so on.

This was a way of exploring with Suzy. When she could connect with her body, I would ask her to give names for her sensations. She learned to distinguish parts of herself that felt numb, such as her legs, and to identify other parts where she felt lukewarm or cool, such as her hands. This helped Suzy to link body sensation and naming and began to address the emotional overload. We focused especially on the body sensations that accompanied the delight she felt when working with children. These were key ways of working with her safely. However, I had to be sure that I was attuned with her; otherwise she would be angry with me for being out of contact with her and tell me (quite rightly) that I was "doing to her" when she wanted me to "be with me."

The domain of physical sensations is the domain of Gendlin's (1981, 1996) "felt sense" and Damasio's (2000) "somatic markers." It is the domain of hunches and gut feelings. These are what tell us that the house we look at is not for us, even though it ticks all of the boxes. Damasio's somatic marker hypothesis proposes that emotion and reasoning work together. Somatic markers are collections of sensations that accompany thinking, feeling, and imagining. They underlie decision making and the process of looking at imagined actions and the likely consequences. This body-sensation level of experience is at the center of feeling embodied. This captures theoretically both Suzy's and Peter's difficulties.

In the late 1960s, Gendlin recognized the significance of the felt sense if psychotherapy was to be successful. Clients who could tune into the felt sense could be predicted to use psychotherapy successfully using outcome measures (Gendlin, 1996). Further questions to elucidate body sensation awareness in clients are these:

- "As you are speaking, how does it feel in your body?" This invites a shift from talking to sensing. Some clients will require more guidance to sense their particular body parts.
- For these clients, questions could be: "How does it feel in your chest right now? How does it feel in your shoulders right now?" (see Chapter 4).

Peter benefited from these sorts of questions. He would talk about the argument going on in his head about marriage, the pros and the cons. I would ask him to put the pros and cons into words and notice what he was experiencing in his body. He would say, "Jackie wants to marry me." He would answer "tight" as the corresponding body sensation. I would ask where he was feeling tight, and he would point generally at his chest, not really sure. As our work progressed and he got more proficient at sensing, he would name tension in the abdomen, tight shoulders, sometimes a jittery feeling his abdomen. It made no difference whether he was speaking about a pro or a con at first.

I would ask him to relate the sensation to his dilemma. He would speak in various ways of feeling trapped and yet feeling obligated to his girlfriend. The "honorable thing would be to marry her." The difference in these sentences and how he spoke in the beginning of psychotherapy was that they reflected his body sensations and were not just his "thinking speaking." His body was becoming generally more mobile as he spoke, and his voice carried more feelings. He was beginning to connect moving, sensing, feeling, and thinking. Generally by the end of a session, he felt somewhat less tight in his abdomen. While reducing his physical discomfort was not an aim, it did indicate that when Peter voiced his feelings, not only "the argument in his head" lessened, but also his physical tensions.

The shift from talking about an emotion to sensing the experience of it can be elicited with the question, "As you are talking about feeling sad, how does it feel physically?" This can be followed up with more specific body-focused questions. The shift from the conceptual level of speaking to the sensing level can be elicited by asking, "As you are thinking about that decision, how does it feel physically?"

The idea is that these sorts of questions are so embedded in the therapist that they arise spontaneously in the moment out of the curiosity of the therapist. The switch from talking about something to experiencing it is a shift from relatively more left-brain talking to relatively more right-brain talking.

As noted in the introduction, the exploration will go nowhere if the therapist is just using the questions as if following a manual. It will elicit a left-brain-to-left-brain dialogue. The idea behind all of these suggestions for further exploration is taking the client into sensing through the physical body, and then, as the client does this, staying in contact with him or her. Thinking, feeling, imagining, and so on are always accompanied by bodily sensed experiences. Once clients "take a step through the door" into experiencing body sensations, it opens up possibilities for discovering more dimensions of experience. More awareness brings more information, builds a different relationship with oneself, and enables more rooted choices. Each new experience offers further possibilities for experiencing and discovering more. Peter was beginning to become more aware of his bodily sensations and his feelings.

TALKING TO INNER EXPERIENCE USING IT LANGUAGE

Notice that the questions are posed using *It-language*—how does *it* feel? The therapist guides the client into inner experience without specifically saying she is doing so. The tone of voice and the delivery of the question carry the suggestion that it is okay to go inward, take time, and explore. There is no fixed, premeditated answer. The form of the words is important for connecting with spontaneous impulses and "talking to the right brain." As noted in Chapter 4, asking "How are *you* feeling in your chest right now?" would not guide the client so directly to an inner experience. Even gently saying, "Let *yourself* go inside and see what is happening" can leave clients feeling too self-conscious and watched to let go into inner experience. Instead, they are likely to stiffen and just become overly compliant or resistant. This is because the level of consciousness being addressed in the client by the words "you" or "yourself" is more at the interpersonal level.

Exploring feelings deliberately uses It-language initially (Southwell, 1999; Westland, 2009a). It shifts the client from thinking about a concept to experiencing it. Using It-language takes the client away from a being a person with an ego relating interpersonally. The "it" that is being referred to is deliberately left vague. *It* can refer to feelings, movements, sounds, sensations, and energies. The therapist uses descriptive, nonpersonal words. These speak to the inner processes of clients and especially the right-brain, less-conscious, non-verbal aspects. As the therapist speaks, her voice tone goes down the musical scale, and is slow and evocative. The therapist is receptive to the client's non-verbal responses. Here are some examples of therapist suggestions:

- let it come.
- feel how it wants to move.
- let the breath come.
- let the sounds come.

A variant that keeps the dialogue more verbal and more at the talking-about level, but begins to name an emotion, is, "There seems to be anger around." In this phrasing of the words an emotion is named and can be explored, if the client can relate to it. This is especially useful, for example, when the atmosphere of the consulting room is experienced as angry. The anger is neither the therapist's nor the client's. Neither of us has to become defensive about who is angry. We are both in it, and neither of us is at fault. One of us may have initiated the anger, but it may be unclear which one. We want to cultivate a joint exploration of anger.

Sometimes It-language takes clients into more universal states, where the boundaries of self and others are indistinct. No words can describe these states. It-language contrasts with "I-you" language, which involves someone who is experiencing a feeling and owning it. For example, "*I* am angry with you." This takes us into you-and-I talk. Sometimes we want that, but not in the early stages of exploring imperceptible feelings. Deepening into the emotional life of the client requires a stance of identifying with the client's inner world. It involves diminishing the conscious sense of two people in the room, a "you" talking to a "me."

Recognizing Emotions

The collection of physical sensations gradually becomes recognized as an emotion and then becomes named. Happiness, anger, sadness, and so on, all have particular sensations that can be recognized and named. Happiness, for example, goes with feeling softer and warmer, feeling an inner glow, and feeling more peaceful. The muscles are less taut; the body feels bigger, with more sense of inner space; the breathing is more expansive; alertness is reduced; the posture feels more open, and there may be a sense of an inner smile throughout the whole body, and especially dancing around the mouth and enlivening the eyes.

Some individuals, however, cannot name their sensations to themselves, recognize their feelings, and express them. Such individuals have *alexythymia*. McGilchrist (2009a) explains that in these the right brain is not communicating with the left brain. Additionally, there are also individuals whose parents misnamed their emotions when they were children. For example, the parents may not have been able to tolerate anger in their toddler and misnamed it to the child as "upset" or "making a fuss" or "naughty."

The adult client may then fail to know that she is angry or mis-name her experience as "upset." Similarly, adult clients may drip a tear from the corner of the eye but do not know that they are feeling miserable. Sometimes they may not even know that a tear has fallen. Physiologically the client is responding but is not aware of it. Eliza (Chapter 4) and Peter were both somewhat alexithymic individuals.

Naming Feelings

The process of naming feelings puts them into a form that can be communicated to another person in spoken language. In nam-ing a feeling, it becomes possible to reflect on it, and to explore the sensations of it further. While putting feelings into spoken words is valuable, they never fully capture the whole experience of and various tones of our feelings. Parents who could not name the emo-tions of their baby may also have been unable to manage their own emotional states. Perhaps the parent became a bit panicky at the baby's cry, and instead of attuning to the expression of the emotion within the crying, with its rising and falling contours, the parent may have gone up the intensity and contour scale. This may have left the child "unmet" and with uncontained energetic movements. Naming experiences can be very containing for clients flooded with feelings, who had this sort of parenting. "Words alone make con-cepts more stable and available to memory" (McGilchrist, 2009a, p. 114). Naming an experience lets clients have some distance from their emotions.

This proved to be the case with Suzy. Suzy could only manage some moments of being in touch with her body and its sensations. However, once she was in contact with her body sensations, it was strengthening for her to say, "confused," "desperate," or "frightened." At first she found simple one-word answers to my questions but, as our relationship developed, she would be able to elaborate on "frightened." For example, one day she described feeling "uneasy." She linked this with the anticipation of her mother's forthcoming visit. Her mother would be "critical" and the visit something to "endure." She was then able to elaborate on what it was about her mother that made her feel uneasy.

Therapists benefit from having a large emotional vocabulary to help clients develop or broaden their repertoire of words for feelings. The choice of the "right word" and how it is spoken makes a difference. The sounds of words for feelings make a difference in whether clients feel therapists are resonating with them. In Chapter 4, Eliza and I were in tune with each other when we found the word "lonely" together to describe her feeling. The sound of the word "lonely" and how I said it felt just right to her.

I asked colleagues to come up with a list of words for sadness. The list included distressed, glum, gloomy, blue, unhappy, miserable, melancholic, sorrowful, discontented, dejected, grief-ridden, grief-stricken, hurt, not nice, bad, low, despondent, nostalgic, wistful, regretful, doleful, and so on. Sadness also easily slips into depression, a sense of longing, hopelessness, and helplessness. It can also be mingled with shades of anger, hurt, and irritation. You might try saying some of these words out loud to get a feel for their different resonances. Each word has a distinct feel to them, when spoken to resonate with the emotion that they convey.

Finding the Object of the Feelings

The next phase of the experience is feeling the movement direction of the feelings, reflecting on it by thinking and sensing, and then discovering who the emotion is directed toward. It is strengthening for clients to name the person in this way. So asking the question, "Who are *you* angry with?" supports clients in bringing their inner experience toward another. They can take the question inside and find responses. "Who am *I* angry with? I am angry with myself, the world, you, my father." Note the word shift here from *it* to *you* when addressing the client.

When Peter became bolder in our relationship, he told me with feeling that he did not like me looking at him. He felt scrutinized in the same way that his father scrutinized him. The possibility of us relating interpersonally was developing. I welcomed this.

Expressing or Containing Feelings

The next phase is a decision about containing the emotion and expanding into it to feel it more, or to express the emotion, or an edited version, of it to another. This phase demands the capacity to reflect on and think about feelings, to imagine consequences, to hold the emotional intensity and depth of a feeling by choice. In this phase, clients have the choice to give voice to their discoveries or not and to sense the physical responses and reactions in their body.

Suzy and Peter both had difficulties in this domain. Peter did not want to hurt his girlfriend but hardly knew what he felt when he was with her. Suzy was terrified of her feelings and could not contain them when she touched them. As with Peter, she could not easily tell another how she felt.

BOUNDARIES

Underbound or Overbound and the Metaphor of Water for Emotional Flow

Being able to contain feelings or be flooded by them depends on boundaries. Water is a useful metaphor for thinking about emotions. Using words such as *drips, drops, rivers, streams,* and *oceans* for emotions builds a scene in the imagination, about the liveliness, flow, quantity, and intensity of feelings. *An illustration of this is thinking about Peter's emotional life as a faint trickle with the odd drip of rain. Gradually Peter's trickle of feelings had become a stream and at times a strong waterfall. He was actually a passionate man with deep feelings.*

For emotions to be experienced, they have to be contained. The more intense the emotions are, the stronger their container has to be. If we stay with metaphorical thinking, the flow of emotions is like a river (Figure 6.2). A river has banks that hold the water in place and guide the direction of flow. If the banks are too flimsy and the emotions are torrential, flooding can occur. Clients fitting this description are described as *underbound. Suzy was an underbound client. When she touched her feelings, she had no way of containing them and so spun out of her body.*

If the banks are too thick, they may restrict the flow of emotions and it may be hard to know any emotions are there. These clients are described as *overbound. Peter was more overbound than underbound, but his riverbanks were somewhat brittle. His feelings were somewhat more available to him than Suzy's, but again he was frightened to feel more fully because he might not be able to contain his feelings.*

Ideally the banks of the river are able to contend with the pres-

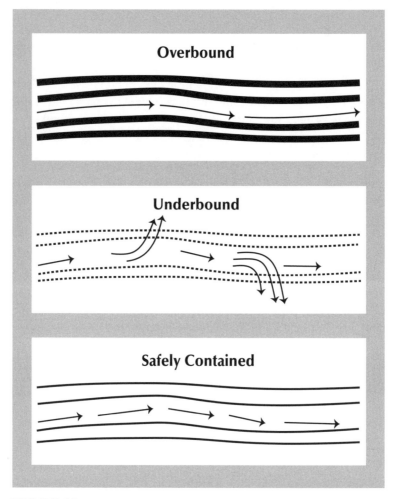

FIGURE 6.2 BOUNDARIES: OVERBOUND, UNDERBOUND, AND SAFELY CONTAINED.

sures coming from torrential rain, when our feelings are in full flow, through to tranquil periods of the river burbling along. The terms *under-* and *overbound* were coined by Keleman, who observed that overbound folk take on and "maintain aggressive attitudes . . . either directly or just below the surface" and underbound types give in and appease others in present relationships, but originally it was a protective reaction to the neglect, abuse, shock, or trauma of early parenting (1989, p. 6). Overbound bodies lack space for "motility." Nothing gets in or out. The therapeutic task is to explore and become aware of the body's rigidity. Exploratory movements, such as those described with Peter, are one way to do this. Over-bound individuals can be deceptive for therapists because they seem to function well in the world, but being overbound can hide very fragile individuals. Tony (Chapter 3) was like this.

Suzy was easily invaded by others. She also "leaked" energetically and emotionally into others and was experienced by others as too demanding and needy. She gave her partners the impression of being independent, but they were disappointed as they got to know her. The banks of her rivers were porous, letting too much in and out. She tried, often very successfully, to contain herself through repetitive thinking. When she was more over-whelmed or flooded, she fled further out of her body, particularly when she was in the presence of others and in a confined space. When she was most overwhelmed, she looked at the landscape, trees, the clouds, or clear sky to hold herself together and prevent herself from disintegrating. She did not feel safe with people. This cost her a lot of energy daily just to keep going, and she was exhausted.

A Sense of Self

Being overbound or underbound is closely related to a sense of self. The physical embodiment of boundaries gives a sense of "me" and "not me." This is especially important in relationships with oth-ers. Boundaries are formed by appropriate contact in babyhood and childhood. Boundaries are maintained literally in the thickness of the skin, muscle consistency, the capacity to adjust physically to the emotional demands and physiological requirements of what is happening in us, and in relationships at any time. Being "thick or thin skinned," "having a backbone," or "being spineless" capture the sense of particular sensitivities, and the ability to "stand up" or "buckle under" in adversity.

Overbound individuals are more hard bodied and are able to deal with the world quite successfully in conventional terms, but they often have difficulty contacting their inner life, including body sensations, and can find intimate relationships boring and unfulfilling. They have limited flexibility in situations because their bodies lack flexibility. Underbound individuals tend to be soft bodied, and in relationships confuse themselves with others as they easily become merged with others. The underbound person acquiesces and fits in because she really does not know what is her and what is not her, so that she cannot know what she wants. Her boundaries are underdeveloped. Underbound individuals also tend to be hypersensitive.

Securely attached babies experience being contained and having their physiological and emotional states fairly consistently attuned with and modulated. This builds flexible boundaries and a sense of feeling at home in the body. Babies who were invaded or who were emotional extensions of their caregivers, or who were repeatedly startled or shocked, lose this sense of being at home in themselves and have reduced sense of self and adaptable flexibility with others.

Being Grounded

Boundaries are linked with grounding, centering, and facing. Grounding was first introduced in Chapter 3. Being grounded means being present, being able to root and keep rooted in the way that a tree does in spite of changing weather (mostly). Any child who has been neglected, deprived, invaded, or shocked is likely to manage the situation by becoming ungrounded or may have only weakly developed the capacity to be and stay grounded. Being ungrounded involves upward energetic movement in the body to get away from the inhospitable environment. Ungrounded people have their "head in the clouds," whereas grounded people have their "feet on the ground" and can "stand up for themselves." Clients are often unaware of being grounded or ungrounded. With training, therapists can see the state of groundedness in clients. Lack of groundedness can be experienced as feeling a bit spaced out. Grounding oneself means sensing the contact with the ground through the feet, feeling the arm of the chair with our forearms, and feeling the back of the chair through our back.

Suzy's frightening childhood home led her to move up into her head and lose contact with the rest of her body. Most likely she never came into her body fully as there was little invitation to do so from either of her parents. She sought refuge outside herself and in the natural environment. She could not feel her legs. She spoke of liking the calmness of the consulting room and my "softly spoken voice." "It makes me feel calm. It's safe enough for me to stay." She liked the firm boundary setting of the therapeutic frame. "It's a relief that you have said I may not keep checking my phone and we can explore how that feels. You are giving me permission to not respond instantly to my friends, although they expect that." She enjoyed the strength that rubbing her feet together gave her. When she did this, she felt that she "had her feet to stand on."

Closely linked with grounding are centering and facing. Centering is the experience of sensing the breath and feeling it go down to the abdomen. Being centered gives a sense of inner balance. When centered, neither the sympathetic nor the parasympathetic nervous system is overactivated (Boadella, 1987). Facing involves the eyes making contact with the world and the face expressing authentic feelings. It involves being able to stand and face another, both to give feelings and to receive the feelings of others. *Peter and Suzy obviously had difficulties with grounding, centering, and facing. Their eyes and faces were not very expressive. Over time, their eyes and faces became more expressive. As that happened, more genuine contact passed between us. Peter gradually came to be able to look at me for longer periods of time without feeling scrutinized, and his face became more mobile. His gaze became directed toward me and his eyes showed his feelings. Peter was able to do this as the therapy developed because I accepted that looking at me was fraught in the beginning. I did not put him on the spot and insist that he look at me. Being in the room with me was frightening enough already for him.*

FURTHER GUIDANCE ON SPEAKING TO EMOTIONS

Emotions and Evocative Language

Our clients' emotions respond to evocative language. "In evocative language, words are chosen to resonate in felt experience. *If words "reach us," they are felt as "true," "deep," and "powerful." Words— evocatively spoken from the practitioner's own embodied self awareness— can enhance and amplify feelings*" (Fogel, 2009, p. 248, emphasis in original). Speaking evocatively and reaching the client happen only when the therapist has a direct, felt connection with the client's emotional being. If it is merely a theoretical idea, knowing that it would help a client if his emotional life was "matched" will fall short of the mark.

For the client to feel felt, the therapist must spontaneously communicate that she is in contact with the client through her choice of words, the inflections and music in them, the use of sounds such as *umms* and *ahhs*, silence, the messages coming through the eyes, gestures, posture, and general demeanor. Thinking about talking evocatively will not bear fruit. It has to come more spontaneously through tuning into the emotional tones of the client non-verbally. This can only be done through knowing our own emotions physically and being at ease with them.

Music and Talking With Clients

Music offers some guidance and parallels with how to talk with clients. The therapist's "music" is the music of the voice and the rhythms of body movements and breathing. Fried (1990) advises that music that is more meditative and relaxing has fewer tones, and the melody will progress with steps, not skips and jumps. The rhythm is smooth and flowing, with no sudden changes. The tempo is slow to moderate. Silence is equal to one breath. The tonal quality is "light strings" and the texture of the music is simplified. If we apply this to psychotherapy, speaking simply with few words, and with pauses between sentences and phrases, is likely to be calming. If we want to keep a client's arousal down and maintain calmness, it means not changing topic or tempo without any warning and finding a way to segue elegantly from the previous words and phrases to the words about to come. This reduces the likelihood of the client being startled by a sudden switch of tempo and topic. Ways of doing this might be, for example, saying, "May I change the subject?" followed by a pause. "I would like us to leave that topic. How would that be for you?" Pause. "If you have you finished [talking], may I ask something?" Pause.

Music can also excite the emotions. Musical complexity is exciting, and some music creates a dynamic energy, which can have a sense of pressing forward, sweeping us along to the inevitable resolution and release. So speaking quickly will increase the tempo and the excitement. Irregular rhythms create alertness and attention as they jar with what we are expecting. If this is the intention, then speaking more quickly, with a more upbeat tempo, will bring more liveliness into the dialogue.

Choosing Words to Excite or Soothe

Poets and storytellers understand the power of specific words and lyrics. Words are soft or hard to the ear, and some are neutral (see, for example, Kindborg, 2013). Soft words calm and soothe us and lower our levels of excitement. Hard words wake us up and stimulate the sympathetic nervous system. The vibrational quality of words affects our physical being, and the inherent sounds of a word can be harnessed to guide emotional rhythms and modulate them. So we can choose our words carefully to stimulate or calm our clients. Kindborg suggests that the word *stretch* is hard, and *float* is soft. You might try saying words out loud in your own language and getting a feel for whether they are hard or soft. How does the sound of the word leave you feeling? The reader might also refer to Chapter 4's comments on masculine and feminine language.

CONCLUSION

In this chapter we have looked in general terms at how to increase or decrease the intensity of emotions by the way that we speak to clients, by the way that we hold the therapeutic relationship, and how we relate to different domains of experience. I recommend Rothschild (2000) and Ogden and colleagues (2006) for more on how to work with traumatized clients. Traumatized clients like Suzy in this chapter are usually emotionally overwhelmed and highly aroused. In Chapter 7 we shall hear more about Peter and explore the non-verbal communication involved in deepening emotional connections.

Chapter 7

FREE ASSOCIATION
THROUGH THE BODY

GUIDING IMPLICIT COMMUNICATIONS OF
CLIENTS TOWARD FULLER EXPRESSION

Peter (Chapter 6) arrives for his session. He is now in the third year of psychotherapy and we have a solid working relationship. He is much more at ease with himself. He breathes and moves more freely and can look me in the eye as he speaks. Peter comfortably moves around the therapy room now—standing, walking, lying down, sometimes sitting on the floor instead of in his chair. He is aware of when he is becoming ungrounded and less present. Sometimes he spontaneously gets up from his chair and walks around the room to increase his awareness of his legs and to get himself more grounded and present.

We had been through a phase of Peter wanting to miss his sessions, ostensibly because of work commitments, and tussling with that. I remained firm with him on the importance of attending to maintain the continuity of our relationship for it to develop and deepen. He grudgingly continued to attend regularly. Over the next several weeks, he spoke angrily of his dependence on me and his feelings of being trapped. He could see the parallels with his relationship with Jackie and his early mothering. What was important for him was being able to disagree with me (i.e., bring his feelings) and that we continued to have a relationship. You will remember that he is a strong thinker, but less in touch with body sensations and feelings. Peter's pattern of relating hitherto was to avoid difficulties in relation-

ships. It marked a huge change that Peter could express his feelings to me, particularly his hostility.

Peter's relationship with his girlfriend, Jackie, remained a theme of his sessions. He had not married Jackie, but he did spend more nights at her house. He used his own home as a place "to get away" and have time by himself. Generally he felt under less pressure from Jackie for more commitment. His work continued to go well, but he had concerns about a plan to promote him to project manager. The work tasks were no problem; the proposed management of people was.

Peter usually sat in his chair at the beginning of sessions and talked. Either of us, at some point, would refer to his body sensations as he spoke. He often felt tense in his shoulders, neck, jaw, and diaphragm. Peter might recount an event from his week and then describe his immediate physical sensations, which brought him to present experience of himself. He knew that explorations of these body sensations usually bore fruit.

VEGETOTHERAPY

As Freud developed his understanding of how to reach the unconscious, he stopped using hypnosis and used "free association" instead. In free association, the patient was asked to lie down on a couch, which loosened up her more guarded daily way of being, and then to "associate" in words around whatever came into her thoughts.

We know from earlier chapters that the psychoanalyst Reich became interested in how the unconscious showed itself in posture, gestures, and habitual movements (Reich, 1970, 1983) and this is a contemporary interest in psychotherapy, which includes the nonconscious (for example, Ogden, et al., 2006). Darwin observed that much can be controlled by the will, but more autonomic responses are less easily controlled: "those muscles which are least obedient to the will, will sometimes alone betray a slight and passing emotion" (1892/1998, p. 79). Reich was also aware of this and developed the method of "free association through the body," which he called vegetotherapy. The vegetative nervous system is the Germanic term for the autonomic nervous system. Thus vegetotherapy works closely with the processes of the autonomic nervous system.

Primary communications, also called primary impulses, are spontaneous movements that are not controlled by willpower. They carry emotions and basic vitality. They often flicker briefly, like a distant light, and usually clients are not aware of them. Primary communications become overlaid by secondary communications, which inhibit the expression of primary communications. *Secondary communications* manifest in restricted breathing and inhibited movements. These secondary patterns protect clients from the difficult and painful feelings contained in the primary communications. Both primary and secondary patterns are evident in psychotherapy. The idea in vegetotherapy is to make contact with the primary communications and to support their stronger manifestation in the therapeutic relationship, and to explore the secondary protective patterning. Both sorts of communications and their interplay are important to be aware of, although at different times either primary communications or secondary patterning will be in the foreground.

Vegetotherapy has continued to be developed in schools of body psychotherapy since Reich. This has kept self- and interactive regulation as a main focus in body psychotherapy. In vegetotherapy, the psychotherapist resonates with "passing emotions" and their energetic qualities. Quite often the energetic quality comes first (see Chapter 6) before an emotion is nameable. The emotions lie hidden in clients behind the "social mask" and the "obvious" portrayed in the face and body to create a self-image. The client's spontaneous, expressive movements are encouraged and welcomed by the therapist, who continues to resonate non-verbally with the client's vitality, physiology (especially breathing), movements, and emotions. Words (and sometimes touch) are used by the therapist to communicate with the encoded implicit processes in clients.

Some psychotherapists get a feel for vegetotherapy quite easily and seem able to get onto this "wavelength" with clients. The skills involved are similar to those of relating to babies, having an affinity for spontaneous dancing to music, or playing musical improvisation with others. There is a requirement for flexibility, being prepared to enter into "not knowing," that is, not always conceptually understanding the emergent process. Trusting the client's inherent healing capacity (see introduction) and his or her unique way to do that requires more right-brain skills such as intuitive responses (see Marks-Tarlow, 2013). Vegetotherapy does not always lead to deep emotional processes. It can be much less emotional and more mundane, but nevertheless effective. It can also be quite subtle, taking clients into universal, "oceanic" levels of consciousness (Southwell, 2010). However, when highly charged powerful emotions along with autonomic nervous system reactions do occur, they can take the uninitiated by surprise. Vegetotherapy, therefore, can be quite challenging for the untrained and inexperienced. For this reason, I recommend basic training in working with the stronger emotions in vegetotherapy before working directly with clients.

In this chapter I describe how to deepen the emotional expressions of our clients through vegetotherapy. We learn how to relate to clients so that they "let their bodies speak." This is a very direct way of "one body talking to another body" non-verbally. This does not, of course, preclude using language to communicate information alongside it and keeping in mind other ways of relating with clients. With Peter, as an example, I (verbally) drew parallels with his internalized, unconscious relationship with his childhood mother and our relationship, *and* we communicated non-verbally. All of the skills learned so far in this book are applicable in this chapter. The vasomotoric cycle is used to guide us in how to relate to clients at different stages of the cycle.

The invitation to the client is to let the body speak and involves *resonating with the deep emotional level of consciousness* within predominantly *long rein holding of clients*. Words, sounds, and sometimes touch are employed to communicate with a client's movements, breathing, energy, and feelings. Closely attending to breathing and autonomic nervous system signs (levels of excitement and calm) also guide the process from moment to moment. So if a client looks as if his breathing is going too fast, he might be asked, "Feel what your breathing wants to do." Or he might be told more directly, when it looks like he is beginning to overbreathe (hyperventilate), "Slow your breathing down" (matter-of-fact, short rein). The therapeutic qualities of clarity, compassion, and spaciousness using the model of inquiry presented in Chapter 3 are reflected on from time to time to keep the therapeutic relationship on track.

The relational resonance or contact with a client contains the process. Ongoing process adjustments to the holding (long and short rein) and to the contact are made *without thinking* about them in response to clients being more or less emotional. In so doing, therapists can raise the emotional charge or bring it down, depending on the intended therapeutic trajectory for individual clients. This regulates the intensity of feelings and the level of physiological arousal accompanying them. It-language plays a key role in guiding the early phases of the therapeutic process and keeping the relating going on. Later on, "you language" becomes important.

Combining all of these elements with clients who are open to this way of working brings their early insecure attachments into sharp focus. These attachments are enacted in the present in their bodily processes. Non-verbal patterns of interaction (breathing, moving, looking, sensing, feeling), particularly from the time when the client was a baby and had no words for self-expression, are experienced, amplified, and expressed. In doing this, bodymind processes are reconfigured; new interactional patterns emerge; old patterns die away; and healing occurs. The expression of feelings is not the goal per se. Rather, it is about becoming aware of old patterns of interaction and latent energetic potential (the primary impulses) contained in the secondary patterns becoming available. In the process, clients feel more alive and move more freely in their bodies. *Peter's physical ease and flexibility in the consulting room showed me that more of his potential was available to him.*

Peter was a client suited to deepening into his emotional life and working in this way because he could hold an awareness of the present and simultaneously explore spontaneous movements, which often took him to retrieving past events. In other words, he could hold dual awareness. The events felt vivid and alive to him, and yet he knew that the past events were not actually happening currently. He was also robust enough not to be overwhelmed by the intensity of the feelings that could arise. Sometimes he would let his body move and he might feel angry, lonely, or frightened and so on without any clear memories. At other times, he had clear recollections and feelings. These movement patterns and feelings derived from his early parenting. From these bodily explorations, he became physically freer and had more vitality. He gained embodied understanding about his current relationships and, over subsequent weeks, he reported daily life relationships becoming less restricted and more satisfying. Our relationship also changed. He was learning to stay present with me and to deal with difficulties in relating rather than retreating.

Early Experiences

At this point you may wish to remind yourself about implicit memory (introduction, Chapter 1) and also infant development (Chapter 2). Briefly, to recap and provide you with some additional information, early memory is implicit and encoded subcortically. These early implicit memories begin to be laid down before birth in movements and sounds (for example, the mother's voice, the mother's heartbeat, and noises from the environment generally). The mother's voice carries emotional states and "sounds emerge from memory through evocation" (Maiello, 1997, p. 158). In the therapeutic process, as we resonate with clients, we evoke these early implicit memories.

Early Movements

The German embryologist Erich Blechschmidt (1904–1992) writes, "the development of a human being, from the earliest stages onwards, can be interpreted, in a dynamic and biological sense, as *a performance specific to the individual*" (2004, p. 62, emphasis added).

Blechschmidt describes how the fertilized egg is whole from the beginning and functioning in its environment at each stage of its development. It is not something becoming whole. He describes the process of embryo development as "movements in a metabolic field." These movements are ordered and always occurring against resistance. Positional and structural development occur together "and it is only in harmony that they bring about development in general" (Blechschmidt, 2004, p. 61). But what happens when there are subtle or perhaps less subtle disharmonies even at this early stage of life? It has been suggested that in adults, observable patterns of movements that lack fullness of flow, pulsation, and coherence (secondary patterning) begin to arise from the earliest stresses on the developing embryo (for example, Boadella, 1987; Sills, 2009; Southwell, 2010). Thus the embryo, the baby, the child, and then the adult grow into physical form with some loss of overall coherence and loss of a sense of wholeness. This is not just lack of wholeness of movement, but also wholeness in all of the systems of the body.

Babies move with purpose (intention; see Chapter 8 for a description of baby Logan and his movements). While babies do make some reflex movements, other movements are far from random. Babies regulate their state of arousal, make contact with and explore the environment, and relate to others through their movements. Babies move their eyes to look at someone, reach out to touch, and move their faces to engage and keep the attention of their caregivers. One of the first things that an unstressed newborn baby does is to look around the room and at those in it. Babies feel welcomed or not by how others respond to them. If those around miss these moments because they believe babies are not interested in anything at this early stage, some precious moments of relating are lost. In small ways, then, such babies begin to be less interested in the world and to retreat into themselves. Of course there will be many opportunities for contact, and these lost moments of connection with others are not irreparable. What is crucial is the patterns of interaction over time.

Opportunities for attuned relating come in normal everyday mundane moments, during feeding, diaper changing, dressing, and washing. They are at the heart of secure development and the development of movement patterns with their associated breathing, physiology, energy quality, and feelings. They are not just moments for performing functional tasks but opportunities for dialogue and play.

Movements are made by striated or voluntary muscles, mostly without any awareness. Stern (1985) describes how movements, other than reflexes, are preceded by a "motor plan," and that they give a baby a sense of volition or will. The motor plan is what makes the movements seem like "self acts" and are the earliest beginnings of a sense of self with self-agency. Any movement is accompanied by proprioception, giving constant feedback through bodily sensations on one's position in space and movements. Again, proprioception is mostly out of conscious awareness. Stern points out that any movement initiated by and involving only the baby gives constant proprioceptive feedback and reinforces the sense of agency. This also reinforces the movements. Movements are often made with accompanying sounds and even if the baby is babbling by herself, she will feel the resonance of the sound inside in her chest. Those movements involving others may only sometimes be "received" by others.

Peter's mother had been depressed after his birth, and again after his brother was born 18 months later. He came from a traditional family, and although the Truby King method (see Chapter 2) of baby care was less in vogue when he was born, his parents followed this style. Peter's mother was his main caregiver and she seems to have offered him functional rather than relational care. We can infer that she did not respond to or stimulate his expressive movements and babblings. Peter's lack of body awareness and his difficulties with communicating his feelings to others seem to go back to his early insecure attachment. Peter's father was a distant figure. We know from Chapter 6 that Peter found him critical. Later on I learned that his father was a "buttoned up" man who was not emotionally demonstrative.

Before we move on, I want to reiterate that communications (including movements) from babies, when they are not received (misattuned with) by caregivers, remain in the body as undeveloped possibility. These intentional, unreceived communications from babies are primary communications and carry energetic, physiological, and emotional messages (e.g., Reich, 1970, 1983; Boyesen, 1980). When babies receive misattuned interactions, for whatever reason, their primary communications get physically overlaid by their responses to misattuned interactions, forming secondary patterning. The primary and overlaid secondary elements reveal themselves in muscle and breathing patterns, loss of vitality, and inability to regulate physiological arousal and emotions. These are the physical manifestation of the psychological aspects of baby-caregiver interactions coming into present relationships. The overlaid secondary communications correspond with Reich's (1983) muscle armor (1970) and Boyesen's (1980) tissue and organ armor (1980). The muscle tensions of armoring "protect an individual against painful and threatening emotional experiences. They shield him from dangerous impulses within his own personality as well as from attacks by others" (Lowen, 1975, p. 13). These patterns are also the physical counterparts of Winnicott's (1960/1990b) false self and true self.

To illustrate the development of primary and secondary patterning (communications) in Peter, let's suppose, as a newborn, he looked at his mother (primary impulse) and she was disinterested. Perhaps she was already depressed or the birth had left her physically spent. Next time Peter looked at her, she was also disinterested. Then he started to look at her less often and more hesitantly; on repeated occasions, she was not just disinterested but hostile and resentful, perhaps because she had to look after him or he reminded her (unconsciously) of someone she hated. Baby Peter, in those circumstances, chose to look elsewhere, and especially at objects in the room for his security, and avoided eye contact with his mother. This way of relating generalized into other relationships and became his mode of relating.

My experience of meeting the adult Peter was that he found it hard to look people in the eye, and when he did look his eyes seemed to pull away in fear (secondary patterning). His head tilted to one side and backward (secondary patterning). He breathed shallowly, and his body was stiff and awkward (secondary patterning), giving the impression that he wanted to be invisible and to get away from a dangerous and terrifying world.

Movement Patterns

Primary communications and secondary patterns are part of signature patterns of interaction, which are formed in early attachments and are unique to individuals (see introduction). Particular patterns of movement in signature patterns of interaction have been called motoric fields (Boadella, 2000b). Thinking about motoric fields helps therapists to observe and explore the habitual movement patterns of clients. Boadella took inspiration from Laban's movement analysis (see, for example, Laban & Lawrence, 1974), Blechschmidt's work, and Sheldrake's (2011) morphic fields hypothesis. Boadella makes historical connections with the concept of motoric fields and Pierre Janet's movement attitude, motoric memory, and motoric self (Janet, 1929, cited in Boadella, 2000a); Piaget's sensorimotor schemas (Piaget, 1952, cited in Boadella, 2000a); and Stern's affecto-motoric schemas (Stern, 1985; Boadella, 2000a).

Motoric fields describe specific movement patterns paired with their opposite movement. The paired movement patterns represent someone's capacity for relating. The motoric fields (explained below) are absorption and activation, flexion and extension, traction and opposition, and rotation and canalization. Impairments in the full range of our movements in these different fields and their flow are observable in most of us.

Absorption is about being able to take in, and activation is the impulse to move. Absorption involves stillness and corresponds to the final phases of the vasomotoric cycle (Chapter 6). Some of us are frightened to be still and just be. In contrast, depressed clients find it difficult to get moving (activate). Becoming activated can be pleasurable, but for many, pleasurable movement is replaced by tense, driven movements and is the unhealthy norm.

Flexion is when muscles bend toward the body, as in placing a piece of fruit in the mouth with the hand. Extension is the opposite movement away from the body. Psychologically and emotionally, flexion of both arms means something like "come to me," and extension with the palms facing outward is something like "that's far enough" (for example, Marcher & Fich, 2010). Traction involves pulling, and opposition involves pushing. Combining traction (pulling) with flexion of the arms involves pulling someone or something toward us. Pushing (opposition) involves taking personal space and resisting invasion. Rotation is going toward something indirectly. Rotation movements are circular and meandering. Canalization is direct and focused, as when walking with purpose to a meeting with no time to spare. Pulsation integrates all of these movement styles. Pulsation, in its whole-body form, is moving out (expanding) toward the environment, followed by moving inward. Pulsation has a regular rhythm and flow to it. As a rule of thumb, the less the movement of pulsation is inhibited, the more flexible is the relationship with oneself and others.

At the beginning of psychotherapy, Peter had difficulties with the full range and flow of the movements of flexion and extension, and traction and opposition. He had no physical impairments limiting his movements, but they did not flow. From an emotional-relational perspective, his lack of mobility showed in him not daring to ask Jackie to be closer because he could not tell her when she was close enough. He feared that if Jackie got close to him, he would have no space for himself. When he was particularly stressed, he retreated home to be in solitude, but then he was fearful of venturing out (activating himself). He tended to be stronger on canalization, such as getting jobs done on time, but did not spend much time doing things like going for a walk without a purpose (rotation). As a whole, his body lacked pulsation. During the course of psychotherapy, Peter's movement repertoire gained more breadth and became more expressive.

Implicit memory includes "learned motor patterns, conditioned reflexes, verbal priming, and innate memory (e.g. reflexive startle to a sudden loud sound)" (Rustin, 2013, p. 60). These movement memories (motor memories) have never been put into a symbolized form and do not have spoken language representing them. They communicate their stories and messages in physical forms rather than spoken narratives. They may also change over time with experiences and relationships that invite the latent tendencies to manifest and modify.

Movement memories are not easily accessed by using ordinary language and words. However, the latent tendencies in the body movements of our clients, with their accompanying expressions (energies and emotions), can be communicated with by using particular forms of spoken language that talk to the right brain. This is coupled with an embodied presence. They may also be accessed through touch and movement. Rustin (2013) discusses how these unconscious, repetitive movements and posture may come into the consulting room and manifest within the present relationship. She reminds us that implicit memories are dependent on mood and are likely to be recalled in a similar state in the future. The therapeutic situation may provide the context for retrieval cues coming either externally, perhaps from the ambience of the room or from the therapist, or internally, from a physical sensation experienced by the client.

We have already seen how Peter's spontaneous movements in therapy took him to experiencing baby states in the present (Chapter 5). As he became safer with me, his movements were frequently an opening for him to access implicit memories. Often the memories would come as fragments from different stages of his life. So feeling out of his depth at work might lead him to a memory of being at a loss at school, which might be followed by feeling lonely as a baby.

PHASES OF VEGETOTHERAPY

The vegetotherapy process follows the overall phases of the vasomotoric cycle (Chapter 6), but I elaborate on specific phases more fully. Also relevant is keeping in mind the breathing cycle. The psychotherapy hour can be construed as an overall vasomotoric cycle containing different phases of the vegetotherapy process. The phases of the vegetotherapy process include smaller cycles (as with emotional cycles in Chapter 6 and breathing cycles in Chapter 5).

Arriving, Phase 1.1

The repeated ritual of arriving and starting the session becomes familiar to clients and their therapists. Both have their usual positions and respective chairs. This way of starting begins the transition from daily life and social relating to coming into the therapeutic relationship. The relating is interpersonal.

Peter took time to make this transition. At the beginning of a session, he functioned socially but did not see me, take me in, and begin to express himself more authentically for a while. Outwardly he looked calm enough, but this masked his high arousal, revealed in his shallow breathing and bodily stillness. I knew that he had "arrived" when his breathing wave expanded and his shoulders became less stiff looking. I did not leave him in silence and generally started with, "How has the process moved in you?" I did not have to prompt him at this stage of our psychotherapy by saying, "What have you been feeling, imagining, sensing, thinking about, and so on? Have any moments stood out for you as you have been going about your life?" This latter question had been beneficial to ask Peter in the earlier years of psychotherapy as it got him noticing that life was not just happening on one note in an emotionally flat way. Generally this predictable beginning and my questions were enough for him to feel less anxious, as long as I did not overwhelm him with the force and vitality of my personality.

As clients talk, in this first phase of a vegetotherapy process, the fleeting primary communication might be a small (nonconscious) movement, a change in breathing, a word with a frisson to it, a glimmer in the eye, or the face flushing as the sympathetic nervous system is activated by a feeling being stirred—showing that something dynamic is happening. Vegetotherapy can be done with clients sitting, standing, walking around, or lying down. The positioning will affect the level of consciousness invited and the therapeutic relationship (Southwell, 2010). The change of positioning may happen fairly quickly, and for some clients, lying down on the mattress, which is placed on the floor, may be the familiar way of being together.

On this particular day Peter arrived, sat in his chair, and described his reluctance to accept the planned work promotion. He knew that he had little choice about it. His company had been taken over; colleagues had already been made redundant or reorganized. I listened. I noticed Peter's breathing was less full than usual. His shoulders were somewhat hunched and pulled back, and I noticed that I had started to think about Peter's dilemma. This was a suitable moment to interrupt Peter's protective secondary pattern, and I asked, "How are you in your body right now?" Peter was aware of "a heavy feeling" in his head, a tight jaw, and some tension and discomfort in his abdomen.

We agreed that it was time to lie down on the mattress. I moved the mattress away from the wall so that I could move around it as needed. I sat beside him on his right side and faced him at a slight angle. His eye line did not meet mine, although he could see me if he chose to. This enabled him to focus on his inner experience. Peter put his knees up, so that his feet were resting on the mattress, to help him to stay grounded and in contact with himself. He experienced me as "with him." It felt "intimate" but with "less demand" than when we sat in our chairs together. He closed his eyes and commented on the growing intensity of the pressure in his midriff.

Positioning: Lying Down and Preparing the Way, Phase 1.2

Having clients lie down on the mattress lets their muscles relax as they feel the support of the ground. It loosens conscious controls and encourages spontaneous (nonconscious) movements to "leak out." Generally clients are asked to wear trousers or leggings for their sessions. They are asked to remove jewelry and watches for safety. Belts and buttons are loosened so that they do restrict breathing and movements. The head lies flat on the mattress, not supported by a pillow, enabling free movement of the head, neck, and shoulders. (see, Heller, 2012). *Peter would have liked a pillow for his comfort, but he could manage without one. Going without the pillow was pertinent for Peter, as his neck and shoulders did not move flexibly.*

Establishing Grounding, Phase 1.3

Grounding and dual awareness are fostered by asking clients to be aware of the points of contact between themselves and the mattress.

Basic Grounding on the Mattress
The instruction to the client is as follows:

- Notice the points of contact your body has with the mattress.
- Notice the back of the head, the shoulders, the bottom, the feet touching the mattress.
- If you cannot sense parts of the body, put some pressure into the body part that you are focusing on (e.g., press your shoulders into the mat-

tress) or try moving that part slightly (e.g., wiggle your toes). Notice how
that is.

- Let or *let* yourself sense your body; take time to scan different parts of
your body.

Notice that the verbal instructions here are more direct when they
start with "notice" and less direct with "let." For less present and
grounded clients, "notice" is appropriate. The word "notice" is harder
sounding, crisper, and less spacious. When clients are more present,
then "let" phrases are applicable. Let can be said in a more definite
manner as in "Let" (capitalized) or said more diffusely, as in "let."
These versions are softer-sounding and more spacious than "notice."

Placing the feet flat on the mattress and having the knees bent
and the legs slightly apart helps clients with dual awareness. It also
enables mobility in the legs and pelvis. Sometimes, clients might
be asked to move their limbs randomly around on the mattress, as
a mechanical exercise, to get the body moving and more active. It
can increase body awareness and activates the sympathetic nervous
system.

Developing Awareness and Inviting Primary
Communications, Phase 1.4

*For this next phase, I became receptive, lengthened and slowed my
breathing, and grounded myself through my sitting bones. I let myself be
spacious and held Peter with a deep, wide-range perceptual focus. This is
something like watching a bird in the garden, while being aware of the rest
of the garden, not wanting to disturb the bird, so being very still and looking
and listening intently, so as not to miss anything.*

*I suggested that Peter breathe into his tension (or imagine the breath
going into the tensions) and letting his body move. "Let your breath go into
the tension in your diaphragm. Let your body move. Feel how it wants to
move."*

These instructions are indirect ones, phrased so that the right
brain is receptive to them. They are delivered slowly, on a full
out-breath, spaciously, with down-going contours, suggesting that
there is endless time. The instructions are like suggestions rather
than commands. The smallest twitches and movements in the client's body are observed. This might be a quiver around the mouth,

a slight finger movement, or a change of color in the face. There might be an unexpected shudder, a yawn, or a mouth movement. The client is guided in what to be aware of and how to proceed, especially when the "dance" gets stuck.

Moving into Some Action and Expression: Phase 2.1

Peter's abdomen expanded, showing me that his breath was going all the way down into it. Peter's foot moved and then it stopped. I encouraged Peter to "do that more." My instruction was vague and directed to his breathing, but could be construed as he liked. Peter's head and neck moved slightly from side to side; his breathing continued to go into his abdomen. His foot moved more definitely and stopped. This was a suitable moment to ask Peter how he was feeling. "How are you?" My holding was long rein and spacious, but my tone of voice neutral. It gave some time out for reflection. Reflection here means putting into words his subjective experiences. I did not intend this discussion to be lengthy, which would have taken Peter away from his inner experiencing.

Peter kept his eyes closed and replied briefly that he was enjoying moving. He continued to move and breathe. His face began to flush and I suggested that he lengthen his out-breath. This was to encourage him to deepen his breathing. A deeper out-breath will usually be followed by a deeper in-breath. Deeper breathing increases overall vitality and amplifies feelings. In Peter's case, his secondary communication tendency, exhibited in his breathing, was to inhibit the out-breath.

Peter was moving both feet now. I told him softly, "let the feet move." He became self-conscious and moved his feet in a perfunctory way. His thinking, evaluative left brain had become more dominant, and he had fallen into his usual habits. Perhaps I had not quite been in tune with him, and the intonation of my voice did not resonate with the energy of his foot movements. I tuned into him again and suggested again, "let them move." Peter's feet movements stopped and started. Some movements looked spontaneous and expressive (with intention) and had a developing rhythm. Then he seemed to become aware of himself moving, and his movements became mechanical. It was like a musician warming up before the main recital. A few bars of a piece were played, then the music stopped and some warm-up scales were played instead.

Next time Peter's spontaneous foot movements appeared, I caught their rhythm. I tapped my hand on the floor in the same rhythm and spoke with the same intonation and speed. This gave him two sources of sound, my voice and the hand tapping, to contact his primary impulses. This time Peter did not inhibit himself. His foot movements became faster and the rest of his legs joined in. I began to feel hot, and Peter's movements looked full of vitality.

Moving Into Stronger Expression and Action, Phase 2.2

Peter's expressions were now at the peak of the first phase of the vaso-motoric cycle and tipping into the second phase. His sympathetic nervous system was activated (and mine). As his leg movements got more energetic and faster, his breathing quickened to take in more oxygen needed for the exertion. From experience, I knew that his movements might become more expressive and larger, so I made sure that there were no hard objects around on which he might hurt himself.

I continued to utilize It-language to communicate predominantly with Peter's energy, emotions, and right brain. I encouraged the dynamic of what was impinging from within to come into being. Peter knew that I was sitting with him in the room, but he was barely aware of me. My instructions to him slipped under his "ego controls," and he followed my instructions without fully (consciously) knowing that I was instructing him. My words drew out his bodily (non-verbal) primary communications, which were pressing to express themselves. I encouraged him to amplify them. The phrases that I used were fine-tuned and nuanced to communicate with different levels of consciousness in Peter.

In this phase of the vegetotherapy process, the language employed may start with phrases using the personal adjective "your" and "your foot." This word usage is for when the client is closer to everyday consciousness and the interpersonal relationship is more in the foreground. Using the personal "your" indicates that there is a "somebody" with a "foot" in the room. It suggests, "I've noticed that and want you to notice that too." This word choice communicates to clients that the therapist is drawn to something of interest happening in their body and hopefully clients get curious too. "That's interesting. I hadn't noticed that as I was talking about my partner, I was doing that. I wonder what might happen if I do that some more?" Conversely, sometimes this response to a client cuts the spontaneous movements dead. Either because the therapist's presence and tone of voice do not quite resonate with and "catch the movement" or because clients become embarrassed, perhaps feels criticized or even ashamed, they might tuck their foot away behind the other foot (see Chapter 3).

Questions that fail to "speak" to these sorts of spontaneous movements and further their exploration include "What is your foot doing?" "Why are you moving your foot like that?" With this phrasing of a question, clients are likely to stop the movement and look at the foot in a slightly objectified way. They will go on to think about what their foot is doing and come up with explanations and reasons for the movement (left-brain activity).

Here are some graded examples of how to talk to the non-verbal parts of clients:

- feel your foot.
- let your foot move.
- let it move.
- umm . . . ummm . . . umMM . . . UMMM . . . UMHER . . . UMMMHER . . . Ummm (making sounds spoken in the rhythm and intensity of the client's movements).

I have used the lower case in an attempt to indicate the way that these words are spoken to communicate with the nonconscious and as nuanced suggestions.

As repressed or latent movement tendencies begin to emerge, clients may experience "peculiar body sensations . . . : involuntary trembling and twitching of the muscles, sensations of cold and hot, itching, the feeling of pins and needles, prickling sensations, the feeling of having jitters, and somatic perceptions of anxiety, anger and pleasure" (Reich, 1983, p. 271). These are autonomic nervous system reactions and indicate the body is finding a new internal physiological balance. These reactions will happen in both clients and therapists in a non-verbal approach to psychotherapy, although therapists' reactions will have a less intense flavor.

As Peter explored his foot movements, he mentioned tingling in his feet, especially in his right foot and leg. His leg movements grew coarser, stronger, and more definite. I observed his arms moving and joining the "music of his legs." I increased the volume of my voice, joined Peter's tempo, and switched to using sounds (rather than phrases) to continue speaking to the movements: "Yes, umm. . . . Yes . . . umm. Um, UM, UM." My sounds were affirmative, saying implicitly, "Do it some more, yes, yes, yes."

The process moved quickly, as if we were dancing vigorously. Peter started to kick his legs away from himself, and I placed large hard floor cushions at his feet so that he could kick into them. The thwacking sounds produced by his kicks seemed satisfying, and he kicked harder. These kicks were primary communications, but I noticed that his arms were moving less strongly, and his jaw looked tight (secondary communication). So I addressed this by saying, "Bring the arms into the movement. . . . Let the jaw loosen. . . . Let the neck and head move."

In this phase (phase 2.2) the energy activation is high. The intensity of the action and expression often builds, subsides for a while after more intense expression, and then builds again. When this happens, the atmosphere feels pregnant with expectation.

Peter's primary communications were in the ascendant, and my words were taken up readily. He moved his neck and head around from side to side, opened his mouth wide, and made different mouth movements. His arms made pushing movements on the mattress. Intending to raise the intensity and encourage him to vocalize, I told him, "Let the sound come. (short pause) . . . Make a sound. (short pause) . . . Put it into sounds." (All said imperatively). Peter readily grunted and made loud, angry roaring sounds. He spat his sounds out with a mean look around his mouth. Suddenly, as the velocity and intensity of the sound increased, he shouted, "Leave me alone! Go away! . . . Go away! . . . Leave me alone!" (Getting louder and quicker). Peter was now fully in the throes of the expression/ action phase of the vasomotoric cycle. His movements and vocalizations were performed by an adult man but had all the intensity and appearance of an angry baby.

In this phase of the process, the client must "stay aware of his adult, here and now self whilst at the same time casting himself into the regressive experience" (Southwell, 2010, p. 11). A client reflecting on this state in his therapy recounts that he was "conscious that I was allowing myself to undergo this experience for therapeutically beneficial reasons. There was also a fully identified part of me that was taken on a journey over which I had little conscious control" (Eiden, 2002, p. 45).

These observations are apt for Peter, but therapists too are required to stay aware of different levels of awareness; the adult and the child in the adult client.

Recognizing Who the Actions and Expressions Are Addressed Towards, Phase 2.3

The next phase (phase 2.3) of the process occurs when the client, in this childlike state, recognizes who he is addressing. It signals the time for the therapist to change the form of her language. Instead of addressing processes as "it," as in "let it," and using it- language, we address the client as "you" and use you language. This evokes sentences in clients starting with "I" and enables clients to take possession of their feelings and actions, in the present as adults. The client may be experiencing the past (childhood), but the recall is in the present.

At the height of his sounds and movements, I asked Peter, "Who are you saying that to?" Instantly he said, "My mom." "Tell her what you want her to know," I encouraged Peter. "I want you to leave me alone.(pause) . . . I hate you! .(pause). . . I hate you! . . .(pause). . . I HATE YOU! .(pause). . . You never wanted me," he bellowed. (Each pause between his words gets shorter and after each Peter gets louder)

This was the climax of this phase, and the atmosphere changed. Peter's movements became less angry, softer, and slower. A new energy and feeling were emerging. His fingers made tiny movements. I encouraged Peter to let his hands move. His fingers, then his palms, made stroking movements on the mattress. "Feel what the hands want to do . . .(pause) . . . Let them move." Peter's arms began to move slowly, dancing in the air in front of him. Tears trickled down his face. He reached out into the air with his arms. "I want my mommy, I want my mommy . . . (pause) . . . Where are you? Why don't you come? . . . (pause) . . . Mommy, where are you?"

At this time, I wanted to align myself with Peter's words to support his experience, so I too said, "I want my mommy. I want my mommy." I spoke in the same tones and rhythms as Peter. I let myself resonate with his feelings. Peter's body was wracked with sobbing. I gently placed a small cushion in his hands and he readily pulled it to his chest. His arms embraced the cushion and his body rocked from side to side. His fingers stroked the cushion lovingly.

In this last sequence, Peter was an adult man expressing the feelings of babyhood. He referred to himself as "I," giving his authentic feelings to another (his mother) "you," and shared with me (as guide). His movements were congruent with his words and feelings. It-language was now redundant and gave way to I-you forms of expression. Peter's expressions had a sense of purpose. They belonged in a relationship with someone.

Comments and questions for this phase of the process include:

- Tell her what you are feeling.
- Say it loudly so she can hear you.
- Tell her what you want.
- Tell her what you feel.
- Let her know that.
- Say it to her with the full force of how you feel it.

It is also possible (through having dual awareness) to ask the client in these states, as an aside, "How old are you? Where are you?" Notice these instructions start with capital letters as they are more emphatically said. *In Peter's case I learned the answers to these questions later in the session. He was a baby, a few months old in his crib, alone in the darkness of his room.*

My alignment with Peter's feelings by repeating his words, "I want my mommy," identifies with his experience and his emotions (see Mahrer, 1983). Liss explains that this form of words using "I-Messages" (a term coined by Mahrer) "intensifies the patient's emotional state, even when difficult emotions that could cause shame, embarrassment or guilt were brought to light" (1996, p. 46). It is based on the therapist intuiting the client's feelings or "feeling potential." The I-Messages should not overwhelm the client but support his expression. Liss advises explaining I-Messages and gaining permission from clients beforehand to avoid confusion and "unwanted imposition." It is a way of working that demands that clients should have a strong enough sense of self to avoid boundary invasions and confusions.

Sense of Satisfaction: Phase 3, and Re-Organizing, Integrating, and Healing: Phase 4

Peter now enters the next phases (3 and 4). His latent primary communications have manifested, and his system has been highly aroused. Now he begins to go into the transition between being very stimulated and becoming calmer. This is not a time for further talk. Peter needs to feel safe with me and let his bodymind find its new way of being. I suggest that he rest on his left side, and I cover him with a blanket. The blanket keeps him warm as his system relaxes, but also gives him a sense of security in his vulnerability. During these phases he may feel an inner satisfaction from having expressed himself authentically; his bodymind finds its new pattern and integrates his experiences.

After some minutes, as the session comes to a close, Peter gets up and says, "I can do this. I might need some help, but I can do it." I assume that he is speaking about his new promotion. The following week, we discuss his experiences more fully, sitting in our chairs. Peter has found a way to take on the new job. "It won't be a walk in the park, but I'm up for it."

Integration Into Daily Life: Phase 5

Sometimes how the changes during a therapy session in a client will translate into daily life are not immediately obvious. In Peter's case he required time to be with himself (resting on his side) and not to go prematurely looking for explanations. (He was more than competent with this.) Skill is required to manage this phase of the cycle. With experience, it is relatively easy to provoke strong feelings with their physical and physiological counterparts. It is another thing altogether to know how to pace and time interactions so that the new sense of self emerging from such cathartic expressions is integrated and reorganized in the physical body.

The main changes in clients' autonomic nervous systems occur in the second half of a session (Braatøy, 1954). This is in the downswing of the vasomotoric cycle, the parasympathetic part. It is important to give enough time for the autonomic nervous system responses to find their new equilibrium. Silence in this phase gives space and lets clients go deeply into just being with themselves.

During and after the session, as Peter's bodymind reorganized itself, the subtle and bigger changes in him were reinforced by different forms of feedback from his everyday relationships. The key moments of the session had been, first, when he told his mother to leave him alone and expressed his hatred, and second, when he reached out with his arms and called for his mother. He may not have been a natural manager at work, but he began to enjoy the challenge, and his staff appreciated the way that he listened to their concerns and thought about them. Peter's life continued to improve.

Work continued to bring its challenges, but Peter rose to them. He and Jackie set a date for their marriage, but they decided to keep both of their houses; they both liked their own space.

CONCLUSION

In this chapter we have looked at vegetotherapy with the focus on emotional deepening. Vegetotherapy comes in a variety of forms depending on the combination of client and therapist. Much of its effectiveness comes from keeping out verbal and interpersonal interactions, which can obscure profound, nonconscious, non-verbal interactions. Vegetotherapy does not require explicit, conscious understanding to be effective. Insights arising from the implicit reorganizations may come later on, although insight is not always necessary for lasting change.

We have been learning about how to recognize and to respond to clients' communications so that they can claim their unused or repressed potential. In Chapter 8, we shall hear more about Tony (Chapter 3) and explore the topic of touch in psychotherapy, a physically direct (non-verbal) form of communication.

Chapter 8

TOUCH

DIRECT COMMUNICATION

Tony, introduced to you in Chapter 3, sat down and his words tumbled out. It was apparent that he had reverted to his old ways of speaking at the start of psychotherapy. He moved swiftly from anecdote to anecdote and I found it hard to keep up. I recognized this reversion to old habits of talking; using his words to hide his feelings, a sign that something was troubling him. He was unusually worked up, and I wondered what was worrying him. Eventually he took a pause for breath and I asked him, "What's happening?" His latest test results were not good. You will remember that he had a form of cancer. His elderly mother was also unwell. He wanted to help her, but said, "She is so difficult."

Tony calmed down slightly as he voiced this information, but then just as quickly he fled into telling me about "being positive" and "getting on with his life." Again he came to the end of his words. He looked me in the eye. His eyes seemed to be searching and asking if he could trust me. The moment was poignant as he told me emphatically, "I don't want to talk anymore. It doesn't help me." He asked about the possibility of having biodynamic massage (see below). He knew that this was part of the form of body psychotherapy that I practice. It was a pivotal moment in our relationship. I understood the subtext of his words to be telling me that he was frightened, and he wanted to find parts of himself that his words so successfully hid, even to himself. Try as he might, he was so proficient at talking as a main form of protection that he did not know how to express his genuine feelings. He could not easily let go of his secondary patterning with his willpower. Bravely, he had decided to try a different communication channel for relating with me. I suggested that we try.

Biodynamic massage is a profound form of communication through touch developed by Gerda Boyesen (1980; see also Carroll, 2000; Schaible, 2009; Southwell, 1988). It is something of a misnomer to call it massage as it is based on Scandinavian physiotherapy methods used with patients in psychiatric hospitals (see, for example, Andersen, 1991b; Braatøy, 1954; Heller, 2007a, 2007b, 2012). Biodynamic massage is both a body (complementary) therapy and a vehicle for intersubjective exploration in body psychotherapy. It is significant in self- and interactive regulation as the tactile messages, passing back and forth within the therapeutic relationship, have an impact on physiological and emotional regulation.

TOUCH IN PSYCHOTHERAPY

Communicating through touch in psychotherapy, accompanied by verbal dialogue or simply non-verbally, is a controversial topic. Nevertheless, it can greatly enhance therapists' repertoire, if they are trained in therapeutic touch and therefore capable of including physical contact with clients at suitable times in the psychotherapy. Without the skills of communication via touch, we lack a significant channel of communication for relating to the implicit communications of our clients.

My position on touch in psychotherapy is that therapists should not be touching clients unless they have had training in how to use touch specifically for communication in psychotherapy (see Westland, 2015). This includes in and out of the consulting room. The beginnings and endings of sessions, both in the consulting room and in the spaces around it such as reception areas, are when and where professional boundaries can loosen and social touching creep in. It is at these times that psychotherapists' behavior can be paradoxical and confusing. An illustration is helping a client put her coat on in the waiting room, while conducting a nontouching form of psychotherapy in the consulting room (see Tune, 2001, 2005).

As well as knowing how to touch psychotherapeutically, therapists must pay due attention to the context in which they are working. This includes any legal requirements or ethical restraints.

Touch: The Closest Sense

Touch is the most proximity-near sense when it involves someone else (Montagu, 1986). Touching another goes in both directions. If we touch a client, the client is also touching us. As we sense clients' non-verbal communications, they often know ours. They may sense if we are using our hands to "listen" to them or are distracted. Equally, with training, we can sense how clients are responding and the intention in their touch. Touch is direct, intimate, and potentially exposing. When touch comes into the foreground, talking often goes into the background for a while. If we are reliant on our words to communicate with others, touch can be challenging and leave us feeling vulnerable. However, as we shall see later, for a client named Julia, not having to talk was an enormous relief.

Reasons to Touch in Psychotherapy

The main reason to include touch in a non-verbally focused psychotherapy is because the client can respond to touch. There are clients with whom the main way to communicate will be touch, perhaps for most of the psychotherapy, perhaps only sometimes or in different phases of the psychotherapy.

The reasons to touch clients or for them to touch us emerge out of the therapeutic relationship and the overall trajectory of the psychotherapy. The outcome of tactile interactions cannot be known before they have happened in the same way that the impact of our words cannot be known beforehand. We can only use our therapeutic experience to conjecture.

More specific reasons to include touch include these:

- Touch is the main channel of communication, of making contact with some clients.
- Touch quickly regulates physiological and emotional states.

- Touch speaks to early attachment physical patterns, both primary and secondary communications, and supports their reorganization.
- Touch can directly address confusions about sexuality and sensuality, and between sexuality and early insecure baby longing in adults.
- Touch can help to differentiate assertiveness from aggression.
- Touch can be a form of relating adult to adult.
- Touch can take clients into profound wordless states of consciousness that are not related to preverbal stages of development.

I return to these topics later, but first I want to make some observations on the position of touch in psychotherapy to give us some context.

Professional Discussions on Touch

Professional discussions on touch provoke strong opinions and charged emotions, tending to follow the lines of whether to touch or not touch. In this atmosphere, it is challenging to have an informed discussion about touch (Westland, 2011). Nevertheless, touch is being reexamined in the light of understanding the therapeutic relationship as a co-created, intersubjective process (see, for example, Fosshage, 2009).

Beneath professional debate lies personal experiences of how we were touched by our own caregivers in childhood.

> Every aspect of our body sense embodies something about our mother's own physicality. If she is awkward and physically reticent, we pick that up. . . . If she fails to touch us in a firm, yet gentle manner, we may become confused or fearful about our bodily sensations. We might not know where our body begins and where it ends. (Orbach, 2009, p. 41)

While we more usually think about clients' touch deprivations, invasions, and abuse, the early touch history of therapists cannot be left out of the dialogue and tends to be quite veiled. Even the most loving of parents may not have been able to touch without some problematic aspect. These early experiences of touch are not easily accessed in talking psychotherapies, and most psychotherapy training does not include any practical training in the skills of therapeutic touch. Knowing and talking about a client's early parenting is not the same as (re)experiencing it through touch in the present with a therapist.

In this professional context, discussion, inevitably, is from a theoretical position put together with some personal experiences of touch taken mostly from daily life. Outside the therapeutic context, the practices of those psychotherapists who do touch and are trained to do so can sound absurd, often worrying, and evoke envy and jealousy. These fears are reinforced and embedded in religious, cultural, and social fears about the human body and touch. Touch is often seen as potentially sexual, abusive, aggressive, or manipulative, especially when gender, age, and cultural differences are in the mix.

Therapists Are Touching

However, far more touching is happening in psychotherapy than is professionally acknowledged and discussed. Surprisingly, therapists may not even recognize that they are touching their clients. David Tune (2001, 2005) found in his interviews with psychotherapists that they did not believe that they touched their clients. It was only when he prompted them further that they recalled episodes of touching their clients, mostly in the social sphere by offering hugs, handshakes, or putting an arm around the client's shoulders. Similarly, Stenzel and Rupert (2004) found in their study of psychologists working in private practice that psychologists were shaking hands outside the actual session, but rarely or never touched in session. Disturbingly, they found that those who did touch in the sessions did not discuss it. They concluded that increased dialogue and research about touch in clinical work could decrease the potential for the misuse of touch. I agree with this, but a safe environment has to be created first of all, whether at conferences or in supervision, so that therapists can speak freely about what they are actually doing in psychotherapy. It is difficult to discuss with a supervisor the touching of clients, if touch is associated with shame and the transgression of the rules of the modality (Pinson, 2002), let alone at a multimodality professional conference.

Touch in Different Psychotherapies

The theoretical position on touch is specific to each psychotherapy modality, but there are even differences within modalities. Whereas touch is a core competency in some forms of body psychotherapy (Boening, Southwell, & Westland, 2012), touch is not part of all body psychotherapies (see, for example, Rothschild, 2000; Young, 2005). With these diverse views of touch in psychotherapy, discussions with other professionals are facilitated when there is clarity around how touch is regarded in the different modalities (Westland, 2011).

The benefits of therapeutic touch are not universally accepted, and the psychoanalytic literature, in particular, from time to time, reasserts the value of not touching (see, for example, Casement, 2002; Schaverien, 2002, 2006). Notwithstanding this, the gradual shift in psychotherapy is toward the advisability or at least acceptability of touching those who have been severely deprived in childhood or are dissociated (for example, Shapiro, 2009, quoted in Sletvold, 2014), or are at risk of self-harm (for example, Kahr, 2006). Janet, Ferenczi, and Reich all used touch in psychotherapy, and there is some re-examination of their work. However, the shadow of Freud stretches far. He may have touched his clients in his cathartic phase (Freud & Breuer, 1895/2004), but the abstinence rule and fears about gratifying clients and acting out still abide. Interestingly, Jung never prohibited touch, but there remains the belief that he did prohibit it (Bosanquet, 2006).

Reasons to Touch in Different Psychotherapies

The reasons to touch in the literature cut across the categories listed above, and different layered effects happen simultaneously in touch. So touching dissociated clients may bring them into the present, calm them down, and connect them with early insecure attachments and feelings about their therapist. Touch is as complex as the spoken word and always multidimensional. So touching the "troubled child" within a client also means touching the adult, and touching the real adult is rarely just that.

There are examples across psychotherapies of therapists using touch with adults who have had insecure early attachments, and this is becoming the most acceptable reason to touch in contemporary literature. Jungian analyst, McNeely, for example, writes of touch for mirroring deprived patients (1987), and Bosanquet (1970), also a Jungian analyst, writes of the importance of touch for symbolic mothering, especially when the client cannot verbalize. Similarly, Jacoby (1986) discusses touch for connecting with the suffering "child within" and reaching "frozen clients," and there are other examples of touch for clients with early attachment problems (Bosanquet, 2006; Woodmansey, 1986; Rosenberg, 1995; Pinson, 2002; Toronto, 2006; Orbach & Carroll, 2006).

Physical touching enabled Eva, a fragile client (with borderline personality disorder) to gain a sense of her own being (Kupfermann, 1998). Touch in Eva's babyhood had been limited. Kupfermann writes of heeding Winnicott's advice to analysts to respond to the patient's need for touch when the patient is in a psychotic state. At Eva's insistence, when she was distressed, Kupfermann stroked her back with her fingers spread wide apart. Eva's urgency to "put on the lines" brought her in touch with her childhood experience of pushing into the bars of her crib with her body to get an experience of her body and to know that she existed (Kupfermann, 1998, p. 167). Touch is, therefore, important for developing a stronger sense of the skin boundary, which fosters individual differentiation and separation (Cornell, 1998). This enables the exploration of relatedness and closeness, and especially discovering that closeness does not come at the expense of loss of autonomy (Cornell, 1998).

Touch puts information into the organism, creates energy flow throughout the body, and thereby increases self-sensation (Davis, 2001). The feedback through touch is part of becoming more embodied and enables clients to stay more anchored in themselves through awareness of body sensations. This is of particular significance with traumatized clients (Ogden et al., 2006). Clients become more contained, enabling more reorienting and reality testing (Mintz, 1969; Hunter & Struve, 1998). In tandem with this goes the collaborative exploration of new actions and postural patterns (Ogden et al., 2006).

Peter (Chapters 6 and 7) struggled with closeness and distance in relationships. We explored this dynamic through standing facing each other, putting our arms in front of us (elbows bent), and placing the palms of our hands together. Peter slowly pushed on my hands, building up the force and gradually moving me away. I responded to the force he gave to me with an equal force. He was instructed to ground himself through his legs and breathe to support him being present. While he looked me in the eye, he retained contact with me as our palms continued to touch.

Peter was in charge of the process in the sense that he could tell me to stop at any time. We also experimented with me initiating firm, slow pushing into the palms of his hands and him telling me when to stop—I was close enough. Peter had agreed beforehand on the limits of our explorations. He was to stop if told to do so, and neither of us was allowed to hurt ourselves or each other. Peter was taller than me and had a wiry strength. Had he become really forceful, he would easily have overpowered me. This would have frightened him. The idea was to stay in contact with each other, slowing down the explorations with awareness to catch the subtleties of our interactions. As we pushed on each other's palms, a frequent question was, "How is that now?" Peter's cold hands became warmer, telling me that he was coming out to meet me. This contrasted with his withdrawal pattern in relationships. He enjoyed keeping the contact coupled with the experience of keeping me at a distance.

Touch has a role in energetic, physiological, and affect regulation, and in healing. It can be part of establishing safe attachment in psychotherapy, and has the potential to accelerate the formation of intersubjective fields (Ben-Shahar, 2012). It can engage with individual and relational "psyche-soma dynamics" for mirroring and coregulating relational tensions (Warnecke, 2009). Touch can reduce fear (Liss, 1974) and "revitalize" a client cut off from feelings (Tune, 2005). Touch restores the body's psychophysiological repair systems (Heller, 2007b; Ogden et al., 2006).

Those discussing the relationship with the real adult see spontaneous touch expressing the therapist's real feelings toward the client. These spontaneous gestures also convey acceptance and self-worth to the client (Mintz, 1969; Smith, 1998), and touch acknowledges clients in postoedipal states (Asheri, 2009). In his discussion of relating to the real adult, Kepner (1987) includes everyday touching such as handshakes and hugs. These everyday social rituals should not be regarded as just incidentals in the therapeutic process. A therapeutic perspective on them must be taken, and they should be discussed with clients in the psychotherapy in the consulting room.

For all clients, the physical body can become a source of plea-surable sensations as the body develops a wider range of move-ments and a higher level of aliveness (Boyesen, 1976; Liss, 1974; Southwell, 1988). This is of particular relevance with abused clients (Ogden et al., 2006), but is significant with all clients with insecure early attachments. The exploration of experiences of pleasure can enable clients to reconnect with their sexual and sensual selves (Staunton, 2002). For some clients, touch enables them to expe-rience more intimacy, but also, importantly, to differentiate emo-tional and sexual intimacy (Cornell, 1998).

Clients with poor personal boundaries, early deprivations, and histories of abuse often have difficulty delineating a spectrum of pleasurable sensations and understanding that it is possible to have pleasurable sensations without acting on them. Feeling one's own strength can evoke pleasurable sensations through the safe explo-ration of self-boundary exercises such as pushing with the hands against the hands of the therapist. The therapist offers reciprocal and matched resistance, and in doing so meets the client's strength (a modified example of this was with Peter above). In working in this way, the client learns at a physical level that it is possible to be assertive (Warnecke, 2009) and stay in relationship. Being asser-tive, which is often confused with being domineering and aggres-sive, does not mean loss of relationship. The controlled exploration of aggression through arm wrestling with clients has also been described (Mintz, 1969). For this sort of interaction, the client and therapist should be matched in strength, with the safeguards men-tioned above for Peter.

And finally, touch can open clients up to mystery and universal states of consciousness. Carroll, for example, writes of her experi-ence of entering "new realms of experience" through biodynamic massage:

> I began to have a sense that someone was sloughing off a layer of me, like a snake invited to shed a skin. And then it felt as if I was becoming the sea; my body was one with the rhythm of the waves. I felt as huge and fluid as the ocean. It changed again. I both sensed and saw an image of a ribbon of light down my body, from my head to my toes. (Carroll, 2000, p. 79)

For a fuller description of touch in psychotherapy see Westland (2015).

The language of touch is wide in its range, and, as we have seen, therapeutic touch does not apply only to states of early insecure attachment experienced by our clients. Touch is an underused form of communication capable of expressing our deepest feelings that cannot be voiced in words.

Touch in Daily Life

Given that touch, more than any other sense, provokes strong feelings, the next part of the chapter explores touch in society, its benefits, and its importance in babyhood. Touch as a channel of communication gets lost in daily life as our senses, including touch, get relegated to a secondary place with verbal communication taking precedence. Montagu, in his seminal work, *Touching: The Human Significance of the Skin*, implores us to notice that

> we have come to rely excessively on verbal communication, to the extent of virtually excluding the universe of non-verbal communication from our experience—to our great impoverishment. . . . We seem to be unaware that it is our senses that frame the body of our reality. (1986, p. xiv)

He equates the senses, especially the sense of touch, with learning to love and be kind. And McGilchrist reminds us that "all artistic and spiritual experience—perhaps everything truly important—can be implicit only: language, in making things explicit, reduces everything to the same worn coinage, and as Nietzsche said, makes the uncommon common" (2009b, p. 6).

Touch and the Skin

Touch is the foundation for all the other senses as it is the first sense to develop. Tactile sensory experiences for a fetus begin with the constant movements of the amniotic fluid in the mother's womb, creating different pressures on the skin. We experience ourselves through our skin and through its contact with the world. Anatomically, the skin develops out of the ectoderm, one of the three germinal layers in the embryo. The ectoderm differentiates into not only the skin but also the whole nervous system, the sense organs of smell, taste, hearing, and vision. Indeed, the skin is a vast communication system (Montagu, 1986), the external part of the nervous system connecting us with the rest of the nervous system and the external environment.

As the skin delineates what is inside us and what is outside, it creates not only a physical bridge between what is inside and what is outside, but also a psychological one. The skin provides literal and metaphorical containment; keeping in what should be kept inside, and keeping out what we choose to keep out and vice versa. We speak colloquially of someone "getting under our skin" when we have not been able to keep someone out or someone being so "thick skinned" that nothing affects them.

The skin seems to have to learn, through experiencing touch, to process sensory information. With this comes the development of a healthy "skin ego" (Stauffer, 2010). Stauffer observes that having a healthy skin ego means that it can be taken for granted that we are safe because the skin boundary is good enough to provide a sense of safety and separateness. None of the clients described so far could take the skin boundary for granted. Eliza (Chapter 4) easily merged with others and so kept herself aloof; Suzy (Chapter 5), living in her traumatized condition, leaked out of her skin and the world seeped in. Conversely, Tony was thicker skinned and he kept others out. Comments to him were like "water off a duck's back," but he could not let his authentic feelings out and not fully feel the care of others. To let feelings come in and out through his skin would be tantamount to loss of power and would give rise to shame and humiliation.

Touch: Our First Language

In Chapter 2 we saw the huge importance of touch for baby animals and humans. Touch is our first language, and merely 49 days after fertilization, when the face of the fetus is lightly touched near its mouth, it responds by moving its head away (Brazelton & Cramer, 1991). Later in pregnancy, when a mother strokes her belly or gently applies pressure to a kicking leg or an elbow pushing on the uterine wall, her baby responds with movements. These are the beginnings of touch conversations, the "Dawn of Attachment" (Brazelton & Cramer, 1991, p. 17). During birthing, as mother and baby work together, the baby experiences enormous pressures, a robust form of touching, as the baby is pushed along the birth canal by her mother's muscle contractions (Montagu, 1986). Then in the first few moments following birth and emergence into the world, the baby is touched skin to skin, perhaps placed on the mother's stomach and, as "touching begins, there love and humanity also begin" (Montagu, 1986, p. xv).

The Sterns, picking up on this theme, describe the exquisite touching that mothers do, getting to know their newborn on the outside for the first time. They do this through fingertip touching, outlining the contours of the baby's face, holding and gazing at the tiny hands and feet. They cuddle their babies close to the body. Touching and gazing are integral to the dance between them (Stern & Bruschweiler-Stern, 1998). A mother communicates something to her baby "in every way she touches him," and it is important that the mother's touch is not tentative. "What a mother communicates to her baby when she holds him with a good firm touch is that he can relax—she's not going to drop him—it's all covered" (Gaskin, 1977, p. 251).

Babies quieten with slow patting and become more alert with faster patting. Faster patting can be exciting and fun, but if prolonged the baby may become distressed. However, too much gentle touch can also be disturbing (Reyna, Brown, Pickler, Myers and Younger, 2012). Animal studies have found that stroking on the front of the body induces more calm than back stroking, with the back being more often associated with defense (Uvnäs Moberg, 2003). There are some differences between the way mothers and fathers touch. Mothers respond to upset babies by containing them, shutting down their movements (motor activity) by touching and holding them. This lowers the baby's arousal, de-escalating the babies' discomfort. Fathers, in contrast, are more likely to engage in arousing play, through jiggling the baby's body, playful poking, and lifting, which takes the baby higher into the air and away from the father's body (Dixon et al., 1981, cited in Brazelton & Cramer, 1991). Babies tend to get more excited with the father's play, and the pattern of the arousal is to go high rapidly and then take a longer recovery time (Brazelton & Cramer, 1991).

Pleasant or Unpleasant Touch

Touch is experienced by sensory receptors in the skin conveying messages to the central nervous system, different receptors registering different information. The receptors rapidly signal whether touch is pleasant or unpleasant. If the touch is pleasant, it activates the "calm and connection system," probably through the release of oxytocin (Uvnäs Moberg, 2003). When the touch is pleasant, it leads to what the Sterns conclude is the "highest point of feeling secure, where one experiences a safe haven." It comes from a chest-to-chest embrace. "A baby held in that way faces the world without fear" (Stern & Bruschweiler-Stern, 1998, p. 162).

In contrast, harsh touch and painful medical procedures are registered by pain receptors, setting off the flight reflex or stress response. Babies born prematurely used to have "minimal touch" as a bid to protect the baby from the consequences of medical interventions, "invasive touch." Medical procedures could lead to the heart rate slowing and reduced breathing (Field, 2003). Not only were these babies isolated in incubators and receiving unpleasant, invasive touch, but there was no compensatory pleasant touch to broaden the range of their touch experiences. Some of our clients will have experienced this sort of touch on entering the world.

Leela was such a client, who benefited from touch. Her overt reason for psychotherapy was to look at a career change. She worked in statistical analysis and wanted to do something more people oriented, but knew that it would pay less. Leela was slight in build and with characteristic features of the sensitive-withdrawn character style of self-protection (consistent with early insecure-avoidant attachment).

Leela was the smaller of prematurely born twins, meaning her early life was spent in an incubator with her twin sister. She found face-to-face contact with me and talking about herself excruciating. We might have found other ways of being together (and we did; see Chapter 9), and, in spite of her early touch history with its medical procedures, we found that she could respond to biodynamic massage. She chose to lie on her back on the massage couch—so that she could see me if she wanted, but she closed her eyes. Her arms rested by her side. When I placed my hands around her hand, it felt hard, taut, and very cold. Her arms, hands, legs, and feet were like a frozen garment stuck in an extended position. She looked like she was frightened almost out of her wits. The first time that I saw this, I was startled myself and almost moved to tears. I had had no inkling of just how terrified she was until I felt and saw it in the tissues of her body. She let me know through her body what she (nonconsciously) lived with.

As I held her hand, my own hands were warm, and she could feel how cold hers was in comparison. She liked me just holding each hand in turn and then each foot. I felt small pulsing, flowing movements coming into her hands. Her hands warmed up as I cupped each one in turn—she was beginning to thaw out. Leela was starting to make real contact with me. She spoke of how frightening it was to think about giving notice at work. She could hear her mother's disapproving voice: "Why throw away a prestigious career for something second rate?"

At the extremes of touch deprivation, we have known for a long time about babies and young children living in institutions developing "anaclitic depression." Deprived of personalized touch, and receiving touch only for physical procedures such as dressing, these infants cried easily, slept and ate poorly, were low in weight, and were susceptible to infections (Spitz, 1946). And more than 40 years ago the lack of touch in childhood was linked with physical violence (Prescott, 1971, 1975.)

The Benefits of Touch

The benefits of touch throughout life are increasingly well known. Field and colleagues at the Touch Research Institute in Miami, for example, have conducted numerous studies on the benefits of touch and massage for medical conditions ranging from anorexia to anxiety, depression, sexual abuse, and headaches, in populations of adults, including the elderly, children, and babies (for adult studies, see Field et al. 1996, 1997). One example of many is the positive effects of "gentle touch" on premature babies. These babies became quieter rather than disorganized and aroused when gently stroked. They also had more wakeful periods, and more mature orientation and motor habituation than the control group (Field et al., 1986).

A further example is research done by Glover and colleagues, working in London, with mothers who were postnatally depressed. They taught the mothers how to touch and massage their babies and found improvements in their interactions with their babies (Onozawa, Glover, Admas, Modi, & Kumar, 2001). We can only speculate how this sort of low-cost intervention might have bene-fited Peter's depressed mother (Chapters 6 and 7).

Touch in Mother-Baby Interactions

In Chapter 2, we learned about touch in each of the insecure attachment categories. Now I write more specifically about touch in face-to-face mother-baby interactions during play with 4-month-old babies as researched by Beebe and Lachmann (2014). They observed the following: attention, affect (facial and vocal), ori-entation and touch (the mother touching her baby, and the baby touching herself, an object, or the mother). Obviously mothers have a wider range of touching at their disposal than babies do. The mother's touch was coded on a scale ranging from affectionate to intrusive touch. By looking at different communication modalities of interaction, they picked up on discordant communication and which modalities the discordance was occurring in. However, they did not neglect the overall picture, which gave a quality dimension, and took account of this through the observation of facial-visual engagement. They used the Mother Touch Scale, which has 11 cat-egories with subcategories, and recorded where the mother touched her baby, the type of touching, and its intensity. Our clients are likely to have received this range of touch. The categories are:

- Affectionate touch
- Static touch
- Playful touch
- No touch
- Caregiving
- Jiggle/bounce
- Oral touch (mother placing finger in baby's mouth)
- Object-mediated touch (touching the infant with an object such as a toy)
- Centripetal touch (touching trunk, face, neck, and head)
- Rough touch (e.g., poking, forcing)
- High-intensity touch (intrusive touch)

Beebe and Lachmann (2014) found dysregulated interactions in those babies who were predicted to have insecure-disorganized attachment. Their mothers had reduced "contingent touch" (touching in response to the baby's behavior to encourage a repetition of the baby's behavior) coordination with the baby's touch. They did not seem to perceive the baby's touch as a cue for tender touch. Future disorganized babies also touched themselves less and had longer periods of no touch. Mothers of future resistantly attached infants demonstrated increasingly less positive touch. In contrast, mothers of future secure infants picked up the cues when infants initiated touch and took it as an interpersonal signal for contact and responded. As well as being aware of and sensitive to infant-initiated touch, the more the infant initiated touch, the more likely the mother was to touch kindly, and vice versa (Beebe & Lachmann, 2014).

Suzy, first introduced in Chapter 6, described a recent visit by her mother, her sister, Karen, and her 10-month-old daughter, Alice. Suzy recounted with vigor what her mother had done when cuddling Alice. Alice was sleepy and tetchy, and Suzy's mother attempted to comfort her, but Alice did not readily snuggle into her body. Suzy's mother insisted on caring for Alice. She made soothing noises and stroked Alice's back in slow rhythmic circles. Abruptly Suzy's mother stopped. She started to rapidly and heavily tap Alice's back. The taps were not hard enough to do physical harm, but Suzy could see that Alice did not like them. Her mother was oblivious to this. She continued to speak tenderly and heavily tap Alice's back, presumably thinking that she was soothing Alice asleep. Alice grew alert and increasingly fussy, confused by the different messages her granny was giving her. Just as suddenly, as the strength of the tapping was escalating, Suzy's mother started stroking Alice's back again. Her voice and her touch were now in tune with Alice, but Alice remained fractious.

Suzy was furious as she spoke. "She's so insensitive. All this play about being a caring grandmother! She can't even see that Alice hates what she is doing!" We cannot know for sure, but it is likely that Suzy had received similar misattuned touch from her mother.

Physiological Arousal and Its Regulation

Touching carries messages between the caregiver and the infant-for both quietening and enlivening. When a baby is able to maintain stability of arousal, she can attend to more of the environment and to the caregiver, in particular. This facilitates further interactions and learning possibilities (Brazelton & Cramer, 1991). In stark contrast with Suzy's description of her mother with her niece Alice is a film of baby Logan.

The Connected Baby is a beautiful training film made by a psychologist, Dr. Suzanne Zeedyk. In the film, 4-week-old Logan is cuddled close by his grandma while they are in the kitchen. His chest and lower body rest on his grandmother's chest and right shoulder. His little head and tiny arms peep over her right shoulder. His body looks relaxed, and he seems secure. He moves his hands together in synchronized movements up and down, regulating his level of arousal. They are not random movements. His hands come down to rest on his grandma's shoulders, and from this vantage point, he gazes around the kitchen.

Logan's eyes become dreamy; he could easily drift asleep. Then he moves his hands again; he becomes more alert and continues to engage with the room and its sounds. Grandma speaks quietly to him, gently stroking his back. She makes downward strokes, starting from his upper back and going rhythmically down his little body. Grandma's hand movements and the soft congruent tones of her voice support his quiet but alert state and give him a sense of safety. She and her daughter, his mother, are obliquely aware of Logan, but their main attention is on their conversation. Grandma and Logan's interactions are positive, synchronized, adaptive, mutual, and rhythmic. They make adjustments in their system together to maintain its balance. Mom also plays her part. Her tone of voice is a background murmur, maintaining the atmosphere in the kitchen. Grandmother and mother support Logan's capacity to be secure with himself. All this bodes well for baby Logan.

TOUCH AS CONTACT: MINDFULNESS OF TOUCH

So far we have looked at how babies are touched and I have described clinical examples of touching, but what is therapeutic touching? How does it differ from everyday touching? Therapeutic touch is a learned skill. It involves learning different ways of touching and reliably letting the touch skills become embedded in us in contactful touch (Boadella, 1987; Westland, 2009a).

This way of touching is described by various authors, who call it by different names. Contactful touch is "listening touch" (Rosen

& Brenner, 2003; Rubenfeld, 2000) and "original touch" (Gaskin, 1977). Contactful touch corresponds to Buber's (1878–-1965) I-Thou relating. I-Thou touch is tender even when robust. Commenting on Buber's work, van Deurzen Smith writes, "The secret of the I-Thou relationship is to give oneself fully over to the experience of the meeting with a preparedness to meet the other" (2010, p. 75). Although it is the hands of the therapist making physical contact with the client, the touching comes from the wholeness of the therapist. Buber also writes about "I-It relating." Functional touch is I-It relating (Buber, 2002). I-It relating involves relating to another with only a part of oneself, rather than the whole of one relating to the fullness of the other. I-It relating is always in the past, and I-Thou relating in the present. In reality, both forms of relating are necessary.

Contactful touch is in the present moment and is likely to occur when therapists are grounded and embodied. It is mindful touch. The skills from Chapter 3 are particularly relevant here for staying aware of the interactions. In mindful, contactful touch, an interactional dance emerges. The therapist listens with his hands and other senses to the client's responses. In turn, the therapist adjusts his touch by perhaps touching the client more strongly, or touching the tissues of the body more deeply. Sometimes it is the pace that has to be adjusted, slowing down or speeding up. The touch can invite the deep emotional level or stay at the matter-of-fact level of consciousness (Chapter 4). The form of touching can change too, perhaps touching with the fingertips for more precise contact or, conversely, touching with the palms of the hands for a fuller contact. Full hand contact can be particularly suited to clients who only knew intrusive poking and prodding in childhood.

The actual ways of touching can include stroking, usually down the body to calm clients, or circular movements, again down the body, which can be energizing if done quickly. For clients with insecure-disorganized attachment and traumatic histories, simply holding the hands on different parts of the body gives time to sense the touch and their feelings about it, as with Leela. Interestingly, contactful touch seldom includes patting clients, perhaps because it can be intrusive, although patting is commonplace for babies.

Contactful touch is intersubjective, exploratory, and to some extent unpredictable. There is a direct resonance with the emotion of the muscle. Contactful touch is accompanied by kindness, curiosity, and not knowing. The clarity, compassion, and spaciousness inquiry brought to experience, now and then, helps to keep the touch contactful. Preplanning touch and thinking about it is no longer contactful. The touch loses connection with the other person or becomes stilted (I-It touch).

As the therapist touches and senses the client's response, awareness is brought to present experience. As in earlier chapters, therapist attention begins with attention to oneself, followed by attention to the client. Bringing attention to the moment of transition from putting attention on the client and back to oneself can often catch nuanced layers of interaction, perhaps with abrupt changes of rhythm or timing. Moments of being distracted or perhaps underinvolved are brought to awareness. It is often worthwhile to explore further moments just before the loss of contact with the client and perhaps discuss them with clients. Tactile conversations can go alongside spoken ones. There can also be pauses—taking some time out for discussion briefly, but keeping in contact physically.

We now come back to Tony and see what happened in his first experience of biodynamic massage. I asked Tony to lie on his front with his arms by his sides and his head turned to one side. I wanted to be able to see his face and have the possibility of talking with him so that we could both see each other. I judged that Tony might feel safer with his back to me. As I began to touch Tony, I felt his tense back muscles, but as I let my hands get to know his back, I sensed his breathing movements becoming slower and widening. I heard his peristalsis and knew that his system was calming down. I asked Tony briefly how he was and he replied, "Fine." I spent a long time "talking with" Tony's back.

I used his breathing to guide me in whether the touch was too strong, too light, or about right. I felt his tight muscles, requiring firm contact from me, gradually soften, and his breathing became much deeper as I touched him in an attuned, contactful way. I sensed his vulnerability and spoke to it with my hands. My touch was definite, kind, and unchallenging. Not speaking about Tony's vulnerability let me communicate with it non-verbally and protected Tony from his shame about it being exposed.

I asked Tony to turn over and lie on his back and indicated that I would be touching his legs next. The difference between Tony's back and his legs was striking. His legs looked like those of a young boy, his back that of a strong man. His back had been warm to the touch; his legs were cooler and both feet were cold. It felt as if no one was home in that part of his body, and the coldness indicated to me that he was ungrounded. No wonder it was hard for him to trust anyone and be vulnerable. I used deep, muscular touch to contact the muscles of one leg, including the foot. The touch conversation was fairly vigorous as I hoped to increase Tony's awareness of his leg. He said that he enjoyed this.

As I finished the conversation with one leg, I asked him to describe differences between the leg that I had been touching and the other one. This is a way to build sensory awareness. Tony was at a loss for words. With suggestions, he was able to tell me, "Yes, this one is warmer, that one colder." I continued in a matter-of-fact way. I moved to engage with his arms and hands. He seemed to like this too, with his peristalsis gurgling along and giving me additional feedback. I finished by making circular movements with my fingertips and long strokes on his head and face. He seemed calm and, unusually, he did not speak. After a brief rest on his side, he got up. As he was preparing to leave, he made two poignant comments. The first was, "I've put my affairs all in order." And the second was, "I'll go to see my mom on the weekend. I wish that I could find a way to tell her that I do love her, in spite of how she is." Both of these statements were "rooted" (see Chapter 4) and left me feeling sad. He was telling me that he knew that he might not have long. I nodded and looked tenderly at him. He knew that I knew without my having to say anything.

Touch can create a non-verbal form of safety and a relationship with the psychotherapist, in which the client is dimly in contact with the therapist, but, more importantly, the client can make a stronger contact with himself and his inner sensations. This in turn allows the internal movements of self-regulation (Eiden, 1998). These comments are apposite for Tony.

Listening for the Client's Response

When we bring touch into psychotherapy, it is important to notice how clients are responding to the touch. "If the hands are too abrupt, or too strong, or held too long, there can be seen a big inhalation, but it is not followed by an exhalation; the breathing stops" (Andersen, 2007b, p. 31). Breathing, as discussed in Chapter 5, is pertinent for reliable feedback on how the client is experiencing the touch. In addition to this, touch gives direct non-verbal feedback from the physical tissues of the client's body.

The bodily tissues can respond with a yes, a no, or a neutral. A yes response might be fuller breathing—often a deeper out-breath, and hard tissues soften. The tissues will become warmer and feel less dense and impenetrable. Tony's back, for example, which was hard to the touch, softened and warmed. His legs, which were cool, also warmed up and went from very pale white to pinkish.

A no response is often conveyed in breath holding and physical tissues tightening and becoming less mobile. Sometimes the tissues also become cooler and paler.

At one point in the session with Tony, he asked me to go more deeply into his muscles. I was not entirely convinced by his request because his words seemed to come from an idea of how he should be touched, rather than his immediate experience. However, I tried what he wanted, and although he said that he enjoyed the touch, his muscle and skin tightened beneath my hand, and he held his breath. Tony was not aware of this, but I took it as a no from his body, and continued to use my own sense of how to contact him through touch.

A neutral response is one without a definite yes or no. The client is indifferent to the touch. As the touch conversation goes on, the idea is to take cues from the client's non-verbal communications. The tissues of the body hold both the primary and secondary communications, and there will be reactions and resonances going on in the touch interactions. When the client expresses a no, one possibility is to hold on the "edge of resistance" (Sills, 2001, p. 236), that is, letting the hands become still and listening for how the conversation develops. Sometimes a no remains a no and the client does not come into contact with us in that part of the body. We just move on. Sometimes, if the client feels safe enough, no becomes a cautious maybe. Unexpressed secondary potential comes into the tissues. That is, the vitality that has been used by the client to keep the defense system (secondary patterning) in place becomes available to them. Then we might linger a little longer to let the primary communication know that we have received it. Then we move on. And of course, where we receive a yes we stay longer but are careful not to overstay our welcome.

Usually it is possible to reach someone through touch somewhere and Boyesen (2006) gives an illustration from her work with a very fearful client. As a 1-year-old, the client had almost drowned in the bath when her mother went to the answer the phone. Boyesen could not find a way to reach the client through touch. Eventually she came to the client's nose and a yes came. The client's parasympathetic nervous system came to the fore and Boyesen heard peristalsis. Boyesen linked this to the client's experience of having water coming into the nose when she was drowning. Boyesen had made contact through her touch with the nonconscious memory of near drowning that was locked in the client's body.

Sometimes a no response comes because the client requires more time to digest the experience and the touch has to be slowed down. At other times the touch needs to be firmer, deeper, or quicker. Sometimes the tempo has to be increased to keep the client more alert and in a yes response; at other times the pace is slowed right down to take the client into a deeply relaxed state, a different sort of yes.

BEFORE TOUCHING IN PSYCHOTHERAPY: TRAINING, SUPERVISION, ETHICS, AND CONTRACTING

Adequate training in therapeutic touching includes having a range of ways of touching. This is like learning a vocabulary and then being able to put it together in a conversation as needed. It means training in discerning clients' responses to touch, especially in the non-verbal realms, and knowing how to discuss touch with clients. A theoretical framework is required to think about touch interactions, and, of course, sensitivity to the context of the work goes without question.

Supervision of touch interactions is also vital, ideally with someone with similar touch training. Without this, supervisor and supervisee may be talking at cross-purposes, or theorizing about the touch interactions rather than deepening into a broader understanding of the touching. For psychotherapists training in a non-touch psychotherapy modality, gaining touch skills is not easy; finding supervision is even more problematic. The solution for some analysts and therapists is to undergo further training in touch via a body therapy such as craniosacral therapy or biodynamic massage.

Touch in psychotherapy should always stay within professional and legal requirements. Touch should conform to ethical principles such as autonomy and beneficence (Calmes, Piazza, & Laux, 2013). And where psychotherapy might include touch, that should be part of the therapeutic contract made at the outset of therapy. The contract should be reviewed and revised at intervals.

CONCLUSION

Touch is the main language of communication for some clients and the main avenue for the repair of insecure attachment patterns, abuse, and neglect. Access to early interaction patterns mediated without recourse to the spoken word and cognitive understanding enables their fuller exploration non-verbally and can be optimal through touch. Touch will be challenging for some therapists, and not every therapist will have the disposition or inclination to touch clients. Psychotherapists, like their clients, have their own preferences, and touch is not for all clients. Nevertheless, the place of touch in psychotherapy can no longer be ignored nor continue to exist in the shadows.

Chapter 9

USING CREATIVE MEDIA
FOR EXPRESSION

Leela, introduced briefly in Chapter 8, found her job even more of a struggle as she realized how profoundly that working with statistics was not what she wanted to do. Her sister had fulfilled the family expectations by becoming a doctor. Although Leela had done well in the eyes of her family, she was not as successful as her sister. She felt like a failure. Leela was going into a crisis. She had taken 3 weeks of leave from work and started taking antidepressants.

Leela sat in her chair and I asked her about her immediate feelings and body sensations. She looked blankly down at her hands and answered monosyllabically and with long pauses between each of her words, "tired," "hopeless," "anxious" As I listened, my thoughts felt sluggish and stuck; my body felt thick and slow. This was the tenor of the session. As we were coming to the end of it, I had a vague memory, from our first consultation, that Leela had enjoyed art at school. In passing, she had told me that she would have liked to have gone to art school, but "that had been out of the question." What counted in her family were the professions. I floated the idea to Leela that we might continue next time by using art materials. She was dubious and could not see the point, but was not entirely unwilling.

Next time I saw Leela, I had arranged various art materials by her chair beforehand. She noticed them as she sat down. I suggested that we both sit on the floor and that she just take some time to look at what was there.

She could arrange the paper, pens, pastels, crayons, and felt tips how she wanted. With some encouragement she moved from the chair to the floor. Immediately I felt some relief that we could be doing something together. I still felt sluggish and stuck, but there was a faint spark of lightness and with it a split second of hope. I sat alongside Leela but was careful not to intrude on her physical space. She lifted the lid off the crayon box and opened up the box of pastels. I felt her interest spark briefly, then go, and then come again.

After an interval, I suggested that she take something to draw with, shut her eyes, and just let her hand do the drawing. I wanted her to "warm up" and get used to the materials. Despite my best intentions, Leela's explorations of the materials stopped. Perhaps I was too quick with my suggestion, or maybe she just needed time to consider it. After a long interval she took a piece of paper, shut her eyes, and her hand moved in circles over the page. She took another piece of paper, and this time she pressed harder and her movements were quicker. Encouraged, I suggested that she show me how she was feeling by drawing whatever came to her. She carefully chose a large piece of gray paper, folded it in half, and took a piece of charcoal. In one corner she drew a sticklike figure lying on its side. It was curled up in a ball with its head tucked down on its chest and the hands encircling its head. The legs were pulled up toward the head. Around the figure she drew a box. The back of the figure was lying along one side of the box, looking toward the rest of the empty paper. She took a while to make her drawing and seemed absorbed in it. I sat watching her work with my holding field wide and spacious so that she would know that I was with her, but not overfocused on her (see Chapter 3).

When she had finished, she sat and looked at her drawing and seemed satisfied. I joined her in the looking and let myself be affected by what I saw. After a while, I asked her to tell me about her drawing and how she felt looking at it now. She turned toward me and looked blankly at me. We both looked at her drawing and, after a time, I gave voice to some of my body sensations, feelings, and thoughts as I looked. I deliberately spoke slowly, using the first person to emphasize my feelings: "As I look, I feel . . ." I spoke of the figure looking very small on the paper. It looked separate from the world. I felt bleak, isolated, and desolate. Privately, I wondered how such an undernourished-looking person, in such an empty void, could find the will to live. Leela seemed to take my comments in, but did not say anything.

INTRODUCTION

In this chapter we look at some more non-verbally focused ways for clients to express themselves. Clients can be invited to use intermediary ways of relating through a variety of creative media such as art materials, as with Leela above. In doing this, clients put their inner experiences outside themselves and come to know and share their experiences. The creative media are the vehicles for self-expression and contain the experiences. Together with the emotional holding of the therapist, it becomes possible to face inner experiences and share them. The forms of self-expressive communication are generally more distant from clients' embodied experience of themselves and their emotional life than putting feelings into words. However, the body is, of course, involved in the communication.

Often clients benefiting from these forms of communication do not find the body a refuge and resource, instead experiencing the visceral nature of the body as alarming rather than safe. They find more safety in using creative media to convey their feelings. Often using creative media is effective when words are hard to find, as with Leela. Sometimes they are fragile clients; they might also be sensitive-withdrawn clients. Generally the clients are more comfortable in the non-verbal realm (without the bodily aspect being overtly brought in) and their communications come more readily in this form than in the spoken word. Where words are part of the dialogue, it is the imagination that is more readily put into words in the form of images, dreams, and metaphors, rather than the words carrying the feelings. Clients' words may have some muted emotional tones, but the clients may have little physical sense of their image as an aspect of themselves.

For these clients, the spoken word does not carry their emotional expression. Perhaps they do not have words to describe their inner feelings to another—such as those with alexythmia. Perhaps putting nuances of tone and inflection in the words is too frightening or potentially overwhelming. Or it might be that for some clients, who have been narcissistically wounded, putting words to their own experiences is a rather dangerous matter. For any client, but especially more fragile clients, where speaking their feelings is not an easy matter, other forms of expression can be the vehicles for self-expression and communication.

The vehicles for communication might be movement as described in earlier chapters but can include "sculpting" an inner state into a body posture. Clients may make sounds and hum or sing. They might speak nonsense words—loudly or softly, fast or slow, putting emphasis on particular words, perhaps "spitting" words out. They might tap out rhythms on the floor or wall, perhaps drum, or stomp and dance. Drawing, painting, and clay work can play a part. Poetry and prose writing, storytelling, and reading out loud is the way for some clients. Others can use and enjoy role-playing, miming, enacting words and phrases, speaking through puppets, or speaking as a friend or imagined friend. Some clients can speak metaphorically through books and fictional characters. Some can use guided imagery. The imagination and metaphor play a large role. Creative media can be mixed. So singing can go with dancing, or painting might go with humming and tapping out rhythms. In the client examples in this chapter, the ways of working often generalize to different forms of creative media.

The forms of communication and the way that they unfold will correspond with the preferences of therapists and their fit with clients with some forms of creative expression speaking to us more than others. Ideally the client's *preferred mode of expression* becomes the vehicle for the expression, but this is sometimes limited by the constraints of the consulting room. Constraints might be lack of space for movement or no facilities to be messy with art materials. I elaborate on preferred mode of expression later in this chapter.

Often these ways of relating hark back to early attachment patterns, in which communication happened through touch, looks, sounds, rhythms of words and interactions, laughter, lullabies, and play. In the present, clients can befriend aspects of themselves that were underdeveloped or truncated in childhood. These aspects can be rekindled and their potential developed. However, the use of creative media is not all about childhood patterns of interaction. It can also be the form for future potential to flower. Creative media also provide the means to express what cannot be put into words—

the awesome, mysterious, and ineffable. Writing in the context of dance movement psychotherapy, Noack observes that some movements have a "numinous quality" associated with awe: "Words are insufficient here and often superfluous, since the experience is one concerning the whole of the person, and in this sense goes beyond words" (1992, p. 194).

These non-verbal communications expressed via creative media are less direct than some of the ways of exploring relationship in earlier chapters, such as touch in Chapter 8. Often the indirectness gives clients a place to hide, not only from the intensity of the interpersonal relationship but from hidden parts of themselves. A client, for example, describing herself metaphorically as "a dead tree" knows faintly, "This is me and not me" at the same time. We can talk about the tree and its characteristics, but the client can feel less exposed than saying something directly like, "I feel dead inside; life does not feel worth living." Expressing through creative media begins to build bridges to feelings.

With Leela, I assumed that she was representing herself in all of her drawing—her choice of paper and the charcoal, the figure, the box, and the expanse of space on the paper. Her drawing was a depiction of her depression, her present emotional state. It held conscious, unconscious, and nonconscious parts of her. It was about Leela's relationship to herself and also our relationship. Leela had been willing to show me through her drawing how desolate she felt. I also thought of her premature birth, and the sticklike figure in the box led me to thoughts of death. The figure's back against the wall of the box seemed to provide it with some connection to something other than itself. This gave me some hope.

Creative media provide a third position that we can orient around with our clients. Client and therapist have something else to focus their attention on, rather than directly on each other. Joy Schaverien, an analytical art psychotherapist has written at more length on two-way and three-way relating. Two-way relating is the client relating to the drawing, with the therapist observing at more of a distance. Three-way relating brings the therapist into the relating. The client relates to the drawing; the therapist relates to the drawing; and the therapist and client relate to each other: client–drawing, therapist–drawing, therapist–client (Schaverien, 1995). Schaverien differentiates two- and three-way relating from two-and three-person relating as described in the psychoanalytic literature.

With Leela, the session above was mostly about her relating to her drawing, with me as an oblique observer (two-way relating). Then there was a period of us both relating to her drawing, but only briefly to each other. We were alongside each other, but not so obviously interpersonally relating. When Leela was drawing and looking at her picture, she was deepening her relationship to herself through the art. It was a visual experience, but also involved movement and touch. She moved her body in making marks on the paper and selecting materials. And the process was tactile; her hand holding the thin charcoal stick, touching the paper as she folded it in half. And while the drawing was a depiction of her inner emotional state, we should not forget that it could never be a fully accurate depiction. This is not because of Leela's lack of artistic skill, but because inner states do not translate directly into outer forms. This is in exactly the same way that words only approximate our feelings.

For those psychotherapists used to working more verbally and conceptually, bottom-up, experience-driven psychotherapies can offer inspiration. Several of the modes of communication listed above have been developed into psychotherapies in their own right, including what are collectively known as the creative arts psychotherapies (for example, music therapy, dance movement psychotherapy, art psychotherapy, and dramatherapy). These draw on the performing arts. Other psychotherapies including the use of creative media are, for example, body psychotherapies, humanistic psychotherapies such as Gestalt psychotherapy and psychodrama, and analytical psychology. "What the performing arts share with psychoanalysis and psychotherapy is a commitment to emotional communication. Practitioners of the performing arts realized long ago that expertise in emotional communication depends on training the body to express emotions" (Sletvold, 2014, pp. 133–134).

So through using creative media we can help our clients to become acquainted with their feelings and to share them with us. While we may not have the expertise of a creative arts therapist, we can use our own creativity to contact the client's main channels of creative expression. When clients express themselves through the various media, we access our own creativity and intuition, and we find ourselves responding to them spontaneously. Staying aware and embodied remains a mainstay in this way of interacting.

FIVE MODES OF EXPERIENCE, FUNCTION, AND EXPRESSION

Earlier I referred to preferred modes of expression. These are aspects of individuals that serve as their main form of communication. Usually the preferred modes of expression are a mixture of genuine expression (primary communication) and inhibited potential and protective strategies (secondary communication). The modes are developed, especially in early childhood. They are what was reinforced by caregivers and what was not welcomed. So we might become strong thinkers, able to communicate complex ideas, but at the expense of our emotional life. Peter (Chapters 6 and 7) is an obvious example.

Nolan (2012) describes *five modes of experience, function, and expression*. These are "body-mind modes" that are "interrelated and reciprocal ways we experience the world, operate in it and express ourselves." The modes are body sensations, emotions, cognition, imagination, and motor activity (voluntary and involuntary muscular and skeletal movements, gestures, and posture). Different psychotherapies tend to emphasize two or three of these modes, but all are present and

> indicate the relational currents at play. By working with all five, we use a wider range of what happens between us and our clients, and keep therapy geared in a more vital way to what is happening in the present moment. This is where our clients learn how to play, become more alive, and change. (Nolan, 2012, p. 114)

The five modes of experience, function, and expression overlap with the domains of experience model (Chapter 6). They correspond also with a model put forward by Boadella (1987) in the 1980s, in which he places domains of experience and expression firmly as body processes (as does Nolan). Boadella draws on embryological development and locates the modes of expression in the different anatomical systems of the body. As we saw in Chapter 8, the embryo metamorphoses into three germinal layers: the ecto-derm or outer layer, the mesoderm or middle layer, and the endo-derm or inner layer. The ectoderm differentiates into the nervous system and the skin, the mesoderm into the muscular and skeletal systems, and the endoderm into the digestive system, including the stomach, liver, pancreas, lungs, and heart. These differentiate into different aspects of ourselves:

- Thinking, imagining, and information processing (from the ectoderm)
- Moving and acting (from the mesoderm)
- Feeling (from the endoderm)

Boadella (1987) relates these anatomical structures to the relational tasks of grounding, centering, and facing (see Chapter 6). So our psychological capacities are related directly to our physical struc-tures. I want to reemphasize here that each of Nolan's five modes of expression are not just theoretical concepts. The modes are more or less embodied by each of us and, to the extent that they are devel-oped and embodied, make a difference in how competent we are in relationships. They are active in our therapeutic interactions even if we do not give them our attention.

Using Nolan's model, we can think of Leela as weak in all of the five modes—embodied (body) sensations, embodied emotions, embodied cogni-tion, embodied imagination, and embodied motor activity. Her strongest modes of expression were cognition and imagination, but she had poor embodied connection with them. So when Leela was talking about an idea, she was aware of few body sensations and emotions going on alongside her thoughts and imaginings. Her motor activity was also minimal. However, one of the ways for her to develop stronger connections with each of the modes was through touch (see Chapter 6), which helped her to differenti-ate body sensations. My hand movements and their warmth invited more mobility in her body tissues (motor activity).

Her emotions began to emerge as I listened and took her thoughts and imaginings seriously. This included her thoughts about a different career and how she imagined her future. Her feelings about that and the body sensations were fostered by resonating with her non-verbally and asking about her ideas. Her imagination, emotions, body sensations, and motor activity developed in her through the use of creative media. We learned how to play together. Sometimes we reflected together on her drawing and our times together. At other times we spoke little, as spoken words felt as if they would intrude on what Leela had shown in her drawings.

CHOOSING THE VEHICLE FOR THE EXPRESSION AND COMMUNICATION

Creative media used in psychotherapy have their own inherent properties. Clients will often have an affinity for one medium over another. Some clients sing or make sounds easily; some can easily translate what is inside into a movement or a drawing. The idea of role-play is bewildering for some clients, but they can readily construct an imaginary story. The main thing for clients to grasp is that these vehicles for exploration are not about being an artist, actor, poet, or dancer. Their purpose is to deepen communication with themselves and others. Once the creative movement is started communications will unfold, taking on a life of their own. They do not have to be known beforehand, or rehearsed and polished.

Each of the creative arts psychotherapies emphasizes particular senses. Art psychotherapy puts internal images onto paper letting the images be seen by clients. They can be reflected back to clients by the expression of the eyes, facial expression, and posture of psychotherapists. This develops a visual sense of self. Singing or vocalizing can be heard and sound vibrations felt in the physical body. Tapping out rhythms with a hand makes tactile contact with the furniture or body part being tapped, and the sounds give an auditory sense of self. Working with clay is tactile and visual and relates to a tactile and visual sense of self.

For the therapist wanting to work with creative media, a selection of props and materials is required. For those wanting, for example, to use art, a selection of papers of different sizes, textures, and colors, and a range of drawing materials, from hefty crayons that have to be grasped with a full hand to pencils and pastels, gives different possibilities for experience. Water paints and large or small brushes allow for more expansive possibilities. Imagination is stimulated by the materials, and each of the materials affords different physical possibilities.

Access to Exploration and Expression of Emotion Through Sculpting, Movement, and Sound

These non-verbal ways of communicating through creative media can be graded in terms of their challenge. They can be adapted for particular clients at different stages in the psychotherapy. For clients who can tolerate more exposure, it can be possible to ask them to take up a body posture, or make a gesture, or start a movement to express their feeling state. For these clients, moving, and being seen to do so, has to be tolerable or tolerable enough. We saw how Peter could use this form of exploration in Chapters 6 and 7. Sometimes making a sculpt, taking up a posture to show current feelings, with the client's eyes closed, will help a more frightened client with feeling less "seen" and exposed. The instruction to the client might be something like, "Let's see if we can find another way of coming at this—perhaps a bit more sideways on," that is, instead of talking. With the client's agreement, the invitation could be something like this (note the lack of capitals again to convey the invitation is a suggestion more geared to the right brain engaging more fully, rather than an imperative):

- let a posture come for how you are feeling.
- let a sound come for how you are feeling.
- tap on the floor with your foot for how you are feeling.
- let yourself move in a way that conveys how you are feeling.

Expressive and Mechanical Communication

In Chapter 4 we considered dead and rooted talking. Similar thinking can be applied to other forms of communication. When a movement, sound, drawing, or communication in any form occurs, it can seem mechanical, preplanned, and thought out in a left-brain manner. It lacks the feel of being improvised afresh and lacks vitality. Sometimes a communication starts mechanically, but then it becomes spontaneous, or sometimes spontaneous and mechanical expressions are mixed. Again, what we look for is whether the expressions move us and resonate with us. This is what we want to encourage and relate to. This alive and spontaneous communication is described by Schaverien (1995), who refers to art causing "ripples" as we view it, and it has continued resonance. In contrast, she writes of "chocolate box" art, pleasing to the individual, but not having an impact on others. In psychotherapy, the creative expressions may not be accomplished in artistic terms, but we hope that they are moving.

Using the Written Word

Some clients find such demonstrative ways of conveying feelings through movement, sound, drawing, and so on far too challenging. Hector was such a client.

Hector was in his early 50s. He was an isolated man whose complementary therapist had recommended that he have psychotherapy. It took a while for me to discover that a relationship had ended, leaving him bereft. He had had a psychotic breakdown in his university years, had taken time out, returned to his studies, and gained his degree. When I met him, he worked from home for a scientific publishing house, which suited him. He took his meals in a local restaurant. He dressed casually but smartly and was always punctual. He was polite but sparing in his words. His body barely moved, giving the impression that he was a mechanical man rather than flesh and blood. Hector would dry up after a few opening sentences of information giving. He had started to edit a new book—he had walked today—he had visited his sister. He looked uncomfortable, and would stare through me in a disconcerting way. I felt embarrassed and awkward. If I asked a question, Hector took a long time to reply. I sensed that he was sifting through a myriad of possible answers to find the right one and maybe also getting lost in his thoughts. My questions felt painfully intrusive and clumsy. Silences were frequent and unproductive.

After the nuts and bolts of daily life, Hector usually continued to speak through references to literary books and poetry. I struggled to meet him in his particular cultural references. Hector had grown up bilingually; his parents were from a different culture and he spoke of literature and poetry from their culture. Some of the works had been translated, but I was not familiar with them. Sometimes he spoke of characters and books that I did know. I saw this as his way of trying to tell me about himself. Our discussion sometimes took off briefly, but soon the conversation would falter. Perhaps another therapist would have been able to deepen into the opening that he offered. Perhaps speaking about books, characters, and the plots in them would have been a way for our conversation to go on. I would have assumed that he was all the while talking in some way about himself. Without being able to do this, I was at a loss. The usual forms of exploration at my disposal felt as if they would be too challenging and too exposing for this extremely diffident, cerebral, and sensitive man.

After a few sessions I told him how I was finding our times together and asked him, how could we do this, how could I understand him? How could he tell me what he wanted me to know? It felt like a big risk to be so direct with him. After a long, thoughtful pause, he replied, "I could write it down during the week and bring it for you to read." This marked the transition into the next phase of our work together.

At first we would exchange a few words at the beginning of our session in the usual way. He had had a walk today or not, and so on. This was part of our opening ritual and seemed to settle him. Then he would hand me his pages to read. At first, I asked if he would like to read it to me. "No, you read it." Over several months of meeting, I would silently read the next episode of a well-written narrative. He would sit and watch me, but I did not feel intruded upon. It felt like being together, but with a lot of space between us. I learned of his lost and only love. Over months I read the story of his love, the start of the romance, their time together, and then her decision to move back to her home country. He had visited and they had tried to keep in touch. He could not move to her country. His family was here; hers was there. Eventually she met someone else and broke his heart.

As the story unfolded in written form week by week, I took my time to read it so that I could catch the tones of feeling in the text. Then I would tell him in unhurried, well-chosen words how I had felt reading it as I tuned into his words. I was tentative and used indirect ways of speaking. I never used "You felt" sentences. "As I read the part at the beginning, when Marie-Anne and you first went for a coffee together, I felt a delight—a tingling in my skin, a sense of hope—a wistfulness—and then a twisting in my heart." I would place a hand in my heart area. "Just here is where I feel it." He would look sideways at me and silently nod.

I kept my excitement and feelings muted. I spoke quietly and with predictable rhythms. I kept myself rather still as I sensed that being too animated would be alarming for him. I gradually found the way to be with him, where some aliveness and feelings could come into the room. After sharing

my feelings, often I would then ask one or two questions to gather informa-
tion, but not to elicit more emotion. "How did you meet? What work did
she do?" While the questions were deliberately information seeking, they
were said from a spacious, rooted place in myself, with slightly down going
intonation in my voice. Gradually the repertoire of our discussions widened.

CONCRETIZATION

Both Leela and Hector gradually expanded their range of emotional expression with me. Hector's process moved very slowly,
but steadily. Leela's range of creative explorations widened more
quickly. She developed more connections both with and between
each of her five modes of experience, function, and expression.
She continued to concretize her inner experiences through her
drawings, and Hector, through his writing. "A concretization is the
psychotherapeutic transformation of a *psychological state* or a psychological situation *into a body state* or a body situation" (Holzberg,
1992, p. 181, emphasis added). Concretization is a way of elaborat-
ing on or entering more fully into an experience for further exploration non-verbally. Abstract notions take on greater physical form,
become more visible, and clients develop more self-awareness in the
process. This switches explorations to a relatively more right-brain
mode of activity. (Note that the term *concretization* is used somewhat
differently in psychoanalysis.)

Concretizations arise spontaneously and creatively out of the
joint relationship between client and therapist. It signifies something of how client and therapist can "play" together. Concretizations provide a bridge between thinking and speaking, to
experiencing and expressing—often non-verbally. The embodied
experience forms the bridge between the spoken word and the
non-verbal. Embodying the experience brings more perspective
and possibilities for further exploration. Usually there are multiple
levels of meaning in concretizations.

Concretization is less appropriate for those clients who think literally and cannot relate to metaphorical ways of describing events.
Concretizations bring therapists into closer spontaneous relating
with their clients, and they have to be more personally engaged
than in some other therapeutic interactions. As with communicating through touch (Chapter 8), concretizations bring more potential

exposure for the therapist. They often demand quick responses from us and an imperative to trust our intuition. This takes us into jointly created moments of the unknown (not conceptualized) and going with the flow of them. The mask of professionalism and the role of therapist have to be less pronounced in these sorts of interactions.

Jumping-off points for concretization may be various words, phrases, or sentences that lend themselves to being enacted. Holzberg gives an example from a workshop situation where he was "not feeling supported." Indeed, his appraisal of his life was that there had never been "anyone to catch me in case I would fall" (Holzberg, 1992, p. 181). The workshop leader invited him to run and jump into his arms. The leader indicated that he would try to catch him. Holzberg did this, and in so doing embodied his words. The workshop leader caught him. Presumably he had not invited this enactment of Holzberg's words before he had gauged that he was strong enough to catch him. Holzberg knew that this experience belonged to his childhood experience of his father. The concretization enabled him to explore further the transferences with the workshop leader and how this generalized to his life.

A client, Jenny provides another example of taking a client's words and making them concrete in physical activity. I had been seeing Jenny for several years, initially because of her difficulties with relationships. On this particular day, Jenny described wanting to "crawl away and hide." This was a feeling that she often had, especially at work. She related it to her childhood experiences with her unstable, explosive mother. As a child, she had often hidden away when she was frightened. When she mentioned this, I suggested that she could hide away somewhere in the room. She was surprised and liked the idea.

We worked out together where she wanted to hide, how to construct her hiding place, and worked on getting it just right. She used lots of cushions and made a sort of nest in a corner into which she crawled. It still did not feel quite right to her, and she constructed a small hole in the cushions and piled more cushions on top of herself. She wanted to see me, if she chose, but did not want me to see her. As her enactment developed she became hot and wanted fewer cushions on top of her. She moved some of the cushions away, which enabled her to move more freely. The atmosphere changed. She peeped out from the cushions and darted back when I looked at her. She giggled and delighted in my seeing her and then not. I joined in by saying,

"Where's Jenny gone?" as she disappeared. Then she surprised me by bursting out and shouting, "Boo!" The game continued. It was fun and exciting. I felt as if, and responded as if, Jenny were a young child.

When the game finished, she spoke of her mom as not always being so frightening. She recalled forgotten times of her mom being "Nice Mommy." "The problem was that you never knew which Mommy you were going to get."

Let's return to Leela now and see what happened in a later session. *Leela's use of creative media became more elaborate as she became more acquainted with her body sensations. She had returned to work, and the antidepressants were lifting her mood. Some months on, she had found an open arts space and had become a regular member of the group using the facilities for her own artwork. She found that she was enjoying clay modeling. Through another member of the group, she heard about a project to do community art with teenagers. They were looking for volunteer help, and she thought she might give it a try. Our sessions together often included biodynamic massage, and her frozen, startled body thawed. We also continued to use art.*

In one particular session, she made a drawing in pastels of what looked like a long figure without clothes with pink-brown flesh. It had wispy swirls of pinks, brown, and green throughout its length. The pastels gave the figure a slightly misty quality to it and the lines of the figure were hazy. The figure was in the center of the paper. Above it was a large, round, yellow ball with a halo of shining yellow light around it. There were other amorphous shapes in the picture, but nothing very tangible. As I looked at it, I felt that it should have been pleasing to me. The colors were subtle, but the ball and the amorphous shapes did not seem friendly, and the central figure looked unprotected.

As Leela signaled that she had finished her drawing, I asked her if she would like to be any part of the picture. She pointed to the figure. She understood that I was asking her to let herself feel what it was like to embody the figure and so concretize her drawing. She told me that she wanted to curl up and moved toward the cushions and mattress.

She felt "raw," that "everything was too bright," and "there was too much noise." Leela made herself a cocoon of cushions. I closed the curtains. Leela experimented with different positions and eventually settled for placing her back along the wall. I was reminded of the stick figure drawing and its back along the box. She looked out into the room, but had cushions surrounding her in front and at both sides. She asked me to sit next to her, but not to touch her. She said that her skin felt sensitive and her head exposed. She asked me to get her woolly hat and place it on her head and over her eyes. She could still see, but the light of the room was less disturbing to her. I had the impression that she was in an incubator—an implicit memory was alive in the present and being enacted. As I resonated with her, I could sense the unbearable sounds, the searing light, Leela's resourcefulness and determination.

I let Leela guide me in what she needed. She put on her wool mittens and wrapped herself in a blanket. Covered in the blanket, surrounded by cushions, and wearing her woolly hat, she looked comfortably tucked up. I sat with her, without speaking, enjoying her profoundly restful state until it was time to start the ending process of the session.

Reflecting on Concretizations and the Depictions in Creative Media

The choice about how much to speak immediately after such experiences as those of Leela and Jenny has to be a professional decision in the immediacy of the moment by any therapist. Speaking can sometimes diminish the experience and be experienced as intrusive. Frequently, clients are best left to make their own sense of their experiences. How much to give words to the experiences enacted by clients is a theme within the creative arts, as well as what form this wording should take. Reflecting on major trauma and its integration at a deep level, Schaverien writes:

> In the pictures the residual effect, or even particular remembered incidents, can be externalized and so seen at a distance by the artist/client. In their picture these may be put outside for the first time. Subsequently there is a choice; if wished the picture can be shown to another person—the therapist. There is then an additional choice; the picture may be spoken about but it can be expressed without the need for words to describe the indescribable. (Schaverien, 1998, p. 158)

Similarly, Noack believes, "There are also many situations when the movement experience stands for itself and a verbal explanation or interpretation would possibly have detrimental effects" (1992, p. 194).

With Leela, I chose not to speak of the experience at the end of the session, but let her leave with the echoes of the experiences reverberating in her body. Leela's profound state of rest that I resonated with seemed more important than talking about her experiences as a premature baby. We did name these experiences in subsequent sessions.

Reflection Versus Mentalizing

Leela's reflections on her experiences correspond with what Ogden (2009, p. 222) refers to as "directed mindfulness." It involves being curious and kind to recollections, and noticing the embodied experience of what has happened as it is revisited in the present moment. Experiences are unpacked and transformed by the looking back, in the immediacy of now. This is embodied reflection. It is not the same as mentalizing (see Chapter 3), but does not preclude it. With Leela, I emphasized embodied-affective directed mindfulness reflection on her experiences to foster connections with each of her five modes of experience, function, and expression.

External and Internal Body Techniques

Concretization is intended as a principle and not a technique (Holzberg, 1992). However, this may not always be so. Drawing on George Downing (1996), Sletvold has described "experiential and internal body techniques" and "external body techniques." External body techniques instruct the client to do something, or involve the therapist directly doing something to the client. In contrast, there are explorations of internal embodied experience and movement (Sletvold, 2014, p. 36). Downing writes specifically about the movement aspects of the body. An external technique might be exaggerating a way of breathing, or taking up a particular body position, for example the vegetotherapy session with Peter (Chapter 7). External techniques stimulate feelings that are not yet conscious. In contrast, internal techniques focus on conscious feelings already present, such as a small movement or gesture (Downing, 2001). Again, we have seen examples of this, especially in Chapter 7.

While I have a clinical preference for relating to movements emerging spontaneously from clients, I also set up structures and provide items such as art materials for some clients such as Leela, and suggest that clients use them to explore their inner experience. This way of working is a collaborative and interactive exploration, rather than doing something to the client (an intervention). As a starting point for explorations, setting up such structures lies somewhere in between Downing's internal and external techniques.

There are also times to use body techniques such as a grounding exercise. This might be necessary, for example, when a client is strongly dissociating. A grounding exercise delivered in a matter-of-fact tone, with short rein holding and from a place of connection with the client, can often bring a client back quite quickly. The grounding exercise can then become a useful resource for the client in daily life. Another use of a body technique is the holding of a particular physical position. Often such positions may involve stretching particular muscle groups and can be used to begin to build some awareness in a numb body (see Rothschild, 2000). Attention becomes focused on exploring body sensations that arise from staying in one position. Once more, it is a question of being suitably flexible with clients. But let's return to Hector and see how his psychotherapy developed.

Slowly but surely, I came to know Hector. I learned that he was his mother's favorite, her firstborn, and boys were special in her culture. She seemed overprotective and cautioned him about all that could go wrong with things that he or others might initiate. He was not allowed to play sports because he could get injured. He had never learned to swim, and his mother had chosen his friends carefully. These friends were never allowed to visit his home and he spent a lot of time alone in his room reading. His mother could be suspicious and get a fixed idea in her head that took her into intense, unpredictable brooding moods. Perhaps she too had breakdowns.

Hector had lived abroad with his mother's family for lengthy periods—"when she had gone away." As a child, he did not know where she had gone. His father worked away a lot, and Hector's younger sisters spent most of their time in their rooms too. I learned that no one in the family spoke directly to another. Feelings were never, ever mentioned. At mealtimes particular needs had to be inferred. "Someone at the table would like the salt passing to them." Or a comment on behavior might be, "Someone in this room has lost their manners." To voice anything personal and directly was extremely rude, and no one ever did it. It felt extremely confusing and terrifying to me as I heard about it.

In the second year of meeting with Hector, his speech had

become more fluid and with more inflection in it. He rarely really looked at me, but his gaze looked less distant. *And he seemed okay enough as he sensed me looking at him. Reading his weekly narratives meant that my attention was indirectly on him and my intuition was that this was important. He could manage this level of regard without being overwhelmed. In this second year, Hector began to bring in photographs. Initially these were of Marie-Anne. He would pass them to me and then explain when they were taken, what they were doing together at that time, and so on. Later he brought other photographs. This meant that I got out of my chair to sit beside his so that he could explain what the buildings and people were. We were in closer proximity, but our attention was on the photographs. As I moved toward him, I moved in an arc and slowly without being menacing in any way. I did not approach him directly.*

Hector was expanding his repertoire in the five modes of experience, function, and expression. He was intellectual and well developed in the cognitive sphere, but very limited in all of the other modes. He had offered me the realm of the imagination in the form of his literary references early on, but I was seldom able to meet him there as I did not know his cultural references well enough, and it was laborious for him to keep explaining them to me. We did find together ways of extending from his thinking, which was disconnected from his body into some motor activity through small changes in his posture and breathing. This in turn brought tiny changes in the emotional expressivity of his speech.

Rhythms of Relating Using Creative Media

A constant theme with this form of non-verbal relating using creative media is working within the window of tolerance. So with Hector, I did not want to flood him with emotional questions or too much direct interpersonal contact. It was important for him that we were in a one-person dialogue. This was true for Leela too, but she could tolerate more direct contact and more emotionality.

When we use creative media, it helps to keep in mind the overall rhythm and musicality of the session. The creative dialogue has four phases. So with Leela and her use of art materials, there was a warming up phase (1), followed by a deepening into internal processes and depicting them on the paper (2), followed by a coming up from that level of consciousness and being more outer focused (3), and completion of the session (4). Each of the phases requires its own time. So part of coming up and completion with Leela, for example, was gathering up the art materials she had used, replacing them in the boxes, and deciding what she wanted to do with her drawings. Sometimes she wanted to take them away; sometimes she disposed of them, and other times she left them with me for safekeeping.

A WORD ABOUT ENACTMENTS

Some of the ways of clients exploring described in this chapter could be called enactments. Enactments are described somewhat differently in various psychotherapies. Moreno, for example, who developed psychodrama, asked patients in his groups to role-play inner conflicts—a reenactment of them. His maxim was "don't tell us, show us" (Holmes, 1992, p. 91). This is closer to the understanding in this book, in the sense of putting the inside outside, so that it can be explored from a different perspective This does not preclude other ways of conceptualizing enactments. Within the context of psychoanalysis, for example, Jacobs (2005) found the term *enactment* when he was searching for a less judgmental term than *acting out*. He described enactments as "communications in the form of behavior on the part of patient and/or analyst that arose out of the transference-counter-transference interactions" (Jacobs, 2005, p. 174). They always include elements of reenactment. Enactments within this understanding of them are inevitable (see for example, Soth, 2009).

Psychotherapists not used to such overt ways of non-verbal communicating through role-play, movement, and creative media may fear that enactments could become unruly. Once more the skills from Chapter 3 help us here. What mitigates against the unruliness of active ways of working is working from an embodied stance, staying with the process, keeping track of presence, and making continual adjustments. A rule of thumb is that if we become too uncomfortable to stay present to what is unfolding, the process is going too fast and must be slowed down. We can keep track of the relational aspects through reflecting, now and then, on the clarity, compassion, and spaciousness inquiry (see Chapter 3) and we also have the constant feedback of our own and the client's breathing (see Chapter 5). Finally, the creative media themselves also provide holding and containment.

In discussing musical improvisation in therapy, the equivalent of bodily free association (Chapter 7), or the free association of psychoanalysis, Helen Odell-Miller highlights the simultaneous nature and importance of both the attuned relationship and musical improvisation in music therapy: "*Musical form and structure* offer access to things which are difficult for the patients to articulate verbally, without descending into 'acting out' and without transgressing the boundaries of the therapeutic relationship" (Odell-Miller, 2003, p. 155, emphasis added).

Notwithstanding, psychotherapy cannot be therapeutic without some risk. When we listen to the detail of non-verbal communication and let ourselves respond actively, we are bound to be spontaneous and creative. It is this direct, genuine responsiveness that reaches clients and is so often repairing.

CONCLUSION

We have considered some more predominantly non-verbal ways for clients to express themselves and to interact with us. The scope of these activities is broad and the choices can be somewhat bewildering. However, if we let our own creativity and intuition flow, it becomes easier to know how to respond to clients.

The use of creative media has tended to be somewhat neglected more widely in psychotherapy because of the high status that the "talking cure" has had. Creative arts psychotherapies have come of age and proved their worth. They are now bringing their own theoretical understanding of therapeutic processes to the wider psychotherapy discussion. They have much to teach us, and we can take up practices from these therapies to bring more balance to the therapeutic process.

CONCLUSION

GOING ON FROM HERE

Some years ago, in the 1980s, when I was in Jungian analysis with the late Dr. Johanna Brieger, she told me that I was trying to understand myself from the wrong part of my brain. She told me that analysis was a right-brain-to-right-brain endeavor, not a linear process. I felt the rightness of her words in my body, and I still did not understand.

Since then, there is far more understanding, through developments in neuroscience and infant studies, of the significance of right-brain-to-right-brain communications with adult clients for the repair of early insecure attachments, especially for those with early traumatic and disorganized attachments. The general trend is for psychotherapy to be less a "talking cure" and more an "affect communicating and regulating cure" (Schore, 2012, p. 85). Early insecure attachments encoded implicitly in our clients in their breathing, moving, gestures, and ways of speaking demand that we acquire new skills to address these non-verbal dimensions of communicating and the difficulties that clients have with regulating their feelings and physiology.

The challenge across the board in depth psychotherapies is to become more inclusive of non-verbal right-brain-to-right-brain communications without losing the usefulness at times of cognitive, left-brain-dominant ways of relating with clients. This means considering psychotherapy as a process that unfolds rapidly from moment to moment. It demands being intuitive and spontaneous in interactions without always knowing why we have suggested something; it means seizing opportunities for improvising and novelty. This often entails being active and playful, and using creative media for expression, and touch in one's repertoire. It includes the basic assumption that in any relating, two bodyminds are always interacting, not just two minds. Working with a non-verbal focus often involves literally changing positions in the consulting room and communicating in an array of ways with clients. This can make interactions both enjoyable and lively, but it can also be confusing to know where to begin and how to proceed.

The focus is on being with clients. This includes prolonging experiential explorations of emotional states without (too) quickly taking refuge in conceptualizations and explanations of processes. Indeed, clients will often accept conceptualizations and interpretations of their experience, after they have felt that we have also felt with them their experiences. The challenge of being with clients as they are communicating disturbing and often highly charged experiences, if they are more traumatized, can be supported by cultivating mindfulness. This disciplined awareness of staying in protracted moments of being present protects us from the vicissitudes of psychotherapy and enables us to take risks. Mindfulness not only offers us support but enables us to thrive.

Developing psychotherapists for the future demands that their training takes into account new knowledge and theories and makes revisions to existing theory and practice. Some long-held theories within psychotherapy may well have to be jettisoned (e.g., projective identification) and other theories drastically revised (e.g., transference and countertransference) or replaced altogether by more contemporary theory until this too becomes redundant. The inclusion of infant studies, the basic neurology of communication, and the regulation of feelings and physiology is pertinent to the training of all therapists. Some experiential learning is essential for developing confidence and the skills of non-verbal relating. Writing on this theme for qualified analysts, Odell-Miller advocates that "actual experience of music therapy in an experiential workshop could help psychoanalytic psychotherapists in the area of attuning to non-verbal responses, and listening with an acute awareness to what lies behind the words" (2003, p. 165). This is not the only way to acquire experiential learning, but any of the creative arts therapies and body psychotherapy can offer inspiration. Contemporaneously with changes in theory and training, supervision of clinical practice may well have to adapt to include experiential explorations of our clients to gain more "lived understanding" (Sletvold, 2014).

The psychotherapy profession is dogged by sectarian rivalries and in any paradigm shift, change is frightening and challenges our familiar ways of offering psychotherapy. As neuroscience and infant studies are relevant to all psychotherapies they provide us with a third (metalevel) position through which we can dialogue with other modalities of psychotherapy. This third position gives us a perspective where we can tackle the reappraisals of our clinical work from more distance and with freshness. An opening question for us to ponder in discussions might be: How is our work changing in the light of new findings? What might be redundant now? What must be included that was excluded? What can be included with a new twist? What are the implications of this for public policy, particularly related to early child care and provision? My hope is that psychotherapy will gradually become less sectarian and less imbued with "schoolism" through respectful dialogue.

In addition to new understanding from neuroscience and infant studies, it has been observed that "mindfulness has potential to link different schools, research and practice and personal and professional of therapists" (Germer & Siegel, 2012, p. 10, citing Germer et al., 2005, p. 20). In fact, "we may be on the threshold of a new, mindfulness-oriented model of psychotherapy" (Germer, 2005, p. 19).

In terms of the polarization of verbal and non-verbal processes, Andersen offers us another way of considering these as "expressions":

Language encompasses all kinds of expressions. Dancing is part of language; so is screaming, hitting, painting, writing, cooking soups—those are all part of my definition of language. There are many other expressions. What they have in common is that language is physical, bodily activity. (Andersen, 2012, p. 31)

For some clients, most of the therapeutic process will involve change at the non-verbal level that is never explicitly known. Indeed, verbalization is not necessary (e.g., Beebe & Lachmann, 2014; Lyons-Ruth, 1998). And, while there is a demand to include non-verbal processes in psychotherapy, it remains important not to lose sight of the contribution of more left-brain-dominant ways of interacting with clients. Gradually, it is to be hoped that in clinical practice there is more integration of verbal and non-verbal ways of interacting with our clients. However, we should keep a close eye on the amount of verbal communication and thinking going on, as it is all too easy for these to take precedence over the non-verbal. Hopefully, this book will make a small contribution to the paradigm shift going on. Ironically, while the subject is non-verbal communication, the form of a book is the written word and the communication of a lot of concepts and ideas.

In the final analysis, psychotherapy is about personal growth, our own and our clients'. If we are to invite the wholeness of our clients, we must become more whole ourselves.

> The basic work of health professionals in general, and of psychotherapists in particular, is to become full human beings and to inspire full human-beingness in other people who feel starved about their lives. When we say a full human being here, we mean a person who not only eats, sleeps, walks and talks, but someone who experiences a basic state of wakefulness. (Trungpa, 1983, p. 126)

GLOSSARY

awareness practices: Practices taken from meditation to cultivate expanded states of consciousness.

bodymind: Term coined by body psychotherapists to describe the unity of mind and body. It challenges dualistic thinking. Usually spelled as one word, rather than two words hyphenated.

boundaries: The experience of being separate from others and the world and in harmony with others. Boundaries are flexible—neither too rigid nor too loose. The flexibility enables others to be closer or kept further away. This includes energetic boundaries that extend beyond the physicality of individuals. Protective or defensive boundaries develop in early caregiver and baby relationships through inadequate attunements.

charge: Increased intensity of excitement in the body through sympathetic nervous system activity, such as breathing more quickly.

concretization: The process of an internal experience—psychological, emotional, conceptual—being made more physical and represented in movement and posture. The internal experience can also be symbolized with objects, sounds, music, and art forms. In doing this, different experiences of oneself are felt, which lead to fuller self-awareness. Also known as an enactment.

constellate: The process of forming the relationship between client and therapist afresh on each meeting. Implicit in this is that each therapist and client form a relationship unique to them.

contact: Being present, connecting with ourselves, connecting with another, and having a direct and immediate sense of another. The absence of contact with others is a palpable experience of alienation and profound loneliness.

dead talk: Talking without vitality and self-expression, a form of protection developed in babyhood.

embodied: Being embodied is a level of consciousness—being aware of our own body sensations and how these continually change with our thoughts, moods, and feelings. Embodied individuals make graceful, flowing movements and look alive. Being embodied fluctuates and includes aspects such as embodied thinking, embodied sensing, embodied feeling, embodied reflecting, and so on. For example, embodied thinking is experiencing thinking through the body and being aware of the bodily counterparts of thoughts and thinking patterns.

enactment: Term used in expressive psychotherapies for putting thoughts, feelings and imaginings into an externalized form such as a posture, movement or sound. See also concretization.

energy: The term has different meanings in different contexts. It is used loosely in this book and it is left to readers to make up their own minds about energy. Energy is a metaphor for breath and movement. It is a palpable force felt by highly trained individuals such as acupuncturists. Terms for it include *chi*, *ki*, and *prana*. In this context, all life is energy. Human beings are massed energy, and we exist in an energetic field. Universal energy is a synonym for the Divine.

essential self: The energetic expression of the soul through the body, also used synonymously with universal energy, God, inherent health, Buddha nature.

grounding: A fluctuating state of being present and in reality, connecting to the world, especially through sensing the legs and feet firmly planted on the ground, but can include grounding through any part of the body touching something external and any of the senses—seeing, hearing, and so on. Being ungrounded is being spaced out, having one's head in the clouds.

mentalizing: Thinking about thoughts and inferring the thoughts of others.

mindfulness: Being in the present moment, as it is, with no preferences for it to be other than it is.

Presence: Universal consciousness cultivated especially through the discipline of regular meditation practice.

psychoperistalsis: Term coined by Gerda Boyesen (1980) for her speculative ideas on the digestive system "digesting" experiences, including emotions and stress.

reflecting: (Embodied) reflecting is being aware of thoughts, feelings, and imaginings by experiencing them through the body.

resonance: Directly experiencing the inner (implicit) processes of others, often, but not always physically felt.

rooted talking: Talking in a lively manner and with whole body movements. The words and phrases of rooted talking express inner states and move us emotionally.

somatic resonance: The direct experience of another's feelings, bodily sensations, and thinking through one's own body.

vegetotherapy: Development of psychoanalysis by Wilhelm Reich, which focuses on regulating the autonomic nervous system

REFERENCES

Ainsworth, M. D. S., Bell, S. M., Blehar, M. C., & Main, M. (1971). *Physical contact: A study of infant responsiveness and its relation to maternal handling.* Paper presented at the biennial meeting of the Society for Research in Child Development, Minneapolis, MN.

Ainsworth, M. D. S., Blehar, M. C., Waters, E., & Wall, S. (1978). *Patterns of attachment: A psychological study of the strange situation.* Hillsdale, NJ: Lawrence Erlbaum.

Andersen, T. (1991a). Basic concepts and practical constructions. In T. Andersen (Ed.), *The reflecting team: Dialogues and dialogues about the dialogues* (pp. 15–41). London: Norton.

Andersen, T. (Ed.). (1991b). *The reflecting team: Dialogues and dialogues about the dialogues.* London: Norton.

Andersen, T. (2007a). Human participating: Human "being" is the step for human "becoming" in the next step. In H. Anderson & D. Gehart (Eds.), *Collaborative therapy: Relationships and conversations that make a difference* (pp. 81–107). New York: Routledge.

Andersen, T. (2007b). Reflecting talks may have many versions: Here is mine. *International Journal of Psychotherapy, 11*(2), 27–44.

Andersen, T. (2012). Words: Universes traveling by. In T. Malinen, S. J. Cooper, & F. N. Thomas (Eds.), *Masters of narrative and col-*

laborative therapies: The voices of Andersen, Anderson, and White (pp. 17–61). London: Routledge.

Aposhyan, S. (2004). *Body-mind psychotherapy: Principles, techniques and practical applications.* New York: Norton.

Asheri, S. (2009). To touch or not to touch: A relational body psychotherapy perspective. In L. Hartley (Ed.), *Contemporary body psychotherapy: The Chiron approach* (pp. 106–120). London: Routledge.

Aviezer, H., Trope, Y., & Todorov, A. (2012). Body cues, not facial expressions, discriminate between intense positive and negative emotions. *Science, 338*(6111), 1225–1229.

Bateson, M. C. (1975). Mother-infant exchanges: The epigenesis of conversational interaction. In D. Aronson & R. Rieber (Eds.), *Developmental psycholinguistics and communication disorders. Annals of the New York Academy of Sciences, 263,* 101–113.

Beebe, B., & Lachmann, F. M. (2002). *Infant research and adult treatment: Co-constructing Interactions.* London: Analytic Press.

Beebe, B., & Lachmann, F. M. (2014). *The origins of attachment: Infant research and adult treatment.* London: Routledge.

Beebe, B., Lachmann, F. M., Markese, S., & Bahrick, L. (2012). On the origins of disorganised attachment and internal working models: Paper I. A dyadic systems approach. *Psychoanalytic Dialogues, 22*(2), 253–272.

Beebe, B., Lachmann, F. M., Markese, S., Buck, K. A., Bahrick, L., Chen, H., Cohen, P., Andrew, H., Feldstein, S., & Jaffe, J. (2012). On the origins of disorganised attachment and internal working models: Paper II. An empirical microanalysis of 4-month mother-infant interaction. *Psychoanalytic Dialogues, 22*(3), 352–374.

Ben-Shahar, A. (2012). A therapeutic anatomy: An historical and theoretical review of body-psychotherapy. *Attachment, 6,* 73–93.

Bien, T. (2008). The four immeasurable minds: Preparing to be present in psychotherapy. In T. Bien & S. F. Hick (Eds.), *Mindfulness and the therapeutic relationship* (pp. 37–55). London: Guilford.

Bion, W. R. (1984). *Learning from experience.* London: Maresfield Library, Karnac.

Blechschmidt, E. (2004). *The ontogenetic basis of human anatomy: A biodynamic approach to development from conception to birth.* Berkeley: North Atlantic. Translated from Blechschmidt, E. (1978).

Anatomie and Ontogenese des Menschen. Heidelberg: Quelle and Meyer.

Bloom, K. (2006). *The embodied self: Movement and psychoanalysis.* London: Karnac.

Boadella, D. (1982). Transference, resonance and interference. *Journal of Biodynamic Psychology, 3*, 54–73.

Boadella, D. (1987). *Lifestreams: An introduction to biosynthesis.* London: Routledge and Kegan Paul.

Boadella, D. (2000a). The historical development of the concept of the motoric fields. *Energy and Character, 30*(2), 18–21.

Boadella, D. (2000b). Shape flow and postures of the soul: The biosynthesis concept of the motoric fields. *Energy and Character, 30*(2), 7–17.

Boening, M., Southwell, C., & Westland, G. (2012, July). *UK body psychotherapy competencies.* Available as a downloadable PDF from http://www.eabp.org/forum-body-psychotherapy-competencies.php and http://www.cbpc.org.uk/

Borofsky, R., & Borofsky, A. K. (2012). The heart of couple therapy. In C. K. Germer, R. D. Siegel, & P. R. Fulton (Eds.), *Wisdom and compassion in psychotherapy: Deepening mindfulness in clinical practice and psychotherapy* (pp. 280–293). New York: Guilford.

Bosanquet, C. (1970). Getting in touch. *Journal of Analytical Psychology, 15*(1), 42–57.

Bosanquet, C. (2006). Symbolic understanding of tactile communication in psychotherapy. In G. Galton (Ed.), *Touch papers: Dialogues on touch in the psychoanalytic space* (pp. 29–48). London: Karnac.

Bowlby, J. (1979). *The making and breaking of affectional bonds.* London: Routledge.

Boyce-Tillman, J. (2005). Subjugated ways of knowing. In C. Clarke (Ed.), *Ways of knowing: Science and mysticism today* (pp. 8–33). Exeter: Imprint Academic.

Boyesen, G. (1976). The primary personality and its relationship to the streamings. In D. Boadella (Ed.), *In the wake of Reich* (pp. 81–98). London: Coventure.

Boyesen, G. (1980). *Biodynamic psychology: The collected papers* (Vols. 1 & 2). London: Biodynamic Psychology Publications. Originally published as a series of articles in *Energy and Character: The Journal of Biosynthesis.*

References

Boyesen, G. (2006). How I developed biodynamic psychotherapy. In J. Corrigall, H. Payne, & H. Wilkinson (Eds.), *About a body: Working with the embodied mind in psychotherapy* (pp. 132–139). London: Routledge.

Braatøy, T. (1954). *Fundamentals of psychoanalytic technique: A fresh appraisal of the methods of psychotherapy.* New York: John Wiley.

Brandon, D. (1990). *Zen in the art of helping.* London: Arkana. (Original work published 1976)

Brazelton, T. B. (1983). *Infants and mothers: Differences in development.* New York: Dell.

Brazelton, T. B., & Cramer, B. G. (1991). *The Earliest Relationship.* London: Karnac.

Brazelton, T. B., & Nugent, K. (2011). *Neonatal Behavioral Assessment Scale* (4th ed.). London: Mac Keith Press.

Bretherton, I. (1992). The origins of attachment theory: John Bowlby and Mary Ainsworth. *Developmental Psychology, 28,* 759–775.

Buber, M. (2002). *Between man and man.* London: Routledge Classics.

Bugental, J. F. T. (1978). *Psychotherapy and process: The fundamentals of an existential-humanistic approach.* London: Addison-Wesley.

Bugental, J. F. T. (1987). *The art of the psychotherapist: How to develop the skills that take psychotherapy beyond science.* New York: Norton.

Bunt, L. (1994). *Music therapy: An art beyond words.* London: Routledge.

Calmes, S. A., Piazza, N. J., & Laux, J. M. (2013). The use of touch in counselling: An ethical decision-making model. *Counselling and Values, 58,* 59–68.

Cannon, W. B. (1927). *Bodily changes in pain, hunger, fear and rage: An account of recent researches into the function of emotional excitement.* New York: Appleton.

Capra, F. (1996). *The web of life: A new understanding of living systems.* New York: Anchor.

Carroll, R. (2000). Biodynamic massage in psychotherapy: Re-integrating, re-owning and re-associating through the body. In T. Staunton (Ed.), *Body psychotherapy* (pp. 78–100). London: Routledge.

Carroll, R. (2009). Self regulation at the heart of body psychotherapy. In L. Hartley (Ed.), *Contemporary body psychotherapy: The Chiron approach* (pp. 89–105). London: Routledge.

Carroll, R. (2011). In search of a vocabulary of embodiment. *Body, Movement and Dance in Psychotherapy, 6*(3), 245–257.

Casement, P. (2002). *Learning from our mistakes: Beyond dogma in psychoanalysis and psychotherapy.* New York: Guilford.

Christiansen, B. (1972). *Thus speaks the body: Attempts toward a personology from the point of view of respiration and postures.* New York: Arno.

Cigolla, F., & Brown, D. (2011). A way of being: Bringing mindfulness into individual therapy. *Psychotherapy Research, 21*(6), 709–721.

Clark, D. H. (1964). *Administrative therapy: The role of the doctor in the therapeutic community.* London: Tavistock.

Clark, D. H. (1981). *Social therapy in psychiatry* (2nd ed.). Edinburgh: Churchill Livingstone.

Cornell, W. F. (1998). Touch and boundaries in transactional analysis: Ethical and transferential considerations. In *Creating our community: Proceedings, first national conference of the U.S. Association for Body Psychotherapy.* Boulder, CO: U.S. Association for Body Psychotherapy.

Cozolino, L. (2002). *The neuroscience of psychotherapy: Building and rebuilding the human brain.* New York: Norton.

Cross, I., & Morley, I. (2009). The evolution of music: Theories, definitions and the nature of the evidence. In S. Malloch & C. Trevarthen (Eds.), *Communicative musicality: Exploring the basis of human communication* (pp. 61–83). Oxford: Oxford University Press.

Damasio, A. (1994). *Descartes' error: Emotion, reason and the human brain.* London: Picador.

Damasio, A. (2000). *The feeling of what happens: Body, emotion and the making of consciousness.* London: Vintage.

Darwin, C. (1998). *The expression of the emotions in man and animals.* London: HarperCollins. (Original work published 1892)

Davis, W. (1984). Working with the instroke. *Energy and Character, 15*(1), 17–25.

Davis, W. (2001). Energetics and therapeutic touch. In M. Heller (Ed.), *The flesh of the soul: The body we work with: Selected papers of the 7th Congress of the European Association of Body Psychotherapy, 2–6 September 1999, Travemünde* (pp. 59–80). Bern: Peter Lang.

Donington, L. (1994). *Core process psychotherapy.* In D. Jones (Ed.),

Innovative therapy: A handbook (pp. 50–68). Milton Keynes, UK: Open University Press.

Downing, G. (1996). *Körper und Wort in der Psychotherapie: Leitlinien für der Praxis* [Body and word in psychotherapy: Principles of practice]. Munich: Kösel.

Downing, G. (2001). Bodies and motion. In M. Heller (Ed.), *The flesh of the soul: The body we work with* (pp. 285–293). Bern: Peter Lang.

Eiden, B. (1998). The body in psychotherapy: The use of touch in psychotherapy. *Self and Society, 26*(2), 3–41.

Eiden, B. (2002). Application of a post-Reichian body psychotherapy: A Chiron perspective. In T. Staunton (Ed.), *Body psychotherapy* (pp. 27–56). London: Routledge.

Ekman, P. (2004). *Emotions revealed: Understanding faces and feelings.* London: Phoenix.

Epstein, M. (1995). *Thoughts without a thinker.* New York: Basic Books.

Esteve-Gilbert, N., & Prieto, P. (2013). Infants temporally coordinate gesture-speech combinations before they produce their first words. *Speech Communication, 57,* 301–316.

Field, T. (2003). *Touch.* London: MIT Press.

Field, T., Hernandez-Reif, M., Hart, S., Quintino, O., Drose, L., Field, T., Kuhn, C., & Schanberg, S. (1997). Effects of sexual abuse are lessened by massage therapy. *Journal of Bodywork and Movement Therapies, 1,* 65–69.

Field, T., Ironson, G., Scafidi, F., Nawrocki, T., Goncalves, A., Burman, I., Pickens, J., Fox, N., Schanberg, S., & Kuhn, C. (1996). Massage therapy reduces anxiety and enhances EEG pattern of alertness and math computations. *International Journal of Neuroscience, 86,* 197–205.

Field, T., Schanberg, S. M., Scafidi, F., Bauer, C. R., Vega-Lahr, N., Garcia, R., Nystom, J., & Kuhn, C. M. (1986). Tactile/kinesthetic stimulation effects on pre-term neonates. *Pediatrics, 77,* 654–658.

Fogel, A. (2009). *The psychophysiology of self-awareness: Rediscovering the lost art of body sense.* New York: Norton.

Fonagy, P., Gergely, G., Jurist, E. L., & Target, M. (2002). *Affect regulation, mentalization, and the development of the self.* New York: Other Press.

Fosha, D. (2009). Emotion and recognition at work: Energy, vitality, pleasure, truth, desire, and the emergent phenomenology of transformational experience. In D. Fosha, D. J. Siegel, & M. F. Solomon (Eds.), *The healing power of emotion: Affective neuroscience, development and clinical practice* (pp. 172–203). New York: Norton.

Fosshage, J. L. (2009). To touch or not to touch in the psychoanalytic arena. In B. Willock, R. C. Curtis, & L. C. Bohm (Eds.), *Taboo or not taboo? Forbidden thoughts, forbidden acts in psychoanalysis and psychotherapy* (pp. 353–361). London: Karnac.

Freud, S., & Breuer, J. (2004). *Studies on hysteria*. London: Penguin Classics. (Original work published 1895)

Fried, R. (1990). *The breath connection: How to reduce psychosomatic and stress-related disorders with easy-to-do breathing exercises.* New York: Plenum.

Fulton, P. R. (2005). Mindfulness as clinical training. In C. K. Germer, R. D. Siegel, & P. R. Fulton (Eds.), *Mindfulness and psychotherapy* (pp. 55–72). New York: Guilford.

Gallese, V., Fadiga, L., Fogassi, L., & Rizzolatti, G. (1996). Action recognition in the premotor cortex. *Brain, 119,* 593–609.

Gaskin, I. M. (1977). *Spiritual midwifery*. Summertown, TN: Book.

Gendlin, E. (1981). *Focusing* (2nd ed.). London: Bantam.

Gendlin, E. (1996). *Focusing-oriented psychotherapy: A manual of the experiential method.* London: Guilford.

Germer, C. (2005). Mindfulness: What is it? What does it matter? In C. K. Germer, R. D. Siegel, & P. R. Fulton (Eds.), *Mindfulness and psychotherapy* (pp. 3–27). New York: Guilford.

Germer, C. K., & Siegel, R. D. (2012). (Eds.). *Wisdom and compassion in psychotherapy: Deepening mindfulness in clinical practice.* New York: Guilford.

Germer, C. K., Siegel, R. D., & Fulton, P. R. (2005). (Eds.). *Mindfulness and psychotherapy.* New York: Guilford.

Gershon, M. D. (1998). *The second brain.* New York: HarperPerennial.

Gilbert, M., & Orlans, V. (2011). *Integrative therapy: 100 key points and techniques.* London: Routledge.

Gomez, V. (1997). *An introduction to object relations.* London: Free Association.

Greenfield, S. (1998). *The human brain: A guided tour.* London: Phoenix.

Hanh, T. N. (1998). *The heart of the Buddha's teaching: Transforming suffering into peace, joy and liberation.* London: Rider.

Hanh, T. N. (2001). *Transformation at the base: Fifty verses on the nature of consciousness.* Berkeley, CA: Parallax.

Harlow, H. F., & Harlow, M. (1966). Learning to love. *American Scientist, 54*(3), 244–272.

Hebb, D. O. (1949). *The organisation of behaviour.* New York: Wiley.

Heller, M. C. (2007a). The golden age of body psychotherapy in Oslo I: From gymnastic to psychoanalysis. *Body, Movement and Dance in Psychotherapy, 2*(1), 5–15.

Heller, M. C. (2007b). The golden age of body psychotherapy in Oslo II: From vegetotherapy to non-verbal communication. *Body, Movement and Dance in Psychotherapy, 2*(2), 81–94.

Heller, M. C. (2012). *Body psychotherapy: History, concepts and methods.* New York: Norton.

Heller, M., & Haynal-Redmond, V. (1997). The doctor's face: A mirror of his suicidal projects. In J. Guimón (Ed.), *The body in psychotherapy* (pp. 46–50). Basel: Karger.

Hesse, E., & Main, M. (1999). Second-generation effects of unresolved trauma as observed in non-maltreating parents: Dissociated, frightened and threatening parental behavior. *Psychoanalytic Inquiry, 19,* 481–540.

Heuer, G. (2005). "In my flesh I shall see God": Jungian body psychotherapy. In N. Totton (Ed.), *New dimensions in body psychotherapy* (pp. 102–114). Maidenhead, UK: Open University Press.

Hick, S. F., & Bien, T. (2008). *Mindfulness and the therapeutic relationship.* London: Guilford.

Holmes, J. (1993). Attachment theory: A biological basis for psychotherapy? *British Journal of Psychiatry, 163,* 430–438.

Holmes, P. (1992). *The Inner World Outside, Object Relations Theory and Psychodrama.* London: Routledge.

Holmes, P., & Farnfield, S. (2014). Overview: Attachment theory, assessment and implications. In P. Holmes & S. Farnfield (Eds.), *The Routledge handbook of attachment: Theory* (pp. 1–10). London: Routledge.

Holzberg, O. (1992). Concretisation: A principle in body psychotherapy. In B. Maul (Ed.), *Body psychotherapy or the art of contact* (pp. 180–192). Berlin: Bernard Maul.

Howell, M., & Whitehead, J. (1988). *Survive stress: A training programme*. Cambridge, UK: Health Promotion Service Cambridge.

Hunter, M., & Struve, J. (1998). *The ethical use of touch in psychotherapy*. London: Sage.

Iverson, J. M., & Fagan, M. K. (2004). Infant vocal coordination: Precursor to the gesture-speech system? *Child Development, 75*(4), 1053–1066.

Jacobs, T. J. (2005). Discussion of forms of intersubjectivity in infant research and adult treatment. In B. Beebe, S. Knoblauch, J. Rustin, & D. Sorter (Eds.), *Forms of intersubjectivity in infant research and adult treatment* (pp. 165–189). New York: Other Press.

Jacoby, M. (1986). Getting in touch and touching in analysis. In N. Schwartz-Salant & M. Stein (Eds.), *The body in analysis* (pp. 109–126). Wilmette, IL: Chiron.

Johanson, G. J. (2014). Somatic psychotherapy and the ambiguous face of research. *International Body Psychotherapy Journal, 13*(2), 61–85.

Johnson, S. M. (1994). *Character styles*. New York: Norton.

Kabat-Zinn, J. (2001). *Full catastrophe living: How to cope with stress, pain and illness using mindfulness meditation*. London: Piatkus.

Kahr, B. (2006). Winnicott's experiments with physical contact: Creative innovation or chaotic impingement? In G. Galton (Ed.), *Touch papers: Dialogues on touch in the psychoanalytic space* (pp. 1–14). London: Karnac.

Kapila, M., & Dixon, M. (1987). *Promoting community mental health: An experience of general practice based relaxation groups. Final report August 1987*. Unpublished document, Cambridge Health Authority, Cambridge, UK.

Keleman, S. (1970). Bio-energetic concepts of grounding. *Energy and Character, 1*(3), 10–19.

Keleman, S. (1979). *Somatic reality: Bodily experience and emotional truth*. Berkeley, CA: Center Press.

Keleman, S. (1981). *Your body speaks its mind*. Berkeley, CA: Center Press.

Keleman, S. (1986). *Bonding: A somatic-emotional approach to transference*. Berkeley, CA: Center Press.

Keleman, S. (1989). *Patterns of distress, emotional insults and human form*. Berkeley, CA: Center Press.

Kepner, J. (1987). *Body process: A gestalt approach to working with the body in psychotherapy.* New York: Gardner.

Kernberg, O. F. (2004). *Borderline conditions and pathological narcissism.* New York: Jason Aronson, Rowman and Littlefield. (Original work published 1975).

Khoury, B., Lecomte, T., Fortin, G., Masse, M., Therien, P., Bouchard, V., Chapleay, M.-A., Paquin, K., & Hofmann, S. G. (2013). Mindfulness-based therapy: A comprehensive meta-analysis. *Clinical Psychology Review, 33*(6), 763–771.

Kindborg, M. (2013). Rosen movements and words. *Rosen Method International Journal, 6*(1), 29–44.

Knoblauch, S. (2000). *The musical edge of therapeutic dialogue.* London: Analytic Press.

Kornfield, J. (2008). *The wise heart: Buddhist psychology for the West.* London: Rider.

Kuhn, T. (1970). *The structure of scientific revolutions.* Chicago: University of Chicago Press.

Kupfermann, K. (1998). Cancer as a factitious disorder (Munchausen syndrome) related to body self-image and object relations in a borderline patient. In L. Aron & F. Sommer Anderson (Eds.), *Relational perspectives on the body* (pp. 139–171). Hillsdale, NJ: Analytic Press.

Kurtz, R. (1990). *Body-centered psychotherapy: The Hakomi method.* Menocino, CA: Life Rhythm.

Laing, R. D. (1977). *The Facts of Life.* Harmondsworth, UK: Penguin.

Laban, R., & Lawrence, F. C. (1974). *Effort.* London: MacDonald and Evans.

LeDoux, J. (1998). *The emotional brain.* London: Phoenix.

Liss, J. (1974). Why touch? *Energy and Character, 5*(2), 1–8.

Liss, J. (1996). The identification method: An innovation in therapeutic language that favors the growing impulse and diminishes interpersonal defenseiveness. *Energy and Character, 27*(2), 45–60.

Lorenz, K. Z. (1953). *King Solomon's ring.* London: Reprint Society.

Lowen, A. (1971). *The language of the body.* New York: Collier.

Lowen, A. (1975). *Bioenergetics.* New York: Penguin.

Lyons-Ruth, K. (1998). Implicit relational knowing: Its role in development and psychoanalytic treatment. *Infant Mental Health Journal, 19*, 282–289.

Mace, C. (2007). *Mindfulness and mental health*. London: Routledge.

Mahrer, A. (1983). *Experiential psychotherapy: Basic practices*. New York: Brunner/Mazel.

Maiello, S. (1995). The sound-object. *Journal of Child Psychotherapy, 21*(1), 23–41.

Maiello, S. (1997). Sound-aspects in mother-infant observation. In S. Reid (Ed.), *Developments in infant observation: The Tavistock model* (pp. 157–173). London: Routledge.

Main, M., & Solomon, J. (1986). Discovery of an insecure-disorganized/disoriented attachment pattern. In T. B. Brazelton & M. W. Yogman (Eds.), *Affective development in infancy* (pp. 95–124). Westport, CT: Ablex.

Malinen, T., Cooper, S. J., & Thomas, F. N. (Eds.). (2012). *Masters of narrative and collaborative therapies: The voices of Andersen, Anderson, and White*. London: Routledge.

Malloch, S., & Trevarthen, C. (Eds.) (2010a). *Communicative musicality: Exploring the basis of human communication*. Oxford: Oxford University Press.

Malloch, S., & Trevarthen, C. (2010b). Musicality: Communicating the vitality and interests of life. In S. Malloch & C. Trevarthen (Eds.), *Communicative musicality: Exploring the basis of human communication* (pp. 1–11). Oxford: Oxford University Press.

Marcher, L., & Fich, S. (2010). *Body encyclopedia: A guide to the psychological functions of the muscular system*. Berkeley, CA: North Atlantic.

Marks-Tarlow, T. (2013). *Clinical intuition in psychotherapy: The neurobiology of embodied response*. New York: Norton.

Marwick, H., & Murray, L. (2010). The effects of maternal depression on the "musicality" of infant-directed speech and conversational engagement. In S. Malloch & C. Trevarthen (Eds.), *Communicative musicality: Exploring the basis of human communication* (pp. 281–300). Oxford: Oxford University Press.

Maslow, A. H. (1973). *The farther reaches of human nature*. Harmondsworth, UK: Penguin.

Maturana, H. R., & Varela, F. J. (1991). *The tree of knowledge*. Boston: Shambhala.

McGilchrist, I. (2009a). The divided brain and the making of the Western world. *Network Review*, Winter, 3–6.

McGilchrist, I. (2009b). *The master and his emissary: The divided brain and the making of the Western world*. New Haven, CT: Yale University Press.

McNeely, D. A. (1987). *Touching, body therapy and depth psychology*. Toronto: Inner City.

McNeur, L. A. (2008). The intimate dance of being, building, body and psychotherapy. *Body, Movement and Dance in Psychotherapy*, *3*(1), 19–31.

Merleau-Ponty, M. (1986). *Phenomenology of perception*. London: Routledge.

Mintz, E. E. (1969). Touch and the psychoanalytic tradition. *Psychoanalytic Review*, *56*, 365–376.

Montagu, A. (1986). *Touching: The human significance of the skin*. New York: Harper and Row. (Original work published 1971)

Montgomery, A. (2013). *Neurobiology essentials for clinicians: What every therapist needs to know*. New York: Norton.

Noack, A. (1992). On a Jungian approach to dance movement therapy. In H. Payne (Ed.), *Dance movement therapy: Theory and practice* (pp. 182–202). London: Routledge.

Nolan, P. (2012). *Therapist and client: A relational approach to psychotherapy*. Chichester, UK: Wiley-Blackwell.

Odell-Miller, H. (2003). Are words enough? Music therapy as an influence. In L. King & R. Randall (Eds.), *The future of psychoanalytic psychotherapy* (pp. 153–166). London: Whurr.

Ogden, P. (2009). Emotion, mindfulness, and movement: Expanding the regulatory boundaries of the window of tolerance. In D. Fosha, D. J. Siegel, & M. F. Solomon (Eds.), *The healing power of emotion: Affective neuroscience, development and clinical practice* (pp. 204–231). New York: Norton.

Ogden, P., Minton, K., & Pain, C. (2006). *Trauma and the body: A sensorimotor approach to psychotherapy*. London: Norton.

Onozawa, K., Glover, V., Admas, D., Modi, N., & Kumar, R. C. (2001). Infant massage improves mother-infant interaction for mothers with postnatal depression. *Journal of Affective Disorders*, *63*(1–2), 201–207.

Orbach, S. (2009). *Bodies*. London: Profile.

Orbach, S., & Carroll, R. (2006). Contemporary approaches to the body in psychotherapy: Two psychotherapists in dialogue. In J. Corrigall, H. Payne, & H. Wilkinson (Eds.), *Working with the embodied mind in psychotherapy* (pp. 63–82). Hove, UK: Routledge.

Ostafin, B. D., & Kassman, K. T. (2012). Stepping out of history: Mindfulness improves insight problem solving. *Consciousness and Cognition, 21*(2), 1031–1036.

Pally, R. (2000). *The mind-brain relationship.* London: Karnac.

Pally, R. (2001). A primary role for non-verbal communication in psychoanalysis. *Psychoanalytic Inquiry, 21*(1), 71–93.

Panhofer, H., & Payne, H. (2011). Languaging the embodied experience. *Body, Movement and Dance in Psychotherapy, 6*(3), 215–232.

Panksepp, J. (1998). *Affective neuroscience: The foundations of human and animal emotions.* New York: Oxford University Press.

Panksepp, J. (2009). Brain emotional systems and qualities of mental life: From animal models of affect to implications for psychotherapeutics. In D. Fosha, D. Siegel, & M. F. Solomon (Eds.), *The healing power of emotion: Affective neuroscience, development and clinical practice* (pp. 1–27). New York: Norton.

Panksepp, J., & Biven, L. (2012). *The archaeology of Mind: Neuroevolutionary origins of human emotions.* New York: Norton.

Pervöltz, R. (1982). Aspects of biodynamic gestalt. *Journal of Biodynamic Psychology, 3,* 123–139.

Pierrakos, J. (1969). The voice and feeling. Lecture II. In *Self-expression: New developments in bioenergetic therapy.* New York: Institute for Bioenergetic Analysis.

Pierrakos, J. (1987). *Core energetics: Developing the capacity to love and Heal.* Mendocino, CA: LifeRhythm.

Pinson, B. (2002). Touch in therapy: An effort to make the unknown known. *Journal of Contemporary Psychotherapy, 32*(2/3), 179–196.

Porges, S. (2011). *The polyvagal theory: Neurophysical foundations of emotions, attachment, communication, and self-regulation.* New York: Norton.

Prescott, J. W. (1971). Early somatosensory deprivation as an ontogenetic process in abnormal development of the brain and behavior. In I. E. Goldsmith & J. Moor-Jankowski (Eds.), *Medical primatology* (pp. 357–375). Basel: Karger.

Prescott, J. W. (1975, November). Body pleasure and the origins of violence. *Bulletin of the Atomic Scientists,* 10–20.

Prior, V., & Glaser, D. (2006). *Understanding attachment and attach-*

ment disorders, theory, evidence and practice. London: Jessica Kingsley.

Rabin, B., & Walker, R. (1987). A contemplative approach to clinical supervision. *Journal of Contemplative Psychotherapy, 4*, 135–149.

Randall, R., & Southgate, J. (1983). Creativity in self-managed groups. In H. H. Blumberg, P. A. Hare, V. Kent, & M. F. Davies (Eds.), *Small groups and social interaction*. Chichester, UK: John Wiley.

Reich, W. (1970). *Character analysis*. New York: Farrar, Straus and Giroux. (Original work published 1945)

Reich, W. (1983). *The function of the orgasm*. London: Souvenir. (Original work published 1942)

Reid, S. (1997). Introduction: Psychoanalytic infant observation. In S. Reid (Ed.), *Developments in infant observation: The Tavistock model* (pp. 1–14). London: Routledge.

Reyna, B. A. Brown, L. F. Pickler, R.H. Myers, B. J. and Younger, J.B. (2012). Mother–infant synchrony during infant feeding. *Infant Behavior and Development, 35(4)*, 669-677.

Robertson, J., & Robertson, J. (1969). *Young children in brief separation* [film]. Ipswich, UK: Concord Films.

Rolef Ben-Shahar, A. (2014). *Touching the relational edge: Body psychotherapy*. London: Karnac.

Rosen, M., & Brenner, S. (2003). *Rosen method bodywork: Accessing the unconscious through touch*. Berkeley, CA: North Atlantic.

Rosenberg, V. (1995). On touching a patient. *British Journal of Psychotherapy, 12(1)*, 29–36.

Rothschild, B. (2000). *The body remembers: The psychophysiology of trauma and trauma treatment*. New York: Norton.

Rowan, J. (1988). Counselling and the psychology of furniture. *Counselling, 64*, 21–24.

Rubenfeld, I. (2000). *The listening hand: Self-healing through the Rubenfeld synergy method of talk and touch*. New York: Bantam.

Rustin, J. (2013). *Infant research and neuroscience at work in psychotherapy: Expanding the clinical repertoire*. London: Norton.

Rustin, M. (2009). Esther Bick's legacy of infant observation at the Tavistock—some reflections 60 years on. *International Journal of Infant Observation and Its Applications, 12(1)*, 29–41.

Safran, J. D. (2006). *Psychoanalysis and Buddhism*. Boston: Wisdom.

Schaible, M. (2009). Biodynamic massage as a body therapy and as a tool in body psychotherapy. In L. Hartley (Ed.), *Contemporary body psychotherapy: The Chiron approach* (pp. 31–46). London: Routledge.

Schaverien, J. (1995). *Desire and the female therapist: Engendered gazes in psychotherapy and art therapy.* London: Routledge.

Schaverien, J. (1998). Inheritance: Jewish identity, art psychotherapy workshops and the legacy of the Holocaust. In D. Dokter (Ed.), *Arts therapists, refugees and migrants reaching across borders* (pp. 155–173). London: Jessica Kingsley.

Schaverien, J. (2002). *The dying patient in psychotherapy: Desire, dreams and individuation.* Basingstoke, UK: Palgrave Macmillan.

Schaverien, J. (2006). Transference and the meaning of touch: The body in psychotherapy with the client who is facing death. In J. Corrigall, H. Payne, & H. Wilkinson (Eds.), *About a body: Working with the embodied mind in psychotherapy* (pp. 181–198). London: Routledge.

Scherer, K. R. (2003). Foreword. In P. Philippot, R. S. Feldman, & E. J. Coats (Eds.), *The role of non-verbal behaviour in clinical settings: An introduction* (pp. 3–16). Oxford: Oxford University Press.

Schore, A. N. (1994). *Affect regulation and the regulation of the self: The neurobiology of emotional development.* Hillsdale, NJ: Lawrence Erlbaum.

Schore, A. N. (2002). Advances in neuropsychoanalysis, attachment theory, and trauma research: Implications for self-psychology. *Psychoanalytic Inquiry, 22*(3), 433–484.

Schore, A. N. (2003a). *Affect dysregulation and disorders of the self.* New York: Norton.

Schore, A. N. (2003b). *Affect regulation and the repair of the self.* New York: Norton.

Schore, A. N. (2003c). Minds in the making: Attachment, the self-organizing brain, and developmentally oriented psychoanalytic psychotherapy. In J. Corrigall & H. Wilkinson (Eds.), *Revolutionary connection: Psychotherapy and neuroscience* (pp. 7–51). London: Karnac.

Schore, A. N. (2011). The right brain implicit self lies at the core of psychoanalytic psychotherapy. *Psychoanalytic Dialogues, 21,* 75–100.

Schore, A. N. (2012). *The science of the art of psychotherapy.* London: Norton.

Segal, Z. V., Williams, J. M. G., & Teasdale, J. D. (2002). *Mindfulness-based cognitive therapy for depression*. London: Guilford.

Shapiro, S. A. (2009). A rush to action: Embodiment, the analyst's subjectivity, and the interpersonal experience. *Studies in Gender and Sexuality, 10,* 93–103.

Sheldrake, R. (2011). *The presence of the past: Morphic resonance and the habits of nature*. London: Icon.

Siegel, D. J. (1999). *The developing mind. How relationships and the brain interact to shape who we are*. London: Guilford.

Siegel, D. (2010). *The mindful therapist: A clinician's guide to mindsight and neural integration*. New York: Norton.

Sills, F. (2001). *Craniosacral Biodynamics, Volume One, The Breath of Life, Biodyanmics, and Fundamental Skills*. Berkeley, CA: North Atlantic Books.

Sills, F. (2009). *Being and becoming: Psychodynamics, Buddhism, and the origins of selfhood*. Berkeley, CA: North Atlantic.

Sills, M., & Lown, J. (1999). Licking honey from the razor's edge. In G. Watson, S. Batchelor, & G. Claxton (Eds.), *The psychology of awakening: Buddhism, science and our day to day lives* (pp. 187–196). London: Rider.

Sills, M., & Lown, J. (2006). "In this body, a fathom long . . . ": Working with embodied mind and interbeing in psychotherapy. In J. Corrigall, H. Payne, & H. Wilkinson (Eds.), *About a body: Working with the embodied mind in psychotherapy* (pp. 199–212). London: Routledge.

Sills, M., & Lown, J. (2008). The field of subliminal mind and the nature of being. *European Journal of Psychotherapy and Counselling, 10*(1), 71–80.

Sletvold, J. (2014). *The embodied analyst: From Freud to Reich to relationality*. London: Routledge.

Smith, E. (1998). Traditions of touch in psychotherapy. In E. Smith, P. R. Clance, & S. Imes (Eds.), *Touch in psychotherapy: Theory, research and practice* (pp. 3–15). London: Guilford.

Solms, M., & Turnbull, O. (2002). *The brain and the inner world: An introduction to the neuroscience of subjective experience*. London: Karnac.

Soth, M. (2009). From humanistic holism via the "integrative project" towards integral-relational body psychotherapy. In

L. Hartley (Ed.), *Contemporary body psychotherapy: The Chiron approach* (pp. 64-88). London: Routledge.

Southwell, C. (1988). The Gerda Boyesen method: Biodynamic therapy. In J. Rowan & W. Dryden (Eds.), *Innovative therapy in Britain* (pp. 178–201). Milton Keynes, UK: Open University Press.

Southwell, C. (1999). *The biodynamic use of "it-level" and "I-level" language.* In *Soul and Flesh.* Unpublished manuscript.

Southwell, C. (2000). *Rooted talking.* Training paper, London School of Biodynamic Psychotherapy.

Southwell, C. (2010, Winter). Levels of consciousness and contact in biodynamic psychotherapy. *Psychotherapist,* 10–11.

Spitz, R.(1945). Hospitalism; a follow-up report on investigation described in Volume I, 1945. *The Psychoanalytic Study of the Child,* Vol 2, 1946, 113-117

Stauffer, K. A. (2010). *Anatomy and physiology for psychotherapists: Connecting body and soul.* New York: Norton.

Staunton, T. (2002). Sexuality and body psychotherapy. In T. Staunton (Ed.), *Body psychotherapy* (pp. 56–77). Hove, UK: Brunner-Routledge.

Stenzel, C. L., & Rupert, P. A. (2004). Psychologists' use of touch in individual psychotherapy. *Psychotherapy: Theory, Research, Practice, Training, 41*(3), 332–345.

Stern, D. N. (1985). *The interpersonal world of the infant: A view from psycho-analysis and developmental psychology.* New York: Basic Books.

Stern, D. N. (1998). *Diary of a baby: What your child sees, feels and experiences.* New York: Basic Books.

Stern, D. N. (2010). *Forms of vitality: Exploring dynamic experience in psychology: The arts, psychotherapy, and development.* Oxford: Oxford University Press.

Stern, D. N., & Bruschweiler-Stern, N. (1998). *The birth of a mother: How motherhood changes you forever.* London: Bloomsbury.

Surrey, J. L. (2005). Relational psychotherapy, relational mindfulness. In C. K. Germer, R. D. Siegel, & P. R. Fulton (Eds.), *Mindfulness and psychotherapy* (pp. 91–110). New York: Guilford.

Tantia, J. F. (2014). Is intuition embodied? A phenomenological study of clinical intuition in somatic psychotherapy practice. *Body, Movement and Dance in Psychotherapy, 9*(4), 211–223.

Tolle, E. (1999). *The power of now: A guide to spiritual enlightenment.* Novato, CA: New World Library.

Toronto, E. L. K. (2006). A clinician's response to physical touch in the psychoanalytic setting. *International Journal of Psychotherapy, 7*(1), 69–81.

Totton, N. (2003). *Body psychotherapy: An introduction.* Maidenhead, UK: Open University Press.

Totton, N. (2014). Embodied relating: The ground of psychotherapy. *International Body Psychotherapy Journal, 13*(2), 88–103.

Trevarthen, C. (2003). Neuroscience and intrinsic psychodynamics: Current knowledge and potential for therapy. In J. Corrigall & H. Wilkinson (Eds.), *Revolutionary connections: Psychotherapy and neuroscience* (pp. 53–78). London: Karnac.

Truby King, M. (1941). *Mothercraft* (2nd ed.). London: Simpkin, Marshall.

Trungpa, C. (1983). Becoming a full human being. In J. Welwood (Ed.), *Awakening the heart: East/West approaches to psychotherapy and the healing relationship* (pp. 126–131). Boston: Shambhala.

Tune, D. (2001). Is touch a valid therapeutic intervention? Early returns from a qualitative study of therapists' views. *Counselling and Psychotherapy Research, 1*(3), 167–171.

Tune, D. (2005). Dilemmas concerning the ethical use of touch in psychotherapy. In N. Totton (Ed.), *New dimensions in body psychotherapy* (pp. 70–84). Maidenhead, UK: Open University Press.

Uvnäs Moberg, K. (2003). *The oxytocin factor: Tapping the hormone of calm, love and healing.* Boston: Da Capo.

van der Kolk, B. A. (1994). The body keeps the score. *Harvard Review of Psychiatry, 1,* 253–265.

van Deurzen-Smith, E. (2010). *Everyday mysteries: A handbook of existential psychotherapy* (2nd ed.). London: Routledge.

van Rosmalen, L., van Ijzendoorn, M . H., & Bakermans-Kranenburg, M. J. (2014). ABC+D of attachment theory: The Strange Situation procedure as the gold standard of attachment assessment. In P. Holmes & S. Farnfield (Eds.), *The Routledge handbook of attachment theory* (pp. 11–30). London: Routledge.

Wallin, D. J. (2007). *Attachment in psychotherapy.* New York: Guilford.

Warnecke, T. (2009). The therapeutic modality of touch and statutory regulation. *Self and Society, 37*(2), 11–15.

Warnecke, T. (2011). Stirring the depths: Transference, countertransference and touch. *Journal of Body, Movement and Dance in Psychotherapy, 6*(3), 233–243.

Watson, G. (2002). *The resonance of emptiness: A Buddhist inspiration for a contemporary psychotherapy.* London: Routledge Curzon.

Wegela, K. K. (1996). *How to be a help instead of a nuisance: Practical approaches to giving support, service and encouragement to others.* London: Shambhala.

Wegela, K. K. (1999). Hospitality beyond ego: Working with exchange. In G. Watson, S. Batchelor, & G. Claxton (Eds.), *The psychology of awakening: Buddhism, science and our day to day lives* (pp. 294–304). London: Rider.

Wegela, K. K. (2009). *The courage to be present: Buddhism, psychotherapy and the awakening of natural wisdom.* London: Shambhala.

Wegela, K. K. (2014). *Contemplative psychotherapy essentials: Enriching your practice with Buddhist psychology.* New York: Norton.

Weiss, H. (2009). The use of mindfulness in psychodynamic and body oriented psychotherapy. *Body, Movement and Dance in Psychotherapy, 4*(1), 5–16.

Westland, G. (1985). Dipping into community mental health: An aspect of the occupational therapist's role. *British Journal of Occupational Therapy, 48*(9), 260–262.

Westland, G. (1988). Relaxing in primary health care. *British Journal of Occupational Therapy, 51*(3), 84–88.

Westland, G. (1997). Understanding occupational stress and burnout. In D. Keable (Ed.), *The management of anxiety* (pp. 213–228). Edinburgh: Churchill Livingstone.

Westland, G. (2006). Personal reflections of Gerda Boyesen 1922–2005. *Body, Movement and Dance in Psychotherapy, 1*(2), 155–160.

Westland, G. (2009a). Considerations of verbal and non-verbal communication in body psychotherapy. *Body, Movement and Dance in Psychotherapy, 4*(2), 121–134.

Westland, G. (2009b). Reflections on touch in psychotherapy. *Self and Society, 37*(2), 24–32.

Westland, G. (2011). Physical touch in psychotherapy: Why are we not touching more? *Journal of Body, Movement and Dance in Psychotherapy, 6*(1), 17–29.

Westland, G. (2015). Touch in body psychotherapy. In G. Marlock, H. Weiss, C. Young, & M. Soth (Eds.), *The Handbook of body psychotherapy and somatic psychology.* Berkeley: North Atlantic.

References

Wilber, K. (1979). *No boundary: Eastern and Western approaches to personal growth*. Boulder, CO: Shambhala.

Wilber, K. (1995). *Sex, ecology and spirituality*. London: Shambhala.

Wilkinson, M. (2006). *Coming into mind: The mind-brain relationship: A Jungian perspective*. Hove, UK: Routledge.

Wilkinson, M. (2010). *Changing minds in therapy: Emotion, attachment, trauma and neurobiology*. New York: Norton.

Winnicott, D. W. (1990a). The capacity to be alone. In *The maturational processes and the facilitating environment* (pp. 29–36). London: Karnac. (Original work published 1958)

Winnicott, D. W. (1990b). Ego distortion in terms of true and false self. In *The maturational processes and the facilitating environment* (pp. 140–153). London: Karnac. (Original work published 1960)

Winnicott, D. W. (1990c). The theory of parent-infant relationship. In *The maturational processes and the facilitating environment* (pp. 37–55). London: Karnac. (Original work published 1960)

Winnicott, D. W. (1991). *Playing and reality*. London: Routledge.

Woodmansey, A. C. (1986). Are psychotherapists out of touch? *British Journal of Psychotherapy, 5*(1), 57–65.

Wright, K. (2009). *Mirroring and attunement: Self-realization in psychoanalysis and art*. London: Routledge.

Young, C. (2005). "To touch or not to touch: That is the question": Doing effective body psychotherapy without touch. *Energy and Character, Journal of Biosynthesis, 34*, 50–64.

INDEX

Page numbers in *italic* refer to illustrations.

Index

Index